The Preparator's Handbook

The Preparator's Handbook

A Practical Guide for Preparing and Installing Collection Objects

Andrew Saluti

ROWMAN & LITTLEFIELD
Lanham • Boulder • New York • London

Published by Rowman & Littlefield
An imprint of The Rowman & Littlefield Publishing Group, Inc.
4501 Forbes Boulevard, Suite 200, Lanham, Maryland 20706
www.rowman.com

86-90 Paul Street, London EC2A 4NE

British Library Cataloguing in Publication Information Available

Library of Congress Cataloging-in-Publication Data

Names: Saluti, Andrew, author.
Title: The preparator's handbook : a practical guide for preparing and
    installing collection objects / Andrew Saluti.
Description: Lanham : Rowman & Littlefield, [2022] | Includes
    bibliographical references and index.
Identifiers: LCCN 2022015280 (print) | LCCN 2022015281 (ebook) | ISBN
    9781538139219 (cloth) | ISBN 9781538139226 (paperback) | ISBN
    9781538139233 (epub)
Subjects: LCSH: Museums techniques.
Classification: LCC AM133 .S25 2022 (print) | LCC AM133 (ebook) | DDC
    069/.4—dc23/eng/20220422
LC record available at https://lccn.loc.gov/2022015280
LC ebook record available at https://lccn.loc.gov/2022015281

Contents

List of Figures and Table

Chapter 6: Two-Dimensional Object Prep

Chapter 7: Case Study: Mounting Scrolls for Exhibition

Chapter 8: Three-Dimensional Object Prep

Chapter 9: Case Study: Simple Fosshape Supports for Textiles

Acknowledgments

What is seen in the presentation in the gallery or collections setting is consistently due to the collective work of many hands. Much like so many experiences across the museum profession, this text represents the cumulative result of collaborative effort with numerous colleagues, mentors, and craftsmen that I have had the true pleasure to learn from, work alongside, and teach.

As a young preparator starting my career in an academic collection, I had the good fortune to learn from and work alongside exceptionally talented and highly skilled individuals who were always willing to make the task at hand a teachable moment—something that became an instrumental part of a greater teaching philosophy that has been core to my academic and professional career. I need to recognize Domenic Iacono, former director of the Syracuse University Art Galleries and Collections, for his leadership, friendship, and shared commitment to the stewardship of works on paper. Iacono's tenure in collections and conservation was influential to me and countless others that worked in university collections as well as the greater print community. Dr Edward "Teddy" Aiken was equally formative with his consistent and undying dedication to academic responsibility and student experience; he has shaped my approach to making the themes of this text as core curricular elements for museology. I would also like to thank my museum studies colleague, Dr. Emily Stokes-Rees, for her support and friendship.

I have been equally fortunate to cross professional paths with a myriad of talented specialists, technicians, and conservators through collaborative exhibition and collections projects, experiences that were formative and influential and, while not directly contributors to this book, have been impactful in my growth as a collections professional and to the development of this text. Of special note are my ongoing partnerships/friendships with conservators David Stokoe, conservation librarian at the Special Collections Research Center at Syracuse University Libraries, and Maria Fredericks, the Sherman Fairchild head of conservation at the Thaw Conservation Center, Morgan Library & Museum, in New York City. I genuinely look forward to future encounters and continuing to learn from all.

This text would also not be complete without the active participation of colleagues from around the country who graciously agreed to contribute narratives of their professional experience, illustrating unique projects that augment the essential practice the book aims to cover. It is with profound thanks that I acknowledge these colleagues.

Warren Bunn is the collections and exhibitions manager for The Corning Museum of Glass in Corning, New York. As the museum's collections and exhibitions manager, Warren Bunn is responsible for managing all aspects of the care and display of the museum's glass collections, including registration, installation, lighting, photography, and the collections management database. He oversees the planning and installation of all temporary exhibitions and displays and manages all loans, both to and from the museum. Bunn came to The Corning Museum of Glass from the Herbert F. Johnson Museum of Art at Cornell University, where he was curatorial assistant and registrar for seven years. He also worked in various art galleries in Upstate New York and apprenticed with a conservation lab while in graduate school.

Donia Conn is an assistant professor of practice for the Simmons University School of Library and Information Science in Boston, Massachusetts, and independent preservation and collection care consultant for small- and mid-sized cultural heritage institutions with over 20 years of experience. Ms. Conn is also a private book and paper conservator and a professional associate of the American Institute for Conservation (AIC). She earned her BA in mathematics from St. Olaf College and her MLIS with advanced certificate in conservation from the University of Texas at Austin. Previously, Conn has worked for the Northeast Document Conservation Center, Northwestern University, and Syracuse University.

Kirsten Schoonmaker, assistant teaching professor of fashion design at Syracuse University, teaches courses in the fashion skills and techniques sequence, including construction and draping, and also teaches theory-driven courses that explore contemporary issues in fashion. Prior to joining the program, she worked as the assistant conservator of textiles at the Shelburne Museum and was a Kress Fellow with the New York State Bureau of Historic Sites. She also worked with the conservation departments at the museum at FIT and the Cooper Hewitt, Smithsonian Museum of Design. Before working as a conservator, she worked in costume construction for the Santa Fe Opera and Opera Colorado. Kirsten's training and background revolve around making the historical construction details of garments accessible and relevant for further study and inspiration. Recent conference presentations include the annual meeting for the American Institute for Conservation of Historic and Artistic Works and the North American Textile Conservation Conference.

Adrienne Stroup pursued a master's degree in museum studies—the perfect synergy between geology, paleontology, art, and education—prior to her employment at the Field Museum in Chicago. As a collections assistant in geology, she oversees the very active vertebrate paleontological collections loan program, keeping track of all specimens coming in and going out to researchers around the globe. Aside from managing loan requests, she has also created a number of artistic paleontological reconstructions (paleoart) for the Field Museum and outside organizations.

Meredith Weimer has had extensive experience in the management and practice of object handling, storage, and installation through many professional and academic experiences. She earned her master's in museum studies and has worked with a range of objects through positions including managing exhibition spaces, as an art handler at USArt, as an art storage coordinator at the Museum of Fine Arts, Boston, and most recently as an associate collections manager at the Portland Museum of Art in Portland, Maine.

Emily Zaengle is the CEO of the Stone Quarry Hill Art Park in Cazenovia, New York—a sprawling 104-acre four-season outdoor art space of conserved land and groomed trails. Zaengle champions the work of nonprofits, big and small, and holds an undergraduate degree in design and environmental analysis and graduate degrees in landscape architecture and museum studies. She enjoys working at the intersection of disciplines, ideas, and sectors. Over the past decade, Emily had the privilege of working for several nonprofits advocating for human rights in housing, independent living, and the arts. In her current role as the CEO of Stone Quarry Art Park, Emily strives to center artists and art-thinking in all aspects of the organization—demonstrating the importance, and the need, for a more broadly shared literacy and appreciation of the arts.

The inception of putting together this text began in late 2019, with the aim to complete the project in late 2020. This original plan, like so many, was derailed in March 2020 with the onset of the COVID-19 global pandemic. I personally struggled in balancing the need to reinvent and implement the way we teach our hands-on curriculum alongside the newfound challenges in supporting my family to successfully navigate the virtual educational and professional environment. Where many colleagues were productive in completing research and publication projects, I was, and continue to be, challenged in maintaining the necessary focus and resolve. This all points to not only an appreciation but a truly sincere and emphatic "thank you" to the team at Rowman & Littlefield, New York, specifically to my editor Charles Harmon and his colleague Erinn Slanina for their (what seemed to be) unwavering patience, guidance, and support throughout this process.

Lastly, I would be remiss to not add loving, appreciative, and requisite thanks to my wife, Jenny, for her partnership and encouragement through the duration of this and so many years of projects that she has endured and supported. Without her by my side as a constant adviser, confidant, champion, reinforcement, and trusted friend, none of this would be possible. Thank you.

Preface

Like so many who have come into the museum profession by way of what might be described as an indirect, an unexpected, and a circuitous route, my own path began while completing my MFA at Louisiana State University, where I was fortunate to take on the position of gallery technician for the School of Art's exhibition space. For many years I had already been gaining foundational experience working in commercial framing, and, as a traditional printmaker, the formal presentation of objects—works on paper especially—was hardwired in my ethos as a part of my own process. There was no permanent collection to maintain; however, the experience of collaborating on such a broad range of installations with colleague artists and other traveling exhibitions set the groundwork for a path that would evolve into a decades-long career in collections, design, curatorial, and administrative roles. And, like so many with parallel resumes, my appreciation and passion for the work—the presentation and preservation of objects of all types and needs—has blossomed into a dedication that involves experimentation, partnerships, and perhaps, most importantly, the mentorship of future preparators and collections professionals.

Working in an academic museum offers unique opportunities for both the professional staff and student population that the institutions engage with. During my time overseeing the management and installation of exhibitions and collections care, I had the pleasure of guiding student workers, graduate assistants, and emerging museum professionals in basic techniques of object handling, preparation, and installation that would prove to plant an invaluable seed for their future careers—not only for those who would continue as preparators but also giving insight and practical experience to those who would find themselves in the all-too-common "jack-of-all-trades" museum situation, where they are often one of few (or alone) in the multitude of responsibilities to manage and maintain their spaces. I found that the hands-on experience that was conveyed to my team members was not always consistent across other "hands-on" experiences. In most museum studies programs, this aspect of the profession is habitually relegated outside the guardrails of academic curriculum and more commonly left to internship, volunteer work, or part-time positions. What I consistently observed was a blatant inconsistency in practice—not necessarily that the supervising professionals lacked the knowledge but that the intern/volunteer experience rarely allowed for an in-depth exploration for the needed best practice techniques and information.

Having taught in a museum studies program for many years, I saw the opportunity, and the real need, to create a course that included an overview of prepatory and installation skills that any emerging museum professional should know and have applied experiences with, regardless of their professional path or concentration. The course has evolved over many years of execution, first being taught out of the university museum's preparation lab, expanding to other satellite galleries throughout the campus, and beyond into the larger community. It has become a core part of the curriculum: a foundational experience that our graduate students could apply to their upcoming internship experiences as well as their professional portfolios postgraduation. The course was (is) neither comprehensive nor an exhaustive training ground for future preparators, rather, an overview of the hierarchal concepts, best practice, and foundational techniques in the areas of object handling, storage, crate construction, gallery preparation, installation techniques and process, and perhaps, most importantly, proper preparation management, designed under the premise that these fundamentals could be applied to any type of object or artifact and to any genre of museum. This text is a direct extension of that curriculum, organized in similar sequence, and includes references and resources for a myriad of object-centered needs and exercises. Considering the abundance of exceptional texts that cover collections care—a critical aspect of both the course and profession—*The Preparator's Handbook* comprises the lesser-documented yet fundamental aspects of preparation work: a practice that had been previously relegated to on-the-job learning or disparate internal publication and manuals.

The aim for this text is to be a foundational resource for any collections-based preparation and installation experience, to provide a reference that could be used across the landscape of professional and academic models in any kind, size, and type of exhibition setting, from the local historical society with a handful of permanent staff to the multitiered collections departments of a major museum. It is imperative to note that this text is in no way meant to replace the necessary specific training and procedures that collecting institutions already may have in place, nor will it take the place of invaluable practical experience and apprenticeship within a genre-specific or focused practice, handling, and conservation. This text is not holistically comprehensive, attempting to outline every procedural approach to any type of object or artifact. Rather, this text intends to be a much-needed foundation for any preparator, gallerist, installer, or museum technician: a baseline to start from and a consistent resource to build experience on.

1

What Is a Preparator?

In the museum field, the important work involved in properly managing collection material is a task performed by many hands—an intricate machine of moving parts that work in unison to achieve a successful end. Much like clockwork, this collaborative dance of museum professionals—curators, registrars, conservators, educators, development officers, administration, and more—relies on each gear moving at the appropriate time, in the appropriate way, to effectively accomplish one of a myriad of actions pertaining to the institution's core: its collection. Safely moving an object in and out of storage, preparing an object for transport, or the installation of objects for public view, these routines are carefully orchestrated and executed by a specially trained, uniquely qualified museum staff to ensure that the preserved well-being of the collection is maintained at all times.

While this stewardship of objects and artifacts is the work of many, there is one core group of specialists that are tethered to these collection procedures, invariably present at each move and each

Figure 1.1. Preparators Framing Objects in Collections Preparation Shop. *Source*: Image credit: Andrew Saluti.

progressive stage of the process. If an object needs to be precisely and securely hung on a gallery wall; if an artifact needs to be cleaned or have a mount or case made to fit its singular characteristics; if there is *any* situation where the object has to be moved, handled, documented, measured, or impacted from its stasis, this is the important work of a preparator.

WHAT IS A PREPARATOR?

You've no doubt heard the term—especially visible in the stream of museum/gallery job postings and internship opportunities. But what exactly is a preparator? The dictionary defines this term simply as "one who prepares specimens or exhibits for scientific study or display."[1] This extremely terse description is not incorrect: the preparator does in fact prepare specimens and exhibits. But to the initiated, those familiar with the roles and responsibilities associated with this title would immediately expand on this explanation to include a laundry list of collection- and institution-specific functions that this all-to-important position carries.

Let us first identify the preparator's position in the schematic diagram of the profession. Collections are under the stewardship of the curator. This role, in many mid-to-smaller–sized institutions and galleries, is many times the shared/multitasked responsibility of a director. In order to manage that collection, you will have registrars to track the location, condition, and documentation related to the objects. Conservators hold a special place in this hierarchy—their specialized training to preserve and repair collection objects and artifacts places them, at times, on an equal, or parallel, position to the curator of the collections, and, in other scenarios, working in tandem with all collections staff.[2]

The preparator's position generally falls within the branches of this framework: working closely with registrars and conservators under the direction of curatorial administration. This rank could easily, albeit incorrectly, be construed as a bottom rung, lowest in the pecking order, worker-bee status. In truth, the preparator is fundamental: the general contractor, the front line for any collection. The preparator can be (and many times is) the first and last member of the team to handle an object from station to station before it is installed, stored, or packed; the staff member solving object-related problems during times of transition and installation; and the trained professional given the ultimate responsibility when an object is in need of handling or transport. Depending on the size and scope of the institution, there may be a separate team of preparation staff under the management and supervision of a head preparator or, in other cases, specific preparators working directly with specific parts of the collection. In many areas, preparation staff are hired as independent contractors—brought on to work exclusively on temporary or short-term collection and/or exhibition projects.

Evidence of this role within major museums is peppered throughout historical records and annual reports, yet the formal position, represented as an established professional component in the field, is a relatively modern phenomenon. As early as 1879 the Museum of Fine Arts (MFA) in Boston, Massachusetts, listed a budget line in the annual report for the contracting of service for the "Transporting and Placing of Works of Art."[3] Once more, the formal professional reference for the role at the MFA, listed as "Exhibitions Technician," was not officially recognized until 1977.[4] One of the earliest uses of the actual title "preparator" can be found in references to Charles De Kempeneer (c. 1852–1884), a Belgian natural history preparator and taxidermist who was associated with Henry Ward, businessman and trader in natural history specimens from Rochester, New York.[5] Today, the term has transcended the science and natural history genres to become a widely recognized role within collections practice.

WHAT DOES A PREPARATOR DO?

If the seemingly simple and innocuous question of "What does a preparator do?" is posed to one currently holding the title, the answer will undoubtedly resemble or imply something consistent with "It's different everyday" or "Everything and anything that is needed," followed immediately by an audible

Figure 1.2. Assembling Diplodocus Forelimb, 1916. *Source*: Anderson, A. E. (photographer), American Museum of Natural History Research Library.

huff or sigh meant to articulate the great range of responsibilities and procedures that are carried on their shoulders. It's very true: the preparator, in a single day, may need to be focused on the meticulous work of mounting delicate works on paper under a window mat, followed by patching and painting a gallery before an installation, only then to transition to carefully packing a centuries-old piece of furniture in a sleigh or crate to be shipped. The job is one that consists of innumerable responsibilities depending on the needs of the collections. To outline a general description, one must first delineate between the preparator's physical duties and the administrative, or the job as it pertains to the object and the job as it pertains to the process.

Handling

One of the core responsibilities that a preparator must explicitly understand and employ is the proper handling of objects. This is a fundamental aspect of the role: to safely manipulate and transport objects while mitigating risk and preserving a relative stasis at all times. As simple and straightforward as this sounds, this facet of the job is one that carries the greatest weight (figuratively and sometimes literally!). Proper object handling includes a substantive level of knowledge and/or experience with multiple object varieties (depending on the collection or institution), experience with the appropriate support materials and tools, and, above all, articulate communication skills.

Matting, Mounting, and Framing

Before an unsupported object (loose photograph, archival document, unframed canvas, case-bound book, or non-standing artifact) can be installed for the public, the preparator is tasked with fitting and reinforcing that object to ensure its stability, security, and preservation. A common routine is the archival matting of two-dimensional works or documents and the mounting process used to stabilize that object in place, and also creating a closed environment in a frame for gallery installation, long-term storage, or safe transportation. Examples of these basic procedures include the fashioning of a cradle mount, so a certain page of bound volume can be presented while also supporting the spine of the book as to not damage the binding, and, in addition, the construction of object mounts, such as the brace that holds a Chinese decorative plate in place to allow the greatest viewable angle while installed but also ensuring minimal movement or abrasion to the object at rest.

Exhibition and Gallery Preparation

Central to the preparator's job, but not directly pertaining to the object, is the preparation of the spaces these objects will be presented in. Working well in advance of the installation of the intended content in collaboration with curators, artists, conservators, and designers, the preparation team must ensure that the physical space is prepared to effectively present, and secure, the material on view. The specifics of the preparator's responsibility are always defined by the installation and deinstallation of whatever is, was, or will be on view. Basic tasks, including the mending, patching, and painting of walls, presentation furniture, and display areas, must be carefully orchestrated to precede the introduction of objects into the space. The removal of previous objects, hardware, graphics, and other exhibition elements have enormous impact on the timely preparation of these spaces. This choreography must also take into account any additional practical construction connected or adjacent to the intended display and, most importantly, cleanup of the evidence of this work long before the staff can proceed to the next phase of installation.

Installation

The installation of objects can be a process as simple as placing an artifact inside an enclosed case or as complex as rigging harnesses and buttresses to safely move and install a 3,000-pound bronze sculpture, carefully assessing the structural load and fabricating furniture for support and presentation. With the installation of collection objects, whether for public display or long-term storage, there are a variety of methodologies, equations, and approaches the preparator considers and applies to ensure, above all, that the object is secure—both during the installation and while installed. One of the most important allies in this process is an attention to and comfortability with mathematics: the meticulous calculations and measurements associated with the object that determine the intended relationship of the object to the viewer and the ideal hardware/mechanism(s) utilized to support and safeguard the object. This detail-oriented process is imperative to the preservation of the object—with all appropriate hardware, mounts, furniture, stands, and cradles determined and fabricated well in advance of the object having been moved from its state of rest or storage.

Lighting

In tandem with the installation process is the proper lighting of objects on display. The preparator is often tasked not only with the physical adjustment of lighting fixtures in a space to present the object in an ideal manner but also to implement all steps and best practice to ensure that the illumination in the space is set to proper conservation standards and levels in order to secure the preservation of the objects on view, having a working knowledge of the institution's capabilities, inventories, and idiosyncrasies when dealing with the lighting.

Fabrication

Devising and constructing the varied physical needs of collections are a common charge to the preparation department. Depending on the level of construction or scope of the project, the responsibility of fabricating object mounts, cradles, stands, pedestals, frames, crates, and more are taken on by the preparator. This role can often expand to include non-collection-related projects as well, such as temporary wall construction and finishing, wayfinding and other graphics/signage, and other genre-specific trade work. Even in the frequent cases where the preparator is not tasked with the actual fabrication of a project, the coordination and supervision of these outsourced tasks are regularly under the direction and management of the preparator.

Packing

Much of the outlined responsibilities of the preparation staff thus far have been to the attention of exhibition and display. However, equally important are the duties and object needs while at rest, in transit, and in storage: creating and maintaining appropriate enclosures, microenvironments and long-term housings for objects, and the appropriate containers, wrapping, and cushion for travel. Preparing objects to leave the secure environment of the institution, whether to a storage facility or a borrowing venue, is often delegated to the preparation staff. Intertwined with the diverse qualifications outlined in the preparator's handling, installation, and fabrication duties, the obligations to proper packing and storage extend to a deep knowledge and understanding of not only materials and methodologies but also how those methods and materials will impact the object over, or be impacted by, long periods of time. It is not uncommon for a preparator to also act as currier—the eyes on the ground from the point where the object leaves its home to when it is installed at the collaborating venue (though it is important to note this is not a role solely under the guise of the preparator and can often be assigned to any representative of the collections staff, including the registrar, conservator, or curator).

Administration and Organization

Independent of the responsibilities directly tied to the objects, archival materials, and artifacts in the collection, the preparator's duties also include a managerial role seldom discussed in collections care manuals and internship experiences: the administration of the preparation process. The knowledge and experience that this position contributes to a professional staff by way of material expertise extend to the management and upkeep of the preparation lab and fabrication shops, the inventories of hardware and archival supplies needed, and the maintenance of tools and equipment used.

This administrative function is many times reflected in the preparator's role as manager: not only in the workflow for the preparation of objects and spaces but also in the management of installations and other collections-based projects. Outlining and tracking project details and scheduling, researching and proposing project budgets, delegating specific responsibilities, outsourcing and quoting contractors when needed; these important supervisory duties will naturally fall to the professional at the center of the hands-on stage of the given project or routine. There are several key components to this aspect of preparation work. Proper time management, as with any project-based role, is of paramount importance and is ultimately required for anyone taking on a leadership position in preparation. Creative, responsive, and informed problem-solving is another core trait that is not only desired but necessary in the discipline—an ability to think innovatively and resourcefully to achieve the desired result, all while balancing the stewardship to the objects and artifacts. In addition, all the previously

POSITION DESCRIPTION
Title: Chief Preparator
Direct Reports: Lead Preparator, Preparators (2)
Purpose: As department head, the Chief Preparator is responsible for planning and managing the preparation of gallery spaces and objects for exhibitions and for planning and managing the fabrication, installation, and de-installation of both temporary exhibitions and long-term installations. The Chief Preparator supervises the Museum's preparators, as well as contract art handlers, on all aspects of museum exhibition, art storage, and art movement.

DUTIES AND RESPONSIBILITIES
Recommend department objectives and priorities and develop a strategy to achieve them consistent with the Museum's vision statement, strategic plan, and divisional goals.
Manage all functions of the Exhibition Services Department, its activities and personnel, including fellows, interns, and volunteers; coordinate department activities with other departments and divisions of the Museum.
Collaborate with the Museum's Exhibition Designer in the planning of the preparation of gallery spaces for exhibition and in planning the fabrication, installation, and de-installation of both temporary exhibitions and long-term installations.
Plan, prioritize and schedule daily activities of preparators in the areas of exhibition installations/deinstallations, graphics installation, gallery and exhibition lighting, exhibition maintenance and art movements within the museum. Set team's job assignments to meet deadlines and priorities; oversee external vendors and contractors.
Prepare and present department budget for approval; monitor department and project budgets within approved limits. Assist in the development of exhibition and special project budgets.
Supervise installation of works of art and oversee production and installation of exhibition graphics, signage, and labels.
Design and fabricate, or oversee the design and fabrication of, display and storage mounts for objects using brass armatures, plexiglass, pliacre forms and stabilizers, foam cor, matboard, ethafoam, wood, steel, aluminum, conduit and piping.
Working with the registrars, coordinate exhibition installation/de-installation schedules as well as internal and external art movements.
Contribute to the development of exhibition schedules and budgets. Serve as a member of project teams for exhibition development and implementation.
Remain current with approaches and developments in materials and techniques used in preparation and display of the museum collections.
Working with the Conservation and Registration Departments, establish and maintain best practices for handling, lighting, crating, and shipping of all collection media
Order materials for art packing and exhibition installation.
Recommend improvements to museum art storage.
Assist preparators with gallery maintenance, including dusting of platforms, pedestals, and vitrines, and assist with museum-wide lighting maintenance as needed.
Serve as a courier for outgoing loans. Travel with objects on domestic and international shipments as required; act as Museum representative as necessary
Represent the museum to various public constituencies in the region
Represent department at various meetings and on internal committees
Perform other related duties as assigned

REQUIREMENTS
Proven management skills, including the ability to work collaboratively and cooperatively within a team, comprising museum staff, contractors, vendors and couriers
Experience managing complex projects: ability to work on multiple projects simultaneously, working to strict deadlines
Ability to prepare and manage department and project budgets
Strong communication and interpersonal skills
Knowledge of art storage and display methods, techniques, and procedures
Good manual dexterity for fine detail work and handling fragile objects
In-depth knowledge of art handling techniques and methods of transporting works of art
Experience in exhibition design, mount-making, crate fabrication, preparation and installation techniques
Ability to lift up to 70 lbs.
Ability to safely work with installation equipment including ladders, scissor lift and scaffolding
Ability to work at heights over 10 feet
Motor vehicle operator's license
Travel required for this position

Figure 1.3.   Generic Example of a Chief Preparator Position Description.

outlined responsibilities, functions, and qualifications of the preparator must converge into a theoretical comprehension and an active commitment to mitigating risk. Everything the preparator does directly or indirectly affects objects, making the charge of mitigating risk when dealing with installation, presentation, transit, or storage inclusive to any and all aspects of the position.

VARIATIONS OF THE PREPARATOR

The title of preparator can itself have a variety of institution-specific duties with it depending on the specific roles that the preparation staff are required to take on. When considering what defines a preparator in the museum, there is a taxonomy of title-specific roles that commonly intertwine with the preparator's position and function.

Art Handler

The art handler is a role that is regularly thought of as being synonymous with that of the preparator, particularly those in the art-centric genre, and associated with what are stereotypically considered as art objects: paintings, sculpture, works on paper, and things in frames. An important distinction between the preparator and the art handler is that the preparator is, in most cases, associated directly with an institution or collection, whereas the art handler is more commonly an independent specialist, working not only for/in collecting institutions but also outside the permanent staff of a museum: for storage facilities, shipping companies, or arts consultancies. The responsibilities are parallel in that both positions require experienced knowledge and training in the proper handling and care of objects and for the art handler a focus on dealing with the packing and transport of these objects. This distinction broadens the scope of what falls under the art handler's scope of work (and perhaps how we define the "art" object) to include objects of antiquity, fine furniture and craftwork, and other objects of cultural significance.

Museum Technician

This generalized title is often used for a museum staff member who may be utilized in multiple capacities associated with object and gallery preparation or is working in the department of a collections staff member of specific rank: collections manager, registrar, or conservator. Museum technicians are typically assistants in the day-to-day of these specialized departments—taking on many of the standard duties under the normal purview of preparator but not necessarily in a preparation department. Alternatively, this title is also given to those multifaceted positions where the responsibilities overlap: registration, preparation, and collections management rolled into one. The technician moniker can also be used to describe those staff members whose primary responsibilities focus on physical plant and facilities maintenance, technical installations, and/or fabrication.

Installer

The installer, like the art handler, is a specific position that largely centers around one aspect of a preparator's charge. The installer will focus squarely on aspects of collection care that pertain to the display of objects. This includes basic handling skills; various hanging and mounting techniques; the fabrication of mounts, stands, and gallery furniture; and also sometimes incorporating lighting. The position of installer is also found in non-collecting institutions and art centers, where the display of site specific artwork and exhibitions is central to the mission or program. Like the art handler, this role can be full-time staff or contract based on need.

Fabricator

In any collecting- or object-based cultural institution there is an inevitable need to create customized housings, specialty mounts, exhibition furniture (including pedestals, cases, and frames), and light construction—from the framing and finishing temporary walls to crate building. In many cases, this work is assigned to outside contractors or companies specializing in such needs. However, the role of fabricator is one that many museums employ on staff, usually working within the preparation or collection departments, depending on the dedicated roles and/or frequency of work. These staff members generally have backgrounds in the trade, as well as a focused experience and expertise in dealing with collection objects and exhibitions.

Chief/Head/Senior/Lead Preparator

The preparation department will many times be a robust team of dedicated staff members compiled of a crew of skilled tradespersons and specialists (including the list of titles previously described) whose focus may be just one of the many tasks and responsibilities in the purview of the preparator. In these situations, a chief or head preparator assumes a leadership role: channeling their knowledge and experience to the organization, administration, and supervision of the larger unit. These positions are generally responsible for scheduling projects and delegating responsibilities; budgeting, ordering, and maintaining an inventory of materials and supplies; and contracting specialists when the needs of the work are outside the scope of their permanent staff. The chief preparator will frequently act as the conduit of communication within the hierarchy of leadership in the collections and curatorial departments, balancing the "big picture" of the multitude of institutional demands and overseeing the workflow and deadlines of concurrent installations, object preparation, and collection-related projects.

Preparator (as It Pertains to Natural History/Science Museums/Archaeology)

The functional role a preparator plays, and the specific responsibilities assigned to that role, is largely dependent on the kind of museum, institution, or collection to which they are a part of. In the genre of the sciences, particularly the natural science museum, the term "preparator" can have unique connotations that extend beyond the practice of those professionals employed in the arts or history. In these cases, the title "preparator" is used to describe a specialist who is engaged in fieldwork: often directly participating in the archaeological dig or the subsequent cleaning and conserving of specimens for study or display. Sometimes further defined depending on the subject (i.e., "fossil preparator" in the case of paleontology or "mammal preparator" in the role of taxidermist), these positions employ the supplemental training and routines associated with that of the conservator—where active modification and treatment is performed on the specimen—in addition to the preservational tasks of preparing the object for display or storage. It was in reference to this genre of preparator that the term has its derivative roots, first discussed at the turn of the twentieth century in publications aiming to identify and explain the techniques of fossil collecting and preparation.[6]

Equally important to defining the roles and responsibilities of a preparator is to also understand and acknowledge what the preparator isn't. It is extremely common at many museums and cultural institutions to have small (some might say *nimble*) staffing—where the full-time staff comprises of 2–3 trained professionals used to wearing many hats within the organization, aided by part-time, contract, or volunteer assistance. In these frequent cases, the one responsible for preparation and installation will many times also be the registrar, exhibition designer, and even curator. These circumstances will largely depend on a balance of two factors: the background and training of the staff member and the needs and capabilities of the institution.

There are many in the museum field that must take on the role of preparator in addition to their central focus—most commonly presumed by registrars and curatorial staff. It is very important, however, to outline that a *preparator is not a conservator*. Though a conservator can (and many times does) take on the responsibilities of the preparation staff, the preparator does not necessarily have the years of training, knowledge, and research in the technical and material sciences to perform the conservator's tasks. Only the conservator has the authority to identify and execute the specialized active care and treatment to physically alter an object—returning it to a previous state, repairing damage, or stabilizing active decay. This distinction will be further examined in this text as the difference between *passive* and *active* conservation of objects. The preparator should never perform any physical change or alteration to an object without direct consultation or supervision of the conservator.

Equally important is to acknowledge that *the preparator is not the curator*. This may seem an obvious distinction, but considering the significance of how objects are installed, the narrative that is created in the progression of objects and how they are presented in a public space, here is a situation where the one installing the works can have a paramount impact on the interpretation and context of what is one's view. An effective preparator is one that understands the importance of this staging to reinforce the narratives presented and acknowledges the authoritative source of that context—the curators, artists, designers, and interpreters telling this story and those creating the experience through the artifacts and objects. Working closely with, *not independent from*, that team to identify the how, where, and why things are placed in a space is vital to a successful exhibition: a collaborative linchpin in the process. The preparator should never assume or decide how objects should be installed without insight from the narrative source.

WHAT IS A PREPARATOR'S BACKGROUND?

The position of preparator within the museum field is unique in that these roles are one of the few key ranks in the profession that (currently) don't come from a specialized or formal academic training, akin to those of curators, educators, collections managers, development staff, or administration. The preparator brings an experience to a staff that can be informed by numerous professions and practice. In the academic realm, those earning advanced certificates and degrees in museum studies are often exposed to the intricate framework of collection's care. There are only few programs that place academic focus on the preparation and installation of objects; most delegate this learning to a practical internship experience. In the arts, preparators often come from the studio—working artists who have inestimable amounts of direct interaction with art objects. Especially those who are trained in traditional studio practice and craft: sculptors, printmakers, and ceramicists; these highly skilled makers have unique insight into how these objects were made, often leading to a passionate drive for preservation. In the sciences, the work of the preparation staff is many times derived from the practical on-site training that coincides with anthropology and archaeology—and the shared desire to preserve the artifacts that inform our histories and cultures. The significant contributions by those working in trades, carpenters, construction, welders, and others, become an essential component to the preparation staff and often bring experiences and points of view seldom considered when inside the bubble of the museum collection.

NOTES

1. This is the common definition, from one of many sources in print and online. This particular definition can be found in *The American Heritage College Dictionary*, Houghton Mifflin Company, Boston/New York, 1993.
2. This is of course dependent on a variety of factors, including the size of the institution, the type(s) of collections maintained by the museum, and whether the institution employs conservators on staff or contracts work on an as-needed basis.

3. H. P Kidder, "[Treasurer's Accounts]." Annual Report for the Year . . . (Museum of Fine Arts, Boston) 3 (1878): 9-10. Accessed November 13, 2020. http://www.jstor.org/stable/43477835.
4. "Staff as of June 30, 1978." The Museum Year: Annual Report of the Museum of Fine Arts, Boston 102 (1977): 75-78. Accessed November 13, 2020. http://www.jstor.org/stable/43481814.
5. B. J. Gill, "Charles De Kempeneer (c.1852-1884), Preparator: One of Auckland Museum's Earliest Employees," *Records of the Auckland Museum* 53 (2018): 77-84. Accessed September 23, 2019. https://www.jstor.org/stable/26564907.
6. The first publications to deal with these early techniques are F. A. Bather's *Preparation and Preservation of Fossils* (1908) and A. Hermann's review *Modem Laboratory Methods in Vertebrate Palaeontology* (1909). These publications appear to have resulted from recognition that a preparator (a term apparently first used in North America) should have certain attributes and no longer needed to have a background in coal mining, quarrying, or stonemasonry. Peter J. Whybrow, "A History of Fossil Collecting and Preparation Techniques," *Curator* 28/1 (1985): 5-6.

REFERENCES

Burcaw, George. *Introduction to Museum Work*, 3rd ed. (AltaMira Press, 1997).
Powell, Brent. *Collections Care* (New York: Rowman & Littlefield, 2016).

2

Object Handling

A PHILOSOPHICAL APPROACH

Proper art and object handling may be the most important, fundamental, and universally shared skill sets that anyone working with collections or in exhibitions must understand and employ at all times. These methodologies ensure that in any situation, whether the collection materials are in transit, on display, or in storage, best practice and procedures should always be engaged to ensure the safety and best possible protection for the identified objects, artifacts, documents, or specimen. Additionally, the care and handling of collections is in no way the sole responsibility of a preparation staff or even just the larger collections and curatorial department: these skills need to be, at minimum, holistically recognized if not regularly put in practice.

Figure 2.1. Preparators Handling and Packing Vessels for Storage. *Source:* Image credit: Andrew Saluti.

Consider an interpreter in the education department, a docent in visitor services, or a development officer: how do the basics of proper handling affect these institutional colleagues, who may not routinely have immediate or direct interaction with collections? Put simply, an understanding of these skills can forge an appreciation and a connection to that which is central to the institution's primary charge—precisely what is to be interpreted, explained, or funded. If, for example, the museum interpreter understands the delicate approach needed to transport a Navajo basket woven of natural willow, the discussion and programing they create around that object will undoubtedly be enhanced—better informed with the knowledge of the physical attributes and detailed care associated with the artifact. If the development officer, tasked as a primary contact between donor and institution, can relay even a rudimentary knowledge about the unique preservation demands of a collection of nineteenth-century albumen photographs, or the significantly particular needs of nitrate films, they will unquestionably have greater success in supporting the acquisition and funding for a collection's growth and safeguarding.

This isn't to say that these colleagues can't or won't also need to readily practice these competencies so they might assist in collections maintenance or exhibition installation. As is common custom in the majority of our museums and cultural institutions, the responsibilities of these and many other positions are routinely shared among singular staffers. This further illustrates the necessity for these fundamentals to be ubiquitous in the larger landscape of museum practice.

It is important to note that there are distinct and considerable details pertaining to the specific media and classifications of collections and their care, going far beyond basic handling methods. This information is essential to inform the handling of each particular object, and while these specific needs and procedures that many objects in our institutions demand need to be identified, this is not the focus or intended purpose of this text. There are many publications and resources that squarely explicate, in itemized detail, the various techniques and approaches to the care and handling of the sundry of media and artifacts under the stewardship of your collections department. Guidebooks like *Collection Care: An Illustrated Handbook for the Care and Handling of Cultural Objects* (Rowman & Littlefield: New York, 2015) provide an exhaustive resource that identify the appropriate media-specific approaches that inform institutional practice.[1] Many institutions maintain and publish their own manuals of collections care that speak to internal policy and procedure and directly to the unique makeup of their collections and archives. Resources for preparators that outline the handling and care of virtually any type of object are readily available and should always be sought out before engaging with objects and collections. At the same time, it would be irresponsible to discuss the preparation and installation of objects without referencing the supreme importance of proper handling and the methodologies that should be employed. Let's instead consider a satellite view of this process: a philosophy of handling practice that suggests a universal outline when dealing with any object and one that then dictates general techniques that offer a communal foundation for the best practice in the handling of collection objects. Guided by these general principles, the preparator—or any staff or professional tasked with engaging directly with objects—will be best armed to deal with any object-centric situation in a basic yet informed and thoughtful approach.

Why is such an approach to object handling so imperative to the preparator in their role within the collection staff? The primary objective in employing proper handling techniques is mitigation of risk to an object, especially when that object is in a transitory state. Understanding this includes, in particular, taking collection material out of its permanent storage or state of rest and introducing it to new environments, transport, or housings and mounts. These situations relate to only a few of the possible hazards that have been identified as major perpetrators of risk. In the mid-1990s, the Canadian Conservation Institute (CCI) established 10 defining agents of the deterioration for collection objects: physical forces; thieves, vandals, and displacers; fire; water; pests; pollutants; light; incorrect temperature; incorrect relative humidity; and custodial neglect and dissociation.[2] For the preparator and collections staff, this rubric provides a broad outline of the range of potential circumstances and conditions that need to be taken into consideration when engaging with objects and artifacts—some within our control and others outside the sphere of practice. While these individual aggressors represent a specific threat or set of risks to objects, rarely is their imposition necessarily siloed nor are the reactive actions taken in prevention. In other words, each possible threat does not always occur independently from another, and these situations don't always demand a discrete approach to each. The implementation of good handling practice and proper object preparation procedures offers the first and best line of defense against many of these elements of risk but won't address a preventative solution to all agents of deterioration.

Of these itemized risks that the well-trained preparator can thwart by practicing effective handling techniques are (1) physical forces and (2) custodial neglect. Physical forces include impact and shock (direct forces against the object and the sudden effects of that impact), vibration and abrasion (imposed movement from an otherwise stable state and the resulting consequences of contact between surfaces), and pressure (consistent force applied to a targeted area of an object). Custodial neglect, one aspect of the CCI classification of dissociation, is the end result of a lack of employing best practices of object handling, in addition to improper storage and non-archival preparation techniques. This agent of deterioration also extends beyond the physical changes and damage to objects that the preceding elements of risk define to include cultural relevance and data-driven valuation, such as incorrect identification and labeling, and deterioration due to educational overuse and/or abuse. Additional factors will come into play when considering preparation and storage techniques, including issues of environment (humidity, temperature, and light) and packing (water and pests).

Equal to defining risk in relation to the philosophical approach to object handling is the definition of the preparator's role within this sphere of collections care, specifically, the distinct difference between *passive* and *active* conservation. As previously stated, the preparator is not necessarily going to be a trained conservator, though a conservator within a collections team will often take on the responsibilities of a preparator. This means that a preparator is restricted in what kinds of activities can be done to maintain an object. Only a trained conservator should perform any action that would physically alter collection material. This includes any repair, cleaning, adjustment, or change needed to restore (hence the term "restoration") an object to its previous and normalized state. The North East Document Conservation Center (NEDCC), the first conservation center in the United States devoted to the treatment of works on paper and film-based collections, outlines three different classifications of collection care as defined by the American Institute for Conservation of Historic and Artistic Works (AIC): preservation, conservation, and restoration.[3]

Preservation: The protection of cultural property through activities that minimize chemical and physical deterioration and damage and that prevent loss of informational content. The primary goal of preservation is to prolong the existence of cultural property.

Conservation: The profession devoted to the preservation of cultural property for the future. Conservation activities include examination, documentation, treatment, and preventive care, supported by research and education.

Restoration: Treatment procedures intended to return cultural property to a known or assumed state, often through the addition of non-original material.[4]

The term "preservation" is often used as an umbrella to encompass any and all collections care activities performed to prevent any loss or physical change to the material. This term is widely used when discussing archival and library collections, where there is generally more direct and active use by entities outside that of collection staff (books and other shared media) and where the information that is relayed by the material is the primary focus of care and the physical object that carries said content is secondary (but still valued). A common example of preservation is the rebinding of books, or digitization of deteriorating media formats, but also includes activities that would be shared with a museum, including the maintenance of appropriate environments, light levels, and creating stable housings for objects. The definition of preservation has grown to also include disaster planning, security practices and personnel, binding and other active treatments, and policies and practice within digital collections, including reformatting, storage, and surrogates of physical collections. In short, preservation is a large term that comprises far more than the focused object-centered responsibilities of a preparator.

"Restoration," on the other hand, is a direct action that returns an object to a previous condition after damage, loss, or degradation—not only to preserve the cultural or academic intent but to return the object back to an original state using materials and techniques specific to that object's need and composition. This term is far more specific and specialized than that of preservation and is equally reserved to specialists with extensive training in a particular genre or medium, that is, paper, paintings, photographs, furniture, and so on.

"Conservation" is a term that lives in between these polarized definitions. Or, instead of using a linear distinction, consider a hierarchy of delineation: an upside-down triangle that describes each term's relationship to the other within a larger context of collections care. If "preservation" is the term used to embody a grand cohort of procedures and policies to "prolong the existence of cultural property," then conservation, a means of preservation, describes the specific techniques employed to achieve that goal. Further, using this framework in concert with the AIC definitions previously presented, conservation can further be broken down by the direct or indirect actions taken in relation to the object: specifically, the difference between preventative care and treatment. If treatment can be characterized as the *active* restoration or conservation of the object, then preventative care would be defined as any activities taken surrounding the object to ensure its preservation with no direct physical alterations or *passive* conservation. This includes maintaining a stasis environment with ideal temperature and humidity levels; keeping illumination within acceptable parameters during prolonged exposure; creating housings, mounts, and storage that will ensure the object's stability and safety; and the implementation of appropriate handling techniques and care—an itemized description of the preparator's role within collections. Both *active* and *passive* conservation require examination and documentation, as defined by the AIC. These coexisting designations are important as they inform the roles within collections and the value that should be placed on the training and experience of the personnel, considering the variance in staffing among museums and cultural institutions. However, the relevant article is, again, the delegation of responsibilities: only a trained conservator can and should engage in active conservation. A conservator's responsibilities may include those described as passive conservation, otherwise designated to a preparator. But a preparator does not (necessarily) have the extensive knowledge and training to perform active conservation. The preparator, in addition to any pertinent collection colleagues (depending on the institution's staffing), should always consult a conservator when active conservation may be necessary or if there is a question about any direct action concerning an object.

Upon understanding the importance of proper handling, the resources available, its purpose in assessing and mitigating risk, and the taxonomy of the methodology and roles within a larger schema of institutional preservation, one can consider a philosophical approach to handling: a common and indiscriminate process that preempts the specifics of media or classification and one that can and should be used as the basis for the direct engagement with objects. When formalizing a system for object handling that is responsive to the wide range of different kinds of objects found in collecting and exhibiting institutions, and one that breaks down an effective and universal procedure that accommodates a multitude of situations and routines that object-centered professionals contend with, one should include a variety of components. The first and most obvious would be the object itself. Moving systematically outward, a natural expansion then is to consider the situation that object is to be placed, the factors that circle this situation, and the concurrent issues that the object will contribute to the situation. The mediators of this handling need to be addressed, as well as our attention to the preceding concepts of risk. When combined and distilled into practice, taking as many factors into account before addressing the specificity of media, three distinct pillars form a structure for an object handling foundation: evaluation, communication, and common sense. These three categories work in tandem to ensure object and staff safety, illustrating a coherent, general guide to maneuvering the handling of objects. They are not necessarily sequential; activity nested in one section may be simultaneously occurring or preceding others depending on specific situations. However, each element is vital to ensuring safe and successful handling.

EVALUATION

Evaluation may be the most complex aspect of effective handling as it includes multiple elements that will inform our process: a thoughtful analysis of the object at play, the details pertaining to the situation, and environmental factors including points of proximity and the pathways and circumstances that may become factors in between. This aspect of handling will also inevitably lead to more in-depth research and analysis—the more information you gather, the more input you will have when consulting conservators, collection managers, curators, and others who will inform how you might proceed (this is also a core competency in the communication category).

Starting with the object itself, the preparator's evaluation should consistently consider the elements that follow.

Descriptive assessment: Put simply, what is this object? Is it a work on paper, a cultural artifact or specimen, or a painting on canvas or board? Is it natural or mechanical? If it is two-dimensional (flat), what kind of support does it have? Is it mounted, matted, framed, or loose? If three-dimensional, what kinds of materials does it consist of? Is this object a single, unified structure or does it contain multiple parts that should be disassembled and handled independently? Especially in the absence of detailed records or immediate consultation, this line of investigation will guide our initial approach in determining how we prepare to engage the object, what kinds of materials and tools may be needed, and what kinds of additional questions may need to be answered by our colleagues or resources. At this point, it is less important to identify the precise processes or classification and more important to assess a general understanding about what the "thing" is.

Condition: There is much that can be gathered from a basic visual inspection. What state is the object in? Can this object be safely handled and moved without incurring any damage? Are there elements of the object that appear frail, brittle, loose, or delicate? Does this object have natural and secure areas to grip and hold? The general condition of the object may be evident through visual inspection but will many times also require additional input from the preparator's collection colleagues, including documented conservation or past condition reports. Evidence of conservation may not always be apparent and, especially in the case of object repair, will be areas of extreme fragility and may warrant special attention.

Scale: How large or small is the object? What are the defining characteristics as it pertains to its size (generalized but measured dimensions are key metrics that can inform basic parameters, such as whether or not the object will physically be able to fit through doorways or necessitate multiple handlers)? Will the size restrict or define the methods employed to achieve the desired outcome?

Weight: Similar to scale, a basic evaluation of the weight can immediately update the initial plan when moving any object, but especially three-dimensional objects and artifacts. If the initial descriptive information does not give conclusive insight into how heavy the object might be, a controlled examination of weight might be considered. Ensuring that the object is stable, has adequate cushion, and can in fact be handled (note your evaluation of the condition), performing a lift test (very slowly and carefully elevating the object just off from its station) can inform the preparator's next steps. Note: the safety of the preparation and handling staff must always be considered in addition to the object before performing any such evaluation of weight. Always follow recommended lifting and handling guidelines as outlined by your institutional safety compliance organization, such as OSHA (Occupational Safety and Health Administration) in the United States.

Attributes: Are there any unique or outstanding physical characteristics, beyond condition or classification, that might demand consideration in the handling of this object? Are there dimensional extremities that will need additional support or care when handling? Does this object have movable parts or parts that should be secured? Does the makeup of the object (the materials, the construction, the condition, etc.) warrant attention? Every different object will have its own idiosyncrasies that may or may not be discoverable in documentation or visual investigation—this is where the practical experience and prudence of a well-informed preparator is essential.

Beyond the physical object, the environment will play a central role in defining what should be considered and what might be needed in order to complete the objective. In evaluating the possible issues that may arise when engaging with objects and specimen, also consider the settings and situations surrounding said artifacts.

Current location of the object: What is the present status of the object: in storage, on display, or in a transitory setting? This information obviously dictates the handler's process and planning but can also inform the urgency of the move—objects in their permanent storage location are best left as is until a move is absolutely necessary and properly prepped. Similarly, objects on display should not be removed or handled until their location (be it permanent storage or transport packing) is ready to accept them without any simultaneous preparation or juggling of materials. Will the object's existing location allow handling to take place? Is there sufficient space to manipulate the object safely or to prepare the object for handling? This detail may result in a simple fix: the temporary displacement of furniture or obstruction or setting up a provisional workspace within the current environment. Alternatively, attempting to manipulate objects around impediments of any kind can be catastrophic: the handler's attention is no longer squarely focused on the safety of the object, but is preoccupied by having to traverse the hurdles of the environment from which the object is being removed.

Path: What are the details that pertain to the chosen route from point A to B? Is there a clear, direct, and unfettered passageway? Is the route free from obstruction or traffic? Are there environmental considerations such as inclement weather or variable road conditions that may force delay or postponement? Have interior factors that can impact the handling of an object been assessed, like the dimensions of egresses and the elevation of walkways? Seemingly small details—such as knowing if there are any closed doors that will need to be held open—can aid in the safe transport of objects.

Destination: Where does the object need to go? Is the destination or transport prepared to accept the object? Is there appropriate padding, bracing, mounts, or hardware in place where the object is to be transported? The ideal is to not be in the situation where you have to deposit the object in a state of provisional rest or temporary holding—every move is another opportunity for risk. The need for temporary housing or placement is sometimes unavoidable and almost always unexpected: the best practice for any collections care professional is to anticipate, to the best of their ability, what may be needed when an object is in transition and be ready with alternate approaches when challenges to these projects arise—at all times maintaining strict adherence to mitigating risk.

COMMUNICATION

The evaluation of the object and its surroundings is only one piece of the puzzle to effective handling and must work in tandem with clear and constant lines of communication. Gathering information about the task through evaluation will inevitably lead to additional questions and research—much of which might be answered by the existing experience and documentation collected by the curatorial and collections staff, or, those closely involved with the situation at hand. Using communication as the second pillar of our philosophical outline for handling, consider the hierarchy of contact that handling might require—from those engaged in direct contact with the object outward to the coordination of the project with external entities and collaborators.

Communication between handlers: The first level of immediate communication that needs to be maintained is that with the direct colleagues physically involved with the task—especially when multiple handlers are managing an object. This includes conversations of a well-defined plan *before the object is manipulated*: articulating every step and action that needs to take place, assigning responsibilities for the duration of the move, ensuring that each stage of the process is accepted and understood by those involved. Much of this discussion and planning will occur simultaneously during the evaluation, but details also evolve from it as information is assessed. This communicative connection is also imperative when the actual handling begins—a constant narration of the move ensures that the right hand knows what the left hand is doing at all times. Mistakes that can lead to calamitous situations will occur if one preparator is not clearly expressing a directional shift, a sudden adjustment, or a warning to alert the partners involved. While seemingly redundant, a continuous, audible account of the active handling of an object will eliminate a trove of possible assumption or misunderstanding.

A common technique applied in this aspect of direct communication is the use of physical gestures and signals to supplement the explanation of proposed action, visually illustrating the particulars of handling the object. There is no standard guide for these signals, and different institutions will develop their own unique series of signs and cues particular to their collections and spaces. There is however common practice among preparation staffs when clarifying basic movements and variations in orientation and axis. One such example is using the hand as a surrogate for the object when demonstrating variations in position, angle, and transition. This method is particularly effective (but certainly not exclusive) when the object is relatively two-dimensional, such as a frame, painting, or panel: extending the hand flat to mimic every variation in position and orientation to eliminate any confusion about the course of action. Additional gestures that can be incorporated into the lexicon might reference height variance (doorways, passages, or other obstructions) and directional position (especially when one handler is forced to travel backward to best support the object). Most importantly, one must always remember to maintain stable control of the object at all times, and that any such gestures can only be done if and when the object is at a stable resting point—never while in transit or being actively maneuvered.

Communication with collections staff: Beyond the clear interaction between handlers, there is necessary conference that must be instigated within the collections department. This communication is a two-way road: the registrar, conservator or curator will many times be administering, supervising, or delegating the details of the project to the preparation staff. At the same time, the handlers and preparators will look to their collection colleagues for insight and answers about the object—before, during, and in response to the evaluative process. The wealth of information preserved in the documentation managed by the registrars, including condition reports, donor records, and original accession worksheets are an invaluable resource for the preparator in organizing a handling assignment. Conservation records, assessments, photo-documentation, and consultation from your conservator will also supplement and inform the approach to handling, preparation, and installation of the object. While the preparators, handlers, and techs may be the institutional professionals physically managing an object, the colleagues of the collection staff play key roles in the process—responsible for determining location, verifying condition, and support and supervision. Handling objects without this communication is like handling in the dark, with no direction or destination.

Communication with other departments: Just as the fine-tuned choreography of the collections and curatorial departments is a key factor in effective handling, a well-informed museum or gallery staff will aid to ensure the safe and successful management of any object-related task. Keeping the administration of the institution up-to-date with the schedule of movement and installation will not only create a supportive infrastructure but may prevent unintended mistakes that can result from siloed departmental decision-making. What are the active projects happening in the colleague divisions of your space? Are their physical plant renovations, on-site contractors, or programs and events that should be considered in your plan and schedule?

Communication with lenders, donors, and makers: Akin to the crucial interaction within the collections or institutional team regarding object-specific documentation and history, a similar coordination with external resources that are closely associated with the object will help to inform the handling of borrowed or proposed donations to your permanent collection. In the case of institutional loans, where the object is being temporarily transferred from one formalized collection to the next, the communication will filter from the designated colleague parties (curators, collections managers or registrars) to inform the "home" staff about any special instruction of object history. In the case of non-institutional loan or donation, while these resources may be less formal than standard institutional reporting, the direct knowledge that can be collected from the current owners and (especially) the makers and artists can be just as relevant, if not more so. In regard to a collector or owner, this communication may not include conservation-level or professional assessment but can/should certainly include information that informs current location and environment, a discussion of (known) provenance, and even photo-documentation to illustrate an objects current state before the handling is initiated. Similarly, from the perspective of correspondence with a maker, the insight about the process of creation, materials used, and specialized instruction regarding the objects in question is invaluable. It should also be noted that the information and instruction that comes from a collector, craftsman or maker is rarely from the perspective of the collections professional, and should be weighed with this distinction in mind: while they may suggest particulars of handling and care, this will not always reflect the same level of best practice that your institution requires.

Communication with shippers and contractors: There will inevitably be external entities that impact the management of objects. These situations can include fine art shippers, crate fabricators, on-site riggers, commissioned scholars and appraisers: there are countless peripheral factors that may need to be addressed in order to mitigate risk to an object in transition. The essential communication in these cases includes active scheduling and coordination but also includes accurate evaluative information and institutional details: for fabricators—Are your object dimensions thorough and accurate? For shippers—Have you clearly indicated points of loading, egress, and pathways? Even if the primary contact person is not the preparator or handler (this correspondence will commonly be delegated to the registrar or collections manager), the information that feeds this consultation will originate from the preparation and handling staff, and the consistency of this communication is vital when the project at hand demands external assistance or consult.

COMMON SENSE

Common sense is the final anchor of an effective handling doctrine. It is the facet of the process that is most often lost or forgotten, as it is not specific to the museum profession but carries equal value to those aspects specific to working in collections. Matters of common sense, in regard to handling and managing objects, are largely an implicit qualification: most institutional professionals consider issues of basic awareness and prudence to be second nature when stewardship of collections is concerned. However, it is the lack of common sense, avoidable mistakes, not being properly prepared for the task at hand, or barreling ahead without proper planning or personnel that illustrate the core relevance and magnitude that this component bears on our handling philosophy.

Don't be a hero: Another way to phrase this would be to use the axiom "There is no 'I' in TEAM." The careful work of a preparator is one that often demands collaboration and practical judgment: If you need help, get help. If there's no help, wait for help. This is especially applicable when considering the principal objective of mitigating risk and the potential harm that might be done if and when deciding to take on an otherwise shared task alone or without consultation. In the sphere of object handling, this can manifest frequently in a variety of scenarios: removing a painting from a wall that is beyond manageable scale or reach; hand-carrying an artifact through doorways and terrain without the assistance of a partner to clear your path; and taking the initiative to clean, mend, or alter an object without consultation or approval. What triggers these lapses in common sense? All too often, this is a matter of time management.

Control the schedule, don't let the schedule control you: Significant aspects of the preparator's responsibilities are tied to a schedule—dates for shipping and transport and deadlines for installation and exhibition (see chapter 4, "Project Management"). One of the greatest contributors to foolish mistakes due to a lack of common sense reasoning is when the operation is rushed or stressed due to the imposed overarching timeline. Internally, installation delays and unforeseen issues with the amount of time techniques may take or access to the appropriate materials will always place a strain on the preparation process, but it is absolutely essential that the needs of the objects are paramount to an imposed schedule, never the reverse. Externally, the time frame may be impacted by the collaborating institution/owners, or the shippers and contractors hired to facilitate aspects of your project, but these interruptions must be absorbed into the overall timetable in relation to the needs of the objects at hand or the responsibility of the institution: if an object crate has been delivered by a handling courier and appears to exhibit damage, it is the responsibility of a representative of the accepting institution to stop the process and investigate. This freeze creates the domino effect of delay, not only with your project but also with the shipper's schedule. The conscientious professional will never allow a cranky shipper to override the need to stop, evaluate, investigate, and confirm that the object is safe. This situation may be uncomfortable but a necessary control, as once a representative of the institution accepts the delivery, that institution is then culpable for the condition of the objects in transit.

Be prepared: If you're going to be dealing with artifacts on external sites or in uncontrolled environments, simple decisions, like wearing the appropriate clothing for the task—no loose accessories or layers that may become a hindrance; choosing closed-toed shoes or even steel-toed boots—can make an enormous difference during the handling of objects. Having the appropriate and necessary tools on hand *in advance*, informed by the evaluative process but before direct engagement with the object, will prevent a disruption in active handling when focus needs to be squarely on the task at hand. If performing an external project, be sure that you have adequate inventories of materials or tools needed, anticipating the possibility of expanding needs or problem-solving. And, in concert with evaluation and communication, being prepared means using the data gathered and asking the right questions to the appropriate resources and colleagues to arm the preparation process with information that can be used to facilitate a successful and safe outcome.

TOOLS AND MATERIALS: OBJECT HANDLING

The well-equipped preparator will always have on hand a few tools that are not specific to the field but integral in the process: a quality measuring device for evaluation (a dual-inch/metric tape measure with a true zero hook is best, as well as a fabric tape measure for sensitive and dimensional surfaces) and an extendable snap-off blade that allows for trimming, cutting, and shaping variable materials. These tools are ubiquitous among many trades and can easily be found at local hardware or home stores. There are also those tools and materials that are industry standard for the specialized needs of proper object handling when working in collections and exhibitions.

Gloves

One of the universal tropes of museum and gallery work is the omnipresent use of white cotton gloves. While it is true that in order to protect objects from harm or damage, particularly from the dirt and oils deposited from the handler's skin, gloves are an essential barrier. However, the decision to wear gloves, and what kind of gloves are most appropriate, is not a foregone conclusion—different kinds of

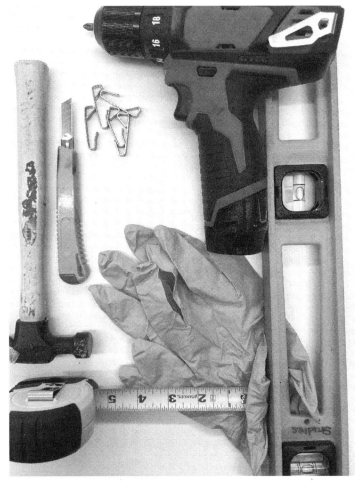

Figure 2.2. Basic Handling Tools: Tape Measures, Knives, Gloves, Level, and Hardware. *Source*: Image credit: Andrew Saluti.

objects will require different kinds of handling, including the decision to wear or not wear protective gloves. The central consideration is informed by the balance between tactility and impact: how much sensitivity to touch is needed to properly handle the object versus the end results and potential effects of using (or not using) the selected protection. The most common and accepted types of gloves are nitrile, cotton, and leather.

Nitrile gloves are the most common, versatile, and widely accepted type of glove when handling most objects. They offer the greatest amount of physical tactility when manipulating a variety of media and will not leave marks or residue. The material is chemically stable, creates an impermeable barrier between the skin and the object, and allows for a firm grip on many surfaces. When selecting nitrile gloves, be sure to select the appropriate size for a snug fit and choose the powder-free option. The drawback to nitrile gloves are durability and sustainability. While they do supply an excellent barrier and touch, they are easily broken and may need to be replaced often. In addition, there is current debate on the ability to recycle these materials, especially considering the disposability and frequency of use.[5] Biodegradable nitrile gloves are now beginning to become more widely available.

Cotton gloves also create a safe barrier between the skin and the surface of the object and will rarely abrade or scratch. While they do offer less tactility than nitrile, cotton gloves are reusable. They are ideal for handling sensitive surfaces and materials including photographs, books, and paintings but are disadvantageous when dealing with objects comprised of fibrous materials, such as wood or natural weavings—the fabric can easily catch on these surfaces. Never use cotton gloves with the vinyl or rubber friction dots, as these can adversely impact many surfaces.

Leather gloves are not always considered in collections care but are essential for the preparation staff and handlers. These common work gloves should always be used for protection and grip when dealing with crates and storage devices, building supplies and materials such as corrugated board, plywood, and acrylic sheets, and gallery and exhibition furniture, pedestals, and bases. These gloves can also provide support and protection when handling exterior sculpture, such as fabricated media and cast metals, where other options would not withstand the stress of the task.

There are also situations where it is best to not wear any type of glove, when the tactility of touch is paramount to the safety of the object handled. This is common in archival collections, when handling various types of documents or volumes. Fragile works on paper may also necessitate the direct feel of your fingers in order to maintain ultimate control during the handling or preparation task. In these cases, *clean hands* are essential—thoroughly washing and drying your hands before any contact with these materials, as well as intermittent wash depending on the task(s) and materials involved, will help reduce any permanent damage to the objects.

There are also gloves that should be avoided when handling objects. Rubber gloves are not ideal for collections or preparation applications. While they can create a barrier between the skin and object, they are chemically less stable than nitrile and quickly decompose or degrade, opening the potential for transferring residue from the glove onto the objects being handled. Similarly, latex and vinyl gloves pose similar risks, as well as the potential for allergic reaction when in contact with the skin.

Polyethylene Foam

In order to provide a secure, yet cushioned environment for any dimensional object, the standard material utilized is polyethylene foam padding and sheeting. Polyethylene is the preferred choice by many collections and preparation staff for its versatility and stability and comes in a wide variety of densities and extruded shapes and sizes. Polyethylene foam is an ideal material for use when handling objects for many reasons. First, these foams are *inert*: they decompose at an extremely slow rate and do not release chemicals into the environment or onto the surfaces they are in contact with. They can be a closed-cell material and are a *hydrophobic*, non-wicking material that repels liquids. Polyethylene materials are generally *nonabrasive*: when placed in contact with object surfaces, they retain their structure and provide a forgiving yet firm support that will absorb shock and impact while still maintaining a durable cradle or base for the object.

Common brand names of archival polyethylene products are Ethafoam® and Volara® and can be purchased from various suppliers of archival products, but generic sheets in variable thicknesses and densities can also be purchased from your local shipping or industrial suppliers.

Polyethylene is most commonly used in two standard structures: dimensional block padding or thinner sheeting. The foam block can be easily cut and shaped to conform to the contours of the object when support is needed in crates, storage devises, or even for display. The foam block can be fused to create larger forms of any size (the standard dimension of the material ranges from usually a 2-inch width at most, 1/4 inch at minimum). The block density is also variable; a 2- to 2.2-pound foam will provide a more resilient support for heavier, less fragile surfaces, while those that require more cushion can be cradled by a 1.5- to 1.7-pound foam block.

Figure 2.3. Two-Inch and One-Inch Polyethylene Foam Block. *Source*: Image credit: Andrew Saluti.

In sheet form, polyethylene provides a customizable protective layer of padding that can literally wrap around an object. In its sheet form, polyethylene foam is an ideal cushion to add a protective layer to flat and glazed objects, act as a wadding to support cavities and crevices, or create a temporary cushion lining around dimensional objects or artifacts. One particularly useful variation is antistatic sheeting: material that retains the same attributes that make polyethylene ideal for objects, with an antistatic additive to eliminate conductivity that is generated from the charge built up on acrylic surfaces from friction and vibration.

Transportation Carts

One of the easiest ways to mitigate risk when handling and transporting objects is to provide a stable and secure structure during the process, taking the potential physical strain off the object as well as the handlers. These devices can take many forms, some object-specific (crates, sleds, and other supports made exclusively for a single object or type) and others intended for a more universal functionality, such as padded utility and A-frame carts. These tools of the trade are indispensable to the collections and exhibitions staff and, together with protective gloves and polyethylene padding, are the core tools and materials for orchestrating effective object handling and care.

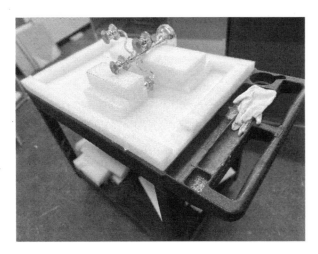

Figure 2.4. Padded Transportation Cart for Securely Moving Objects. *Source*: Image credit: Andrew Saluti.

Top loaded utility cart: These carts are present in most collection-based institutions used primarily for the internal movement of smaller objects from space to space, storage to public display and then back again. Ideally these carts are fully cushioned (with polyethylene or furniture pads/blankets) to accommodate the various needs of that institutional collection. The elevated height of the transport cavity allows the handler an easy transition when manipulating the object between environments, as well as allowing for storage below the object base for additional materials: foam blocking, clean gloves, and other collection-specific supplies. Multiple size-appropriate objects can be cradled and supported with additional foam blocking on the cart bed, allowing for a moderated, cushioned journey between destinations.

A-frame: The A-frame cart is a specialized transport vehicle that is designed to allow two-dimensional/wall-based objects to rest in a vertical orientation on a supported and backed structure. The A-frame is the best way to transport paneled and framed objects, stretched canvas: any object that is meant to be installed on a gallery wall. This tool is especially valuable when there is a need to move or handle ornate and/or delicate frames, as the direct strain of handling (in relation to the weight and physicality of the object) is distributed across the structure of the cart, which can be padded and blocked to protect any embellishments, surfaces, or decorative appendages that the frame or object may have.

Floor dollies and furniture movers: While not exclusively associated with collections care and handling, these common moving instruments are constantly needed when handling large objects, crated, wrapped, or otherwise protected objects, as well as supplemental materials such as gallery furniture, pedestals, casework, and other frequently utilized components in the world of museum and gallery preparation.

UNIVERSAL HANDLING TIPS

The following are general suggestions and best practice for object handling. For detailed instruction for the handling of specific media and objects, refer to your institution's collection care guidelines, consultation with collections managers, registrars, conservators and curators, or published resources for collections care.

When transporting any object, always manage the object with two hands. In the case of hand-held situations, use one hand to carry the weight and one hand to stabilize. The same direction goes for multi-staff handling or when using a vehicle such as a padded cart or A-frame.

Whenever possible, always use a transportation device when moving objects. Hand-held transportation should generally be a last resort depending on the specific situation.

Avoid traversing stairs or inconsistent terrain that might destabilize or distract the handlers from their focus on the object. Always plan paths in advance that will allow for the most consistent and clear movement.

Always separate multiple pieces—never try and handle objects with multiple parts as one whole. Secure small parts on a padded cart and separate with foam blocking.

If transporting objects external to that object's home space, encapsulate the object in a closed and secure environment. When possible, transport the object in its natural orientation (if there is one). This is particularly important when handling works that have been mounted or fixed, especially for objects with extreme dimensions or (in the case of paintings) heavy impasto.

When handling objects, maneuver backward as little as possible in order to maintain a clear line of sight.

Save polyethylene waste when shaping foam blocking for objects; these can be easily reused for object support, elevated object rests, and mounts and cradles.

NOTES

1. Powell, Brent. *Collection Care: An Illustrated Handbook for the Care and Handling of Cultural Objects* (Rowman & Littlefield: New York, 2015).
2. "Agents of Deterioration," Canadian Conservation Institute, Government of Canada website, September 26, 2017. Accessed October 21, 2019. https://www.canada.ca/en/conservation-institute/services/agents-deterioration.html.
3. "Who We Are / What We Do," Northeast Document Conservation Center website. Accessed October 21, 2019. https://www.nedcc.org/about/overview.
4. "What Is Preservation?" Northeast Document Conservation Center website, *Preservation 101*, 2015, Accessed October 28, 2019. https://www.nedcc.org/preservation101/session-1/1what-is-preservation.
5. See the New England Museum Association's online publication "Choices: Gloves for Objects, People, and the Planet," organized by their Sustainable Museums Team in 2015. https://nemanet.org/files/9914/4009/2048/Green_Museum_Gloves.pdf.

REFERENCES

Elkin, Lisa, E. Nunan, and Dieter Fenkart-Froeschl. "Collections Risk Management Program at the American Museum of Natural History." *Collections: A Journal for Museum and Archives Professionals*, Volume 9, Number 1, Winter 2013, pp. 125–138.

"Equipment and Tools." University Products website. Accessed November 1, 2019. https://www.universityproducts.com/equipment-tools.

"How to Select Gloves: An Overview for Collections Staff." *Conserv-O-Gram*, September 2010, Number 1/12. National Parks Service. Accessed October 24, 2019. https://www.nps.gov/museum/publications/conserveogram/01-12.pdf.

"Preventative Care." American Institute for Conservation wiki, updated November 2, 2020. Accessed November 18, 2020. http://www.conservation-wiki.com/wiki/Preventive_Care.

"Preventive Conservation and Risk Management." Canadian Conservation Institute, Government of Canada website, July 31, 2018. Accessed October 21, 2019. https://www.canada.ca/en/services/culture/history-heritage/museology-conservation/preservation-conservation/preventive-conservation.html.

Richard, Mervin, Marion F. Mecklenburg, and Ross M. Merrill, eds. *Art in Transit: Handbook for Packing and Transporting Paintings* (Washington, DC: National Gallery of Art, 1991).

"Storage and Handling/Carts and Trucks." Gaylord Archival Products website. Accessed November 1, 2019. https://www.gaylord.com/c/Carts-and-Trucks.

3

Preparation in Action

PACK IT, BUT DON'T TOUCH IT: A CASE STUDY OF THE TROPE

Meredith Wiemer, Associate Registrar, The Nelsen-Atkins Museum of Art

Being asked to pack an object without handling it is a challenging request that many collections care professionals are familiar with hearing. The increased sensitivity regarding the handling of such an object is typically an indicator that the work's condition is vulnerable in a way that is unique to it. An object is most at risk when it is being moved, and an object with a fragile surface or a delicate component is even more prone to accidental damage during the transitions of handling and packing. The process of safely packing an object that is prone to damage sometimes requires the creativity and expertise of several museum professionals. My experience packing, *Verity* (*magenta blue*), by Nicole Chesney at the Museum of Fine Arts, Boston (MFA), is my personal anecdotal tribute to the trope: "Pack it, but don't touch it."

Verity (*magenta blue*) is one panel of a three panel series created by Nicole Chesney in 2001. Her works are known for their unique surface qualities that seem to change with the light and position of the viewer. The oil-painted surfaces of the panel (edges included) are uneven by design, with some sections presenting as medium rich and others having a less robust effect due to the dilution of the paint. The areas with thin paint coverage were the most susceptible to scratches and abrasion damage from overhandling and were the basis for concern during the packing of this piece. It was requested that the handling of *Verity* (*magenta blue*) was restricted to only essential movement.

In January 2020, *Verity* (*magenta blue*) was deinstalled at the MFA and temporarily placed on a rolling A-frame cart, while it was examined by conservation staff and awaited packing by collections care staff. The piece's riding edge rested on a strip of 4# density 1-inch ethafoam which had been wrapped in a sheet of acid-free archival paper. The selected density of the ethafoam that supported the panel was significant because the temporary riding edge needed to rest on the foam but not sink into it under its weight which would risk damage to the face and painted edges. The acid-free paper acted as an additional protective barrier between the textured surface of the ethafoam and *Verity* (*magenta blue*)'s riding edge.

The packing of this piece was planned by collections care specialists with input and direction from two conservators who were familiar with the work's composition and condition. It was decided that the panel should be packed upright and stored inside a poplar travel frame. A "travel frame" is a term used by art storage professionals that refers to a type of narrow slat crate (typically under 10 inches in overall depth) that are primarily used to house paintings. Poplar is the type of wood that is commonly used to crate museum collections because it is the lowest acid-emitting wood available. This lessens the amount of harmful off-gassing that might occur within the crate as the lumber ages. To protect the painted edges of the panel, *Verity (magenta blue)* would be hung inside its crate using the two pairs of cleats with which it was installed. A layer of 2# density 1-inch ethafoam would be adhered to the floor of the crate as a precaution in case of hanging hardware failure. Light blocking material was also requested as an addition to the crate after packing was completed to protect the object's painted surface from exposure to light which could cause the color to fade over time.

The handling of this work was extremely limited, occurring only twice after deinstallation. The steel installation cleats attached to the back of the panel were largely used for maneuvering these works, sparing the delicate surfaces from unnecessary handling. *Verity (magenta blue)* was permitted to be leaned forward and away from the cart so that a conservator could dust and vacuum the back of the panel and then again a second time when it was leaned forward to provide access to the top cleat which would be employed for lifting the panel.

The set of installation cleats used to install this work would be critical in the handling and subsequent packing of the piece. *Verity (magenta blue)* has two steel cleats adhered to its back; these were added prior to its acquisition by the MFA in 2010. One cleat is located 4 inches below the works' top edge and opens downward. The other cleat is located 4 inches above the works' bottom edge and faces upward. The opposing nature of this hardware would later prove advantageous when securing the panel within its crate. The corresponding cleats that were wall-mounted for installation of this object were fastened to two battens of 1 × 4-inch poplar. These cleat battens would be used to replicate the work's installation on a gallery wall inside the travel frame.

One batten would be used to engage the top cleat and lift the panel, while the other batten would be used to engage the panel's bottom cleat. The battens were cut to a length that extended 6 inches past the piece's side edges, allowing for space to manipulate the battens by hand at a safe distance from the panel. Prior to moving *Verity (magenta blue)* into its crate, the batten that would correspond with the panel's bottom cleat was temporarily attached to the interior back wall of the travel frame. Preparation of the crate also included adding two blocks of 1 × 4-inch poplar to the interior back wall of the travel frame. These blocks would be used to support the lifting batten inside the crate, suspending the panel slightly above the layer of ethafoam on the crate floor.

The process of moving this object into its crate began with two collections care specialists simultaneously lifting the top cleat batten to transfer the weight of the panel onto it via its hanging cleat. A third specialist was present while the work was in transit, keeping their gloved hands close to the object, in case emergency handling was required. After the handlers successfully guided the panel into its upright travel frame, the lifting batten was rested on the two support blocks within the crate, and the batten was screwed into the interior rear wall of the crate. The bottom batten was then unscrewed from its temporary position and guided down to engage the corresponding bottom cleat on the work's verso. Once in place, this batten was also attached with screws to the crate's rear interior wall.

Like with any packing project, our goal was to secure *Verity (magenta blue)* within its crate to inhibit movement in all possible directions. We accounted for upward bounce by using the bottom cleat batten to apply downward pressure to the corresponding cleat on the piece. While forward motion of the face was prevented by the interlocking shape of the two pairs of cleats and the addition of 1/8-inch Volara in the channel of the cleat which improved the seal, any shifting of the panel from side to side in the cleat tracks was avoided by attaching four blocks of poplar to the rear interior wall of the crate that extended from the interior edges of the crate to the end of the cleat tracks.

After *Verity (magenta blue)* was thoroughly secured inside its crate, two 1/8-inch sheets of Coroplast were cut to cover the spaces between the front and back slats of the travel frame to limit the panel's exposure to light. After these sheets were screwed into place, the front slats were reattached, and packing was complete. In preparation for this piece to travel on an art shipping truck, special instructions were added to the exterior of the crate to inform handlers of specific shipping requirements. In particular, we indicated that the travel frame should sit on a sheet of ethafoam in the box of the truck to protect it from the vibration that can be transferred from the floor of the truck to the body of the crate.

Packing an object with specific condition concerns provides an opportunity for collaboration and creativity within the field of collections care. The stewardship demonstrated during the packing of this panel was a result of the advocacy made for its care by MFA staff. Luckily, Nichole Chesney's *Verity* (*magenta blue*) was given a voice by those who cared for it in perpetuity, a voice which demanded a specialized approach and fortified the classic art handling trope: "Pack it, but don't touch it."

4

Preparation Management

As the preparator's core responsibilities largely revolve around all things object and/or collections-related, including standards of handling, installation, and packing, this charge must also extend to the management and administration of that preparation process. Each and every task associated with the preparation of objects carries with it chronological and financial commitments, orchestrated and supervised by an informed and practiced collections professional: from coordinating contractors to overseeing internal staff to problem-solving the inevitable unexpected predicament(s) that are common to the nature of the field. An effective preparator must be equipped to juggle the multiple balls of responsibility all the while continuing to be laser-focused on the needs of the object or installation task at hand.

This administration is an often unseen, and frequently an untaught skill set, sought after and essential for any institution's preparation staff. The challenge is that there can be a multitude of circumstances and conditions that inform and influence effective preparation management. The knowledge of how much time and budget to allocate to specific tasks will often depend on specific extenuating factors and project-specific details. Proximity and access to professional services such as acrylic fabrication, framing and archival suppliers, and packing and shipping services will greatly affect both the timeline and budget for any project. Equally impactful is the number of internal preparation staff to do the work, and whether these colleagues are part-time or full-time, their experience level and/or their specialty or expertise. In smaller to midsized museums, there can be as few as a single staff member dedicated to prepatory responsibilities, and, just as often, these duties might be delegated to collections staffing, maybe with irregular assistance of part-time or contract workers. The institution itself—the capabilities of the facilities—has an enormous impact on what kinds of preparation can be facilitated and controlled internally versus the need to outsource and contract.

In most cases, the experience of past projects will offer the best guidance when forecasting project planning—that is, what your institution or team accomplished in the past will be the gauge for what one can expect moving forward. This is especially significant for those new to the position: leveraging the experience of colleagues and organizational history as a primary resource. In other cases, there will be a need for proactive research and communication between vendors, contract staff, and internal colleagues to estimate timetables and expense. While many tasks are routine, there are equally as many problem-solving situations and the need for creative solutions. This isn't to say that there is no baseline to start from when plotting out projects: the professional best practice standards of preparation work can easily establish the beginnings of a novice administrative calendar and budget.

For the preparator and their larger preparation staff, *time* is one of our most precious commodities. It is a resource that demands to be nurtured, managed, and valued just as efficiently as the calculated use of archival supplies and equally prized as the trusted relationships with craftsmen and contractors that we cultivate. Effective time management will prove to be the difference between opening an exhibition with or without the frenzied last-minute scramble of to-dos and final touches, or the even more distressing scenario of having to open an exhibition to the public unfinished. Improper time management can place objects that are being handled, packed, or shipped at inherent risk, as the stressor of an impending deadline or timetable will inevitably result in a lack of common sense best practice. Properly managing this timetable is also imperative to controlling the project budget, making sure that all tasks are accomplished on a schedule that will (hopefully) not require last-minute shipments or added hourly labor. In museum preparation and installation, the adage does in fact ring true: *time is money*.

SUPPLY MANAGEMENT

In addition to regulating and optimizing workflow, effective preparation management is also reflected in the on-hand readiness and practical use of archival materials. A significant portion of preparation materials are highly specialized resources not easily procured at an instant or available locally, or can also be of a scale that mandates an additional freight or shipping expense. Part of the preparation management equation is having the needed materials on hand, in time. Beyond any one singular assignment, a well-managed preparation space will be equipped with the necessary supplies well in advance of project timeline or will include the procurement of needed materials in the overall scope of project. A regular materials inventory of preparation space supplies should be a common and essential responsibility among preparation teams—making this a routine task (monthly or project to project) can ensure that the team will have what they need, when they need it—and minimize project slowdown or bottleneck (and budget impact) due to the unforeseen ordering and shipping of materials.

Maximizing your archival materials is also crucial. Not only are archival and object preparation supplies not usually locally available, but they also come at a greater expense than most general supplies. Museum-quality mounting boards and mat boards, UV filtered glazing, and other archival-quality supplies need to be treated as a finite resource in the preparation space. An efficient way to minimize waste is *planned use* in prepping materials: mapping the optimum usage for the materials on hand. Forecasting the ideal usage of archival mat board is an excellent example: once the project has been defined and the preparation need has been established, the preparator should consider and strategize how they will prepare the needed materials using the least amount of resource. This can be achieved through a conscious approach to the trimming of material as well as the order in which materials are used: if you know you will need to prepare a number of 20 × 16-inch-sized board for matting, consider that the standard size board (40 × 32 inches), if cut ideally, will result in 4 prepped sheets per board. Add in additional 20 × 24-inch finished sizes; now, depending on quantity, one might consider using half the raw material for one piece of 20 × 24 and the remaining half for two 16 × 20 pieces. Drawing out this materials plan will help to visualize the best outcome with the least amount of waste. Another useful tip specific to cutting window mats: the drop out that is cut away from the top mat (see chapter 7) can be a usable piece of board for smaller objects. When planning a project, starting with the larger objects first and working down through the checklist according to scale will make best use of the archival materials. If an error is made in process (which inevitably will happen), many times the errant material can be repurposed for smaller sizes. This approach is applicable for many other aspects of object preparation and will support minimal supply waste and offset impacts to the preparation budget.

PREPARATION PROJECT MANAGEMENT

When formulating an organized workflow for exhibition installations and/or object preparation in collections settings, there are core variables that are consistent, regardless of the size of the institution or specific details of the project. The following identified elements will consistently serve as the foundation for virtually any kind of preparation-related task. Outlining these factors, specific to the task or project at hand, should be step one in the preparator's administrative duties. Regardless of how these are visualized or applied (i.e., mobile applications, shared spreadsheets, or physical charts), the input data and goals will be the same. Looking outside the museum field to the concepts and philosophies of business and project management, the preparator can best equip themselves to manage any myriad of tasks.

There are existing management methodologies that exist to help inform the unique needs of the collections-oriented projects. The Critical Path Method (CPM) of managing projects, first created by the DuPont company in the 1950s, visualizes the path of any project by linking all the activities needed to reach a final goal as blocks or checkpoints that need to be completed before moving forward to the next stage of the project. Put simply, it is a guide that informs how you get from the A to the B to the C of any project, like arrows directing a path. Using the CPM method enables the project manager to see a map of all the components of a simple or multifaceted job that can also include time frames. This is especially helpful when, much like many of the preparator's duties, there are numerous activities happening at once in order for the project to progress. For example, mounting an exhibition of works on paper might follow a path from (A) unmounted storage to (B) matting to mounting to (C) framing to (D) installation. Using the CPM, a preparator can outline these tasks, according to an estimated timetable for each step, and can be charting the concurrent gallery preparation before installation simultaneously.

Another model that informs the administration of museum or collections projects is the Triple Constraint Method (TCM), sometimes referred to as the project management triangle or the "iron triangle." The TCM is a management concept that specifies three factors that govern the successful completion of an assignment: budget, personnel, and time. Working within these parameters is requisite to running an effective preparation project. While this can be applied to any administered project, including those that are collections-/object-based, a slight augmentation of this model that incorporates the components of the CPM can act as the preparator's consistent guide for outlining the foundation of project management: a new triangle that includes the scope of the project, the timeline according to deadlines, and the available or needed staff.

When employing this project management methodology for gallery installations, handling, or any object-related task, the universal components to consider are the *what*, the *when*, and the *who*.

Scope of Project (What)

This can be a direct list of breadcrumbs that lead to the final result or can be a complex tree of multiple tasks that must be completed before moving onto the next, articulated by the same elements of the aforementioned evaluative procedures of handling: the object and the environment. The most effective way to identify a complete view of all necessary tasks is to organize the project into these two main categories, creating hierarchal outlines derived from each unique object- or environment-oriented circumstance. What has to be accomplished? What are the procedural steps necessary to get to the final outcome as directed by the objects involved and the environment in which they reside or will inhabit?

Specific details to consider in relation to preparation needs:

- Genre or media of objects: How many separate kinds of objects will require separate kinds of preparation? What can be done concurrently, and what needs to be done progressively?
- Condition or state of objects: Does the project require matting, framing, cleaning, or more involved conservation?
- Specific types of preparation for project (exhibition, storage, and shipping): Inventory of supplies.
- Condition and needs of the new environment (particularly in relation to any preceding objects or installation).

A Timeline of the Project (When)

The preparator's duties are commonly dictated by a calendar relating to public presentation or access. This can take the form of the movement of objects in and out of spaces according to the institution's "dark" calendar (when museum and collection spaces are closed to the public) or can be the countdown to when an installation first opens to the public. These scenarios also relate to art and object handling situations, in regard to the availability of controlled access to the objects and spaces in question, for example, coordinating the pickup or delivery of objects to private residencies or commercial spaces around a low traffic, ultimate convenience of, or the absence of residents in a space. In any of these circumstances, the preparator commonly estimates a timeline based on an imposed deadline—a point at which accomplishing the work in an effective way is no longer available or viable. In order to manage this calendar, a reverse (or backward) schedule creates a pragmatic estimation for when certain tasks need to be completed in order to meet the desired target. In tandem, an informed valuation of the amount of time each particular task will take is needed to complete this picture and to suggest the initiation of work. This is best informed by experience, recognizing the capabilities of the staff and institution, but if such institutional or personal knowledge is not available or doesn't exist, the best course of action is to use resources such as professional consultation or networks, especially from independent contractors or colleague institutions.

Most importantly, when developing a timeline for your project, it is best practice to overestimate the amount of time per task, in order to account for unforeseen circumstances, delays, or problems. While there is no standard equation for creating this cushion of time, a common approach is to double the allotted time given to any task. This will reinforce the *common sense* pillar of preparation and handling: avoiding mistakes that will arise from the inflicted stress of a rushed or hastened calendar and can also absorb unanticipated delays or setbacks. In short, this overestimation gives the preparation team and process adequate time to focus on the safe and careful preparation of objects and spaces. Additional considerations on this time frame include the following:

- The shipping of supplies and travel time for contract work: If inventory needs to be replenished or special ordered, what is the lead time on delivery? How long will contract work take to be in hand or on premises?
- Consideration of external or tandem institutional projects: What else is happening in or around the project that might pause, impede, or take attention away from task?

A List of Personnel Involved (Who)

The final core factor that inserts itself into the equation for effectively managing object and gallery preparation is the team of professionals engaged to complete the task. This also happens to be the piece that is most inconsistent and variable within different institutions, entirely dependent on the size, scope, and budget of the space. While the previously noted *what* and *when* components of preparation projects will be relatively consistent elements, the "who" component will be contingent on a variety of variables, including the museum's staffing and the allocated project budget to hire contractors and/or temporary staff, as well as the outlined details (*what* and *when*) of the project itself. Will the project be able to be completed with the full-time preparation staff or are there details of the project that will require skills and labor not present in the current pool of salaried employees?

Equally important when evaluating the staff needed to complete the project is to recognize that even though one might have the skills to carry out the task, does the burden of responsibility outweigh the time it will take to complete? One example might be in gallery preparation: a skilled preparator would certainly be proficient in repairing and painting walls when readying a gallery for a new exhibition; the amount of time that this task takes away from other items on the to-do list may not be financially worth the preparator's attention in relation to more pressing or expertise-related assignments.

Sometimes trying to keep everything in-house, while on the surface may seem fiscally prudent, in reality will cost more due to the amount of time spent and attention diverted. Good preparation management will identify the best use of staffing needs in concert with the necessary duties, most effective use of allocated budget, and the identified timeline. Additional considerations directly related to staffing:

- Is there a budget available to hire contract or part-time assistance to complete the project?

- Assessing the strengths and weaknesses in your preparation team will be an invaluable asset when organizing and outlining the preparation process. Who will be ideal to complete specialized or skill-based tasks most efficiently? Who will need guidance, and who will be able to work independently?

VISUALIZING THE DATA

Once this bank of baseline information is collected, one can input and organize all the exponents of the project into an easy to read and accessible workflow chart—one that combines all three elements into a singular reference that administers *who* should be doing *what* by *when*. This basic workflow chart can be generated and presented in a variety of ways, from something as simple as self-adhesive paper notes on a bulletin board to something as refined as a tailored mobile management application. In any event, the aggregation of this data into a usable and functional management tool for most preparation and installation projects, illustrating and organizing duties and progress, can best be displayed through the century-old business management method of a Gantt chart.

The eponymous technique was developed in the 1910s by Henry Laurence Gantt (1861–1919), a draftsman, mechanical engineer, and later industrial management consultant and theorist. His innovative and visual approach to showing process and progress of industrial production has enormous, worldwide impact in the burgeoning field of project management and was used in monumental endeavors in the United States including the Hoover Dam (1931) and Eisenhower's Interstate Highway System in the 1950s. The Gantt chart not only displays the staffing assigned to specific tasks against the frame of a calendar but also provides a visual monitor that will inform decision-making as the project progresses or stalls, informing the preparation team when and where to reallocate resources and support as needed.

Creating this indispensable management tool is relatively straightforward once the previously outlined details of the project have been gathered and assessed. The next step is to plug all of these elements into a model that assigns responsibilities, delineates workflow, and informs progress. In its most basic form, a preparator's Gantt chart is a planar calendar grid informed by two axis, much like an *x* and *y* line graph but with the inclusion of modular elements. The first vector (*x*), indicating time, is illustrated on the horizontal plane. The second (*y*) identifies the personnel involved in the project. The

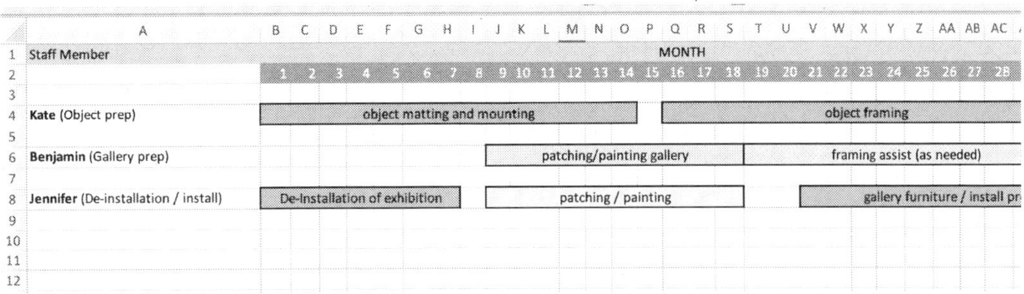

Figure 4.1. Simple spreadsheet Gantt Chart graph for exhibition preparation and installation. *Source:* Image credit: Andrew Saluti.

modules that occupy the interior of the model identify tasks: corresponding vertically (y) in position relating to the appropriate staff member and the width of each module defined by the length of time the task requires in relation to the horizontal (x) line. Once assembled, the preparator has a pictorial aide that allows for a shared satellite view of all the cogs of the machine working toward the identified goal. They can identify which separate tasks can and should be done concurrently, and which parts of the project require a progressive approach or those that can be completed independently. In addition, the preparation staff, and any other colleague or staff member that is involved or affected, has an active (and reactive) instrument that can allow for alteration or intervention, inform needs or bottlenecks in progress, shifts in resources, and ultimately guide the preparation process. These charts provide an essential "communal" access and transparency throughout the preparation process, demonstrating workload on preparation staff as well as illustrating the action plan and progress of the project for any and all colleagues needing insight into the project status.

Consider this example, as illustrated in figure 4.1: the preparation team must turn over a small gallery to install a collection of works on paper. After an evaluative assessment, these objects will require matting, mounting, and framing before the installation can take place. The preparation team has three staff members and has a project timeline of three months. Using the Gantt chart, Kate has been assigned to the object preparation, which is separated into two segments: matting the objects and framing the objects. Each task has been allocated two weeks to complete. At the same time, Benjamin and Jennifer have been assigned the deinstallation of the gallery, the gallery mending, and preparation, with all preparation staff collaborating on the installation of the framed objects, which will include securing the objects on the wall, lighting, graphics, and labels. The chart illustrates how these tasks are simultaneously designated and work concurrently, coming together at the point of installation, using Benjamin as a possible floating staff member between the two tasks that must be accomplished independently in order to complete the installation.

These preparation outlines are implemented in a variety of ways, from the basic hand-drawn calendar to customized project management software. All can be an equally effective tool when there are multiple elements to the project and multiple staff members collaborating to meet the goal. Deciding on what will be the most effective option for your team will be informed not only by the size and scope of the preparation team and the larger institution but also by budget and need: a preparation staff of ten or more who assigned to multiple projects at any one given time may mandate a more robust and interconnected communication solution, while a team of three may easily communicate effectively through a single common chart.

Analog Charts

The simplest and most cost-effective approach for preparation management is using a hand-drawn chart or marked calendar—typically something as simple as a dry-erase whiteboard mounted in or near the preparation space. The key to making this as useful as possible depends on two factors: location and updating. A wall-mounted project planning tool needs to be positioned somewhere where all involved have access and can readily review the tasks, timeline, and progress. This should also be easily seen by collaborators and supervisors to apprise those colleagues of project status and possible need and impact beyond the preparator's purview. The analog chart must be routinely revisited and physically updated by the lead preparator or project manager in order to reflect an accurate forecast of the preparation project. The benefit to using a wall-mounted analog system is not only the cost but also the visibility and presence: a strategically located planning chart can be an omnipresent reminder to all involved depending on scale and position. The downside is the need for constant upkeep and initiation, as well as the singular physical nature of the resource—the team needs to go to it rather than it being with the team. Communicating that changes have been made must be initiated rather than inherent.

Digital Management: Basic Applications

Rather than relying on a physical resource for outlining the tasks, the use of basic computer applications can extend the functionality of preparation management. The same modular outline for task, time, and staff is inherent to the format of a spreadsheet or a word processing table. Automatically generated templates for application such as Microsoft Excel can be modified to include any range of time and assignments. Once created, these files can be updated easily and shared instantly, either through direct methods (email or print) or by using a shared networked drive or cloud folder, allowing anyone involved to access as needed. The digital file can be printed and posted in multiple places, making the team's progress visually present, and the file can also be saved for reference post-project. Using the spreadsheet or table template will initially take some effort and digital ability to reflect all the aspects of the project and will most likely require tweaking to create an optimal tool, but once an initial structure is organized, the template can be reused for future projects.

Digital Management: Free Applications

Note: There are many free and paid subscription workflow and project management applications on the market. The applications discussed have been selected for their known deployment within collections-based scenarios and for the unique quality and contribution they can bring to preparation project management. Institutions and companies may have their own preferred integrated systems in place that will incorporate similar functionality—this text does not aim to promote any one solution over another, rather, aims to introduce the functionality and suggest known solutions.

If a digital management tool is to be utilized and constructing a customized spreadsheet is not ideal or feasible, there are free applications specifically designed for project workflow that can be used. *Gantt Project* (https://www.ganttproject.biz/) is a free desktop scheduling application that will run on any Windows, macOS, or Linux platform. The application is designed as an open fillable Gantt chart template to plan projects over a weekly time frame and outline all resources involved (staffing, contract, etc.) and has additional functionality to illustrate critical path in workflow and PERT chart view (Program Evaluation Review Technique), a graphic modular representation of tasks over time. Another free alternative that connects teams and tasks is the mobile platform *Airtable* (https://airtable.com/), a richly versatile and robust operations, database, and project management platform. Among many other functions, *Airtable* incorporates templated Gantt and workflow functionality that is easy to build, organize, and share with the preparation team. The application allows for the integration of additional applications, including social media, communications, and shared drives that may be a part of the workflow. What makes *Airtable* so effective is that it offers the ability to link the entirety of the project to team members using the application's mobile application—embracing the technology so many have in their pockets—allowing for a seamless flow of shared information from every aspect of the preparation management process. What makes *Airtable* uniquely valuable to object-based projects is the ability to build and incorporate collections management database content into the workflow—allowing the preparation staff to not only organize and confirm related tasks but also update object or project information as the process moves forward, such as condition note or photo documentation. The base application and its functionality are free to use, but there are also premium subscription levels meant for complex integration and data management, depending on the size and scope of the organization or project.

Workflow Applications

Workflow applications can easily be adopted by the preparation process to manage project progress and assignments. Using enterprise platform systems (integrated software that connects multiple applications and databases within an institution) such as *Smartsheet*, *Monday*, or *Microsoft Teams* will tender the needed streamlined flow of communication among team members and project managers and will incorporate the functionality of organizing tasks, time, and team. These applications are commonly meant for full organizational use, incorporated into the larger institutional digital platform. Enterprise software solutions will generally require additional support to deploy, with subscription costs dependent on the institutional size and need.

Customized Museum/Collections/Gallery Applications

If the museum or organization requires unique functionality due to the nature of the programming, collection, or exhibition needs, customized systems can be developed to attend to the specific work-flows and project details within a cultural heritage environment. These solutions can be integrated into industry-specific applications, such as the institution's collections management system, and can be templated and formatted for predetermined routines associated with the museum's functions. Citing a case study from *Curia*, which markets itself as the first workflow planning application designed specifically for museums, and its integration by the Washington State Historical Society:

> The [WSHS] decided it needed to move beyond its spreadsheet-centric exhibition planning process in order to improve efficiency and reduce the time demands created by routine administrative tasks. When researching potential solutions, a key consideration was integration with the Society's existing collections management system.[1]

The result was a system that improved the museum's workflow efficiency, allowing the staff to "take the time we spent compiling spreadsheets and doing data entry, and put it toward creative work, research, and tending to the objects instead."[2] An application like *Curia* eliminates the need for the back end or initial setup that nonindustry applications would require and provides an insightful user experience that is explicitly designed for the collections-based experience. This customization and out-of-the-box usability will come with a premium price, an expense that can be weighed against the time and effort needed to modify and fine-tune other applications for a similar functionality.

Regardless of how this system takes shape, the key to initializing a preparation management tool with the greatest possible benefit is its accessibility to the team: ensuring that all involved can readily access the information, review and update progress and emphasizes one of the previously referenced tenants of handling: clear communication of project responsibility, need, and progress. Whether it be a physical calendar or Gantt chart drawn on a bulletin board or integrated mobile software solution, the implementation of effective preparation management is an important part of a preparator's success.

NOTES

1. Washington State Historical Society Case Study, Curia. https://curia.com/wp-content/uploads/2020/06/WSHS-Curia-Case-Study.pdf. Accessed May 2021.
2. Ibid.

REFERENCES

Britz, Kevin. "A Systemized Approach to Exhibit Production Management." *History News*, Vol. 45, No. 6 (November/December 1990), American Association for State and Local History, pp. 1–6. Stable URL: https://www.jstor.org/stable/42655959. Accessed: September 2020.

Gantt, H. *Organizing for Work* (New York: Harcourt, Brace and Howe, 1919).

"How to Make a Gantt Chart." Gantt.com. Accessed September 2020. https://www.gantt.com/creating-gantt-charts.htm.

Lord, Barry, and Gail Dexter Lord. *Manual of Museum Exhibitions* (AltaMira Press, 2001).

"Present Your Data in a Gantt Chart in Excel." Microsoft.com. Accessed June 2021. https://support
.microsoft.com/en-us/topic/present-your-data-in-a-gantt-chart-in-excel-f8910ab4-ceda-4521
-8207-f0fb34d9e2b6.

5

Preparation in Action

NEW GLASS NOW

Warren Bunn II, Collections and Exhibitions Manager, The Corning Museum of Glass

In 2019, The Corning Museum of Glass (CMoG) undertook an extremely complex and challenging exhibition project, *New Glass Now*. The exhibition celebrated the 40th anniversary of the museum's annual publication *New Glass Review*, a yearly virtual exhibition in print, by building on the precedents of two physical *New Glass* exhibitions at CMoG in 1959 and 1979. *New Glass Now* documented the innovation and skill of artists, designers, and architects around the world currently working in the challenging material of glass. The exhibition was a global survey designed to show the breadth and depth of contemporary glassmaking, and it featured objects, installations, videos, and performances

Figure 5.1. Installation View, *New Glass Now* Exhibition Entrance. *Source*: Image licensed by The Corning Museum of Glass, Corning, NY, under CC BY-NC-SA 4.0 International.

made in the last three years by 100 artists of 32 nationalities working in more than 25 countries. This included a companion exhibition in CMoG's Rakow Library Atrium Gallery, *New Glass Now Context*, which documented the history, process, and impact of the 1959 and 1979 New Glass exhibitions and featured both archival materials and objects that were exhibited in the earlier exhibitions.

The exhibition was the first large exhibition in the Museum's Contemporary Art + Design Wing (CA+D), which opened in 2015. Designed by architect Thomas Phifer and Partners, the 100,000-square-foot CA+D Wing includes a 26,000-square-foot gallery—the largest space anywhere dedicated to the presentation of contemporary art in glass—divided into 5 distinct galleries and a large wraparound "porch" display area. The gallery space, the Material and History Gallery, was chosen for *New Glass Now*, requiring the removal of all existing artwork and display furniture and renovation of the gallery.

The CMoG exhibition core team, comprised of the curator of Postwar and Contemporary Glass, the director of Collections, the Collections and Exhibitions manager, and the director of Education and Interpretation, worked with Wendy Evans Joseph and her team at Studio Joseph in New York City to design the exhibition.

BUDGET

Although having a healthy exhibition budget by many museum standards, it proved challenging to contain costs for such a large and complex project. For example, the shipping budget line seemed appropriately funded until we divided it by the number of artists and quickly realized that we would have to be creative to manage costs, while assuring the safety of the artwork. Manufacturing of exhibition furniture, and walls and decks offsite were brought in, assembled, and finished in place which also drove up costs. The team had to make continuous "cost to benefit" decisions throughout the entire process. Cost reduction solutions included simplifying design/display elements, choosing alternative materials, and sending our collections staff out on the road to pack and transport several domestic loans.

PROCESS/SCHEDULE

Although we typically know what exhibitions we are planning two to three years in advance, the "nuts and bolts" work of selecting objects, requesting loans and the exhibition design happens about a year before the opening date. But the schedule for *New Glass Now* was condensed because of the timing of the publication's selection process. In late July / early August the international selection panel met on CMoG's campus, headed by Susie J. Silbert, curator of Postwar and Contemporary Glass, with the guest curators: Aric Chen, curator-at-large, M+ museum, Hong Kong; Susanne Jøker Johnsen, artist and head of exhibitions at the Royal Danish Academy of Fine Arts, Schools of Architecture, Design and Conservation, Denmark; and American artist Beth Lipman. There were 1,433 designers, companies, artists, and craftspeople from 53 countries around the world submitting up to three works for consideration, with the panel reviewing close to 4,000 images to come up with 100 objects by 100 artist/collectives.

It was only in mid-September, when the artists were notified and invited to submit their work for the exhibition, that CMoG Collections and Curatorial staff could begin to gather all the pertinent information regarding the objects and the loan documentation and to plan and coordinate packing/shipping. This includes all of the object data, insurance values, images, installation instructions/display requirements, packing/crating requirements, pickup location, and so on, that is used for planning the shipment and display of the work.

The existing gallery was closed on January 1 with the exhibition opening on May 9, 2019. Although this is similar timing for our normal Changing Exhibition space, which measures approximately 2,000 square feet, the *New Glass Now* exhibition would end up occupying almost 6,000 square feet, which added to the overall work and complexity.

DESIGN

CMoG does not employ an internal exhibition designer, so we maintain a list of designers with whom we have had fruitful collaborations or whose work we have seen and whom we are interested in engaging. In this case we benchmarked several exhibitions that had complications similar to *New Glass Now* (varied scale, materials, themes, etc.) and then identified a designer we thought had resolved these challenges into successful exhibition designs: Studio Joseph. Having chosen a design firm, we faced significant hurdles:

- Adjusting to a new designer's work style and process;
- Formulating a unified design scheme for very different and unseen works and for an untested temporary exhibition space;
- Inadequate space for the overall scope of the project.

Working with a new exhibition design team always adds some complexity: work for hire negotiations, different work styles/processes and levels of involvement, and so forth. Once hired we met with their team to help them understand the goals of the exhibition, glass as a material, the nature and breadth of the work, the strengths and limitations of the gallery space, and the "vision" of the exhibition. There were numerous workshopping sessions, both in person and virtually, to begin to plan and design the space and display furniture (decks, walls, barriers, and casework).

The main design challenge was to create a cohesive exhibition from the varied and disparate pieces selected for the exhibition (scale, material, and technique), in a large space that had never housed a temporary exhibition. This was further complicated by the fact that, in many cases, it was not clear exactly what was coming until well into the design phase, meaning we were designing display spaces without knowing exactly what would go in them. This required designing casework and decks with flexibility, making educated guesses, and making plans that could be easily modified if issues arose.

We also determined early on that there just wasn't enough space for everything to be presented well, so we identified other suitable "satellite" display areas to exhibit some of the work. Given the exhibition was set in the context of the whole contemporary gallery with a variety of access points, another challenge was helping our visitors understand where the exhibition began and where it ended. This was achieved through creating compelling "sight lines" to pull visitors in specific directions, a strong graphic identity and labeling strategy, and a unified color palette, which was also employed in the "satellite" spaces.

The CMoG and Studio Joseph teams worked with our local general contractor, Streeter Associates, to refine the design, to create all new display furniture (including a large central island with discreet display spaces and walls of varying heights), and to create places where works could be viewed on their own and/or in conversation with other works but with views and sight lines to create moments of discovery for the visitors.

GALLERY PREPARATION

Since the exhibition was not in the usual Changing Exhibition Gallery and would occupy the largest of the galleries in the new wing, along with a large section of the outer hallways and satellite spaces, gallery preparation was much more labor-intensive. It was no minor task to remove the existing artwork and display furniture, which had been designed and built to safely display our collections

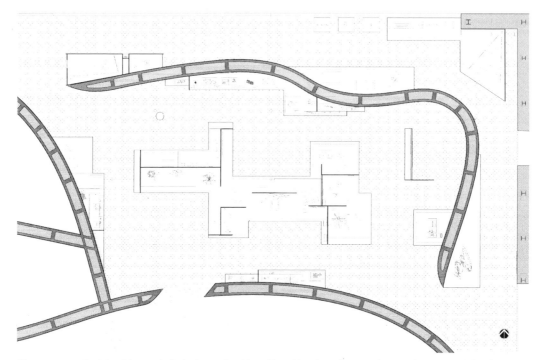

Figure 5.2. Graphic Plan with Sight Lines for *New Glass Now* Installation. *Source*: Courtesy of Studio Joseph, New York, NY.

but not intended for easy removal. All of the existing artwork was documented (photographed and installation/deinstallation notes added to the collections database), deinstalled, packed, and safely moved to our offsite storage facility, and the decks, barriers, and walls were dismantled and removed. Once the gallery was emptied, our operations team put in a huge amount of work to get the floors back in good shape, as they showed staining from the deck materials and visitor traffic, since they had been in place since the new wing opened. We suspected that it might need some work but were surprised at just how much.

CONTAINMENT/CONSTRUCTION

Secure construction walls were built at all three gallery entrances, with double doors, to make sure that building materials, exhibitry, crated artwork, lifts, and tools could all be easily moved into the gallery space throughout the installation.

As this was our first large exhibition project in the new wing, we quickly learned how challenging it would be. Due to the CA+D Wing's architecture, which features large gallery doorways and open-work concrete beams, we realized early on that it would be difficult to contain the construction dust and noise. This required that we manufacture much of the exhibitry offsite and then bring it in for assembly and finishing, which was more complex and expensive but lessened the impact on our visitors and collections in the adjacent galleries.

COORDINATION/COMMUNICATION

The challenges of gathering loan and shipping documents from 100 living artists were not insignificant and at times exacerbated by language issues. Artist follow-through on providing documentation and completing detailed paperwork was inconsistent, and some required additional coordination and encouragement.

CMoG's registrars and curatorial team set up a central communication channel to maintain consistency and clarity throughout. But there were still quite a few surprises when artwork arrived. In some cases, artists had submitted an idea or prototype of their submission when applying for inclusion in the exhibition, but the final work was much different; while in other cases, the artists "supersized' their work for the CMoG show.

Although almost every artist indicated that they preferred to be there to install their work, it just wasn't logistically and/or financially possible. It fell to the exhibition team to identify what works needed that level of artist involvement and to coordinate artists' assistance with the installation of their work. In one case, the artist hand paints his phone number on all the display surfaces, which required that we bring him from Sweden to assist with his installation. In other cases, artists provided installation videos or photographs of how to manage and install their work, while in others it fell to the curator and installation team to make those decisions.

PACKING AND SHIPPING

As noted, we had to develop creative solutions to getting everything safely to Corning. In some cases, it was as simple as digital transfer of a file, and in others it took much more effort and expense. To better manage the safe packing and shipment of the artwork, our team divided the works into three categories:

- Works the artist could easily pack and ship.
- Works that CMoG staff could go collect, pack, and transport back to the museum.
- Works that would require professional art handlers and/or custom brokers.

CMoG collections staff was concerned about artists' ability to safely pack their works, so took the opportunity to work with our digital team to create a series of best practices packing videos, which we not only made available to the artists but also posted on the museum's website and YouTube channel. We also created a handy Tools and Materials Source List (figure 5.3), which listed museum-quality supplies, as well as alternative supplies if the "good stuff" wasn't readily available. These proved to be excellent resources and received great reviews from artists, conservators, and museum colleagues.

Another challenge for collections staff was the sheer volume of crates and packing materials that needed to be managed. The team planned the installation by the complexity of the artwork and a logical progression through the space and had to be creative and organized with bringing works into the gallery in stages, tracking their locations, and organizing them by installation location. During the run of the exhibition, we had to store all the crates, boxes, and packing materials at our offsite storage facility in an organized way without impacting the care of our collections and other work being done there.

ELECTRICAL/DATA

Numerous works in the exhibition required data and electricity, and although there is a grid of power and data outlets in the floor of the new galleries, the exhibition design made it difficult to access many of them. This required creative solutions in bringing power from above and effective coordination with the contractors, as well as with our digital team to make sure that all the pieces with digital components would run as intended.

CORNING MUSEUM OF GLASS SOFT PACKING: TOOLS AND MATERIALS SOURCE LIST

TISSUE PAPER
Use for cushioning/wrapping objects, to cushion around objects within a packing box.
Museum-grade & conservation approved: unbuffered, acid free tissue
- Gaylord Archival: www.gaylord.com

Acceptable: Plain, undyed tissue paper
- Blick Pure White Tissue Paper: www.dickblick.com
- Hallmark White Tissue Paper: www.amazon.com or similar

TYVEK
Tyvek protects objects with particularly delicate surfaces, and is also used as lining in the cavity packing method. We use a soft, museum-grade Tyvek (as opposed to that used in the construction industry).
Lightweight, waterproof and durable, museum-grade, conservation approved:
- Gaylord Archival Standard Weight Tyvek Roll (TR60100): www.gaylord.com

Acceptable: Disposable Tyvek suit, such as:
- Trimaco Non-Woven Laminate Paint Protective Coveralls:
  www.lowes.com/pd/Trimaco-3XL-Non-Woven-Laminate-Paint-Protective-Coveralls/50281811
  Note: This Tyvek may be stiff, so you may opt to wash it on gentle cycle with no detergent and allow to air dry before using.

FOAM
Available in different thicknesses and densities. In this video, we've used a highquality, chemically inert polyethylene foam, which is quite expensive, and locally sourced. Practical and more affordable alternatives are readily available that will provide adequate protection during shipping. *However, due to their chemical make-up, these foams are not recommended for long term storage of art objects.*
Acceptable:
- FoamTouch Upholstery Foam Cushion: www.amazon.com
- Airtex High Density Foam, in rolls or by the yard: www.joann.com

VOLARA
Volara Polyethylene Foam: www.universityproducts.com, comes in different thicknesses
Acceptable:
- White Foam Closed Cell 1/8" High Density Auto Crafts Upholstery 60"W Volara from www.amazon.com, sold by the yard

STURDY CARDBOARD BOXES
Preferably double-walled corrugated boxes.
- Staples: www.staples.com
- Lowe's: www.lowes.com

WOOD CALIPERS
By ZIJIA-INC, Set of 3, available from www.amazon.com

Figure 5.3. Soft Packing: Tools and Materials. *Source*: Image licensed by The Corning Museum of Glass, Corning, NY, under CC BY-NC-SA 4.0 International.

INSTALLATION

As with many exhibitions, the refinement of the design, construction, and gallery preparation can cause the installation schedule to run behind. The collections team ended up having less time than planned for the installation but rose to the occasion and worked hard to get everything installed safely, aesthetically, and with a high degree of finish. The range of scale and materials and the very fragile nature of the glass as an artistic medium required creative solutions using all the tools in our tool kit, from rigging and lifts to good old-fashioned elbow grease. Collections staff did an excellent job collecting and documenting installation instructions and videos from artists, when available, and we referenced those before installing each work to minimize potential damage.

SAFETY AND SECURITY

At CMoG we have a very well-developed safety program, so all design and installation decisions were weighed against the safety of our staff, visitors, and collections. We worked with the exhibition designer to maintain wide enough passages for safe visitor flow during our peak summer visitation. We also must protect those inherently fragile works from the irresistible temptation to touch them, so objects are always displayed in secure cases or behind sturdy barriers. This protects not only the artwork but also our visitors.

Figure 5.4. Preparators Installing *New Glass Now*. *Source*: Image licensed by The Corning Museum of Glass, Corning, NY, under CC BY-NC-SA 4.0 International.

For *New Glass Now*, the exhibition design team wanted to maximize sight lines from the entrances, so we were asked if we would consider using lower barriers. To compromise, we researched and identified a LIDAR sensor system with audibe alarms, which allowed us to incorporate lower barriers in certain areas while still alerting security staff if visitors got too close, thus ensuring the safety of the artwork and the visitor. We did find that during very busy afternoons, the alarms would go off continually, so we feel that this syetem still needs some refinement.

The *New Glass Now* project was one of the most complex challenges our team has ever faced. It pushed our staff to their very limits, but the final exhibitions were a huge success and a watershed moment for the institution. All the museum's programing revolved around the exhibition, from the show's artists participating in our Hot Glass shows and teaching at our Studio to our annual Seminar on Glass, which featured timely presentations and panel discussions on art-making in glass, as well as on issues of identity, gender, and inclusion.

The exhibition received excellent press and reviews, and as with the 1959 and 1979 exhibitions, the museum acquired a large group of objects (approximately half of the exhibition), capturing a snapshot of the state of contemporary glassmaking and documenting *New Glass Now* for the future.

Looking back, we identified and documented several "lessons learned" and things that could have been done to make the process easier, from narrowing the scope and number of objects to adjusting the dates to give more time for larger complex projects. Moving forward we now better understand the complexities of doing large exhibition projects in the Contemporary Art + Design Wing.

6

Two-Dimensional Object Preparation

The proper preparation of objects, for storage, transit, or display, may be the most vital responsibility that the preparator carries out for an institution (*it's even in the name*). One can argue that the practice of installation and handling carry equal weight, though neither of these roles can be separated or successfully accomplished if the object or artifact is not properly prepped for such action.

While it is vital to recognize that there will commonly be necessary input, direction, and many times action taken by specialists, conservators, curators, and other collections professionals, there are standard procedures and practices that should be included in the preparator's lexicon of skills. This chapter elucidates on several basic methodologies that correspond to the physical attributes or categories of flat collection objects: works on paper and two-dimensional wall-mounted elements (i.e., paintings on panel or canvas and framed objects).

WORKS ON PAPER

A substantial population of any art, history, or archival collection will be works on paper. On average, 50–60 percent of an art museum's collection will comprise paper-based objects, with more significant majorities in history and special collections.[1] The range of media types can run the gamut from documents, news clippings, and maps to prints, photographs, or original drawings and paintings. As a support, paper-based objects inherently carry a host of advantages and specific challenges for the collections team. The following is a general methodology for properly preparing a broad range of works on paper.

MATTING

One of the most fundamental and rudimentary housings for flat objects is the hinged window mat. It's a vital preservation and presentation tool in any collection's arsenal. When done well, proper matting can prove to be the linchpin that enables safe and secure exhibition, heightens a viewer's engagement with the object, and provides needed protection and support while the object is in storage, in transit, or on view. Equally, improper matting can accelerate or exacerbate the object's deterioration and can distract from the intended interpretation.

Before exploring the basics of matting and mounting flat objects, it's important to define the function of the mat and its role and application in collection care. The window mat was first introduced in the mid-nineteenth century at the British Museum, an institution that set the standard for paper-based collections practice. The window mat, aptly titled for ability to see the object (or portion of the object) while encapsulated within the housing, has two main functions. The first, and primary in the hierarchy of importance in the preservation of the object, is safety: the mat provides a secure housing and support for the object. This is vital for all aspects of collection usage for the specific work on paper, whether it be storage, handling, or transport. As a storage device, the mat can act as a physical safeguard when stacking objects in a flat file drawer or in portfolio cases. When using the appropriate archival materials (to be defined in this chapter), the housing will ensure (and promote) a stable environment in terms of both regulating the atmospheric conditions and a physical support that mitigates any direct contact with the sheet or object and protects against adverse and damaging handling. Once matted and mounted, the object is by far safer and more secure in transit, opposed to the manipulation and packing of a sheet as a loose object—the housing creates a vehicle that allows for the sheet's natural flat orientation. When presented for inspection or research, as so many collection objects will inevitably be, the matted object can be safely handled and displayed, unframed, independent of (or in buildup to) the exhibition installation process. For the more formal and public presentation in the gallery/exhibition scenario within a frame, the mat creates a cavity of space between the glazing of the closed package and the surface of the object—an important consideration when encapsulating in a closed, sealed environment.

The secondary function of the archival window mat is presentation—an important device for providing an aesthetically supportive format to engage with works on paper of any size or kind. The window mat directs focus to the central visible content area of the object, while also creating a visibly neutral margin to reinforce that direction. The mat can heighten the intimacy or grandeur of the object through margin scale and tone. Depending on the needs of work or material (both in preservation and presentation), different techniques and methods can be utilized to add emphasis, including a thicker ply to create a more dramatic depth or cavity and tiered and multiple window top mats to facilitate object juxtaposition and correlating content. Although a secondary function, the presentation utility of the archival mat can have pivotal impact on how the object is perceived, interpreted, and understood.

How will the acknowledgment of function inform the matting process? When the preparator understands the hierarchy of these considerations, and how they will impact the object and the process, the decisions that are made in creating the window mat housing become clearly defined:

Will the choices pertaining to presentation support the primary role of preservation?

How will these guidelines inspire what can be created to enhance the visual experience of the object?

With an understanding and acknowledgment of function, the preparation staff must then consider the appropriate matting and mounting materials to meet the task. Mat boards come in a variety of grades and variations, but many of these selections would be inappropriately deemed archival for collection-based practice.

All mat board is made up of and measured in layers called plies. The standard board is a 4-ply board; meaning the makeup of the material physically consists of four layers, depending on the type of board. This is also the measurement used to describe the thickness of the material and identify how much space it will create between the object and something else (such as other matted objects or the glazing of a frame). According to best practice, the least amount of spacing that a window mat needs to provide inside the closed environment of a frame is a 4-ply board. This creates the minimum adequate cavity between the object surface and glazing of the frame. There are a variety of board plies, from single ply (essentially a heavy paper sheet, akin to Bristol board or heavy printmaking paper), 2-ply (half the thickness of standard 4-ply), 8-ply (twice the thickness), and so on. Each of these variations can be utilized for specific functions, both for matters of preservation and presentation. For example, while it will not give the equal amount of rigid support as the standard 4-ply board, the 2-ply mat is a wonderful solution for matting objects that are not intended on being framed but still require the safety and support of a housing. Using 2-ply for a housing rather than 4-ply takes up less space within storage units (an important factor for museum and archival collections) while still providing the necessary preservation attributes. For objects that have sensitive surfaces or comprise fugitive media that may not be fixed or cured on the paper surface, an 8-ply mat or greater will create a greater separation and security for the object surface. In addition to the varied thicknesses of mat board, the composition of what creates the finished board will fluctuate based on the intended use or quality of the material.

Paper Mat

This is the lowest grade mat board, found at craft and art supply stores and used in commercial frame shops as an inexpensive alternative to an acid-free material. This board will be commonly found in on-the-shelf picture frames sold in stores and in many prefabricated framing kits. The composition of this board is wood pulp core sandwiched in between a backing sheet (usually white) and a top layer—many times pressed with a linen texture or other unique surface, also in a large variety of colors. This material is acid bearing and will deteriorate over time, in addition to placing archival or collection materials at risk for acid migration. Evidence of the paper mat can easily be identified by examining the bevel cut of the window or the edge of the mat board, where you will see a dull brown or yellowing of the core material—this signifies that the board is not acid-free and is not appropriate for archival use.

Acid-Free Mat

The next grade of mat board is the acid-free mat. This board is similar to the paper mat in that it is a commercial grade mat used in frames shops for residential framing. Like its cheaper alternative, the acid-free mat is constructed of a base sheet, core, and top layer that will come in a variety of colors, textures, and laminate surfaces. The plies are a wood pulp material, however, the acid-free mat is buffered to create a neutral pH board. This can be identified by a bright white core—the indication that there is no degradation of the material. While these boards will not deteriorate as quickly as the paper mat, or pose the same immediate risk to objects, they are not considered best practice for archival housings.

Archival Mat

The highest quality mat board and best choice for the preservation of collection objects is the archival mat. This designation includes different styles and types of boards, all consistent in their composition and quality of material. The archival board, unlike lesser grade mats, is composed of a naturally acid-free cotton "rag" pulp rather than a wood pulp. These boards are consistent in their layers—no top and bottom sheet encapsulating a core, rather, every ply of the archival mat is the same rag layer. Unlike the commercial mats, archival boards do not come in a grand selection of colors or textures, as they do not utilize any dyes or alternative materials and finishes. They generally offer a selection of natural tones, whites, and sometimes black and grays—this also reinforces the nature of the archival mat's function. These boards will mimic the existing tones of the paper support, creating an extension of that object rather than complimentary embellishment, directing all emphasis on the viewable area of the object rather than attempting to match a color palette or corresponding design.

DETERMINING THE WINDOW

Once the appropriate boards have been selected, one must determine both the overall size of the housing and the nature of the window. There are two basic variations of the window mat: the *overmat* and the *float*. The overmat is the most common (and most secure) style of window, providing a physical overlap of the archival board on top of the object—acting as brace that aids in the stability and security of the sheet housed within. This method should be considered when the object has margins that do not need to be seen and/or will facilitate the sheet's ultimate physical stability once matted. The overmat prevents the object from possible movement forward or release, aiding the mounts that hold the sheet in place.

The most common variation, the float, is the same structure of housing but different in that the top window does not overlap or cover any aspect of the mounted object, rather, the sheet is mounted with hidden hinges to present the object in its entirety inside the parameter of the window area. This approach is employed for a variety of reasons, such as when the object has no or minimal margins to cover or when there are markings or information close to the sheet edge that should be seen. While a float mat still provides the same structural support and separation from surface contact as the overmat, the object is somewhat less secure in that the window is not providing the same physical hold over the object. This may also be a preservation decision depending on the condition of the object being matted—a float mat may be the better scenario if the object being mounted is too fragile or at some potential risk of damage if the window is an overmat.

MAT CUTTING TOOLS AND MACHINES

The cutting of a window mat can be accomplished using a variety of tools. A simple and functional window can be created by simply using a handheld blade to remove a section of board; however, the standard for most window mats is to create a regressing beveled edge along the opening of the window, drawing the viewer's eye toward the intended content while also cascading debris away from the object. In order to create a professional presentation, specialty tools are employed and range from handheld cutting devices to computer-guided, mechanically driven machines. The most common of the mat cutting tools is a tabletop cutting machine that has an arm-mounted cartridge to cut a beveled edge on a fixed axis. Some of these mat cutters also have a straight cutting blade option, allowing one to both trim material and create the beveled window using the same tool. This standard piece of professional equipment is one of the core tools in a preparator's workshop and can range in size from a 30-inch cutting length to as large as 60 inches. Alternative to the larger mat cutting machines, the handheld mat cutter is an economical choice that can deliver the same quality presentation as its higher-end options when used by a practiced hand. Using a straightedge or metal ruler to guide the cut, the handheld mat cutter will create a window mat that is indistinguishable from that of other devices and machines. They allow the preparator to create housings larger than the mat cutting machine's size and can also cut irregular shapes and curves depending on the guide used. Independent from a fixed arm or cutting edge, the handheld mat cutter is a compact, affordable, and a versatile option for occasional or specialty use. The opposite side of the mat cutting spectrum is the computerized mat cutter (or CMC), first introduced in the mid-1990s. Similar to industrial computer-guided equipment, these cutters will mechanically cut mats from coordinates entered at a PC and can cut openings of any designed specification, including irregular shapes or patterns, with precision, consistency, and speed. These machines are more commonly found in commercial framing shops or institutions that require high levels of output for these housings.

Process

Step 1: Evaluation

The first step on any rehousing or object preparation is an evaluation of the object, specifically, the details that will determine how you proceed: What is the condition? What are the physical characteristics? In the case of matting flat or loose objects, what is the primary support—paper type, board, or canvas? Does the object have margins that can be covered that will allow for overmat, and are there markings that should be visible once mounted in the housing? The evaluation can be informed by basic visual inspection but may also include information gleaned from curatorial or conservator communication and collaboration (if you don't know, or are unsure, ask).

Step 2: Determining Final Housing Size

Next you will need to determine the overall size of the housing. This determination is based on two factors: the overall size of the object and the desired finished size of the mat. The mat housing must accommodate for the object's scale and provide adequate space to protect the object from damage. The object should never be too snug inside the housing, as this can lead to potential risk when handling or enclosing within a frame. It is good practice to allow for a minimum of 1 inch between the object edge and the finished mat size (this is variable depending on the scale of the object). You should never trim or cut an object to fit inside a mat. Additionally, many collections-based institutions will create mat housings that fit a standard frame size rather than a custom size unique to the object. This is a pragmatic approach: one that allows museums and cultural institutions to maintain a bank of standard-sized frames to use for a multitude of objects in their holdings. Proactively considering these standard sizes when determining the final size of the housing can help offset the cost of eventual framing needs, more efficiently using collection resources.

The preparator needs to cut two sheets of archival board to size: one for the top window and the other for the backing support to mount the object onto. An important tip when cutting archival board: while you should always try to make one pass with the blade when cutting the window opening, it's better practice to not try to cut through the board in a single pass when trimming down to size—this will eliminate unforeseen mistakes such as the board jogging out of position causing a miscut and allow for a cleaner cut—no need to muscle through the material on a straight trim cut. It is important that both sheets of board are square and identical in scale for this hinged housing.

A Note on Standard Sizes

Common imperial (US) frame sizes
12 × 16 inches
14 × 18 inches
16 × 20 inches
18 × 24 inches
20 × 24 inches
22 × 28 inches
24 × 30 inches
24 × 36 inches
32 × 40 inches

Common metric frame sizes
30 × 40 centimeters
40 × 50 centimeters
40 × 60 centimeters
45 × 60 centimeters
50 × 60 centimeters
50 × 70 centimeters
60 × 80 centimeters
61 × 91.5 centimeters
70 × 100 centimeters

Step 3: Determining the Window Size

Once the final size of the mat is determined, the next step is determining the window size and margins. Regardless of the type of window mat, the opening will determine the margin sizes for the housing, which will guide the cutting process. If preparing an overmat, it is customary to allow some space between the image area and the window opening, leaving some of the object margin visible. There are a few reasons for this: it allows for a visual buffer in between what should be a square window and a possibly out-of-square image area. This also provides space for any markings close to the image, such as a signature or publication information near the plate mark of a print. Allocating this perimeter of space will comfortably present the image or document within the mat avoiding any hampering or encroachment from the housing. In the case of a float mount, this aesthetic rationale also becomes an issue of preservation: creating a window too close to the object edge could result in unintended contact with the window mat and can potentially negate the housing's function of separating the object from other surfaces. The amount of space allotted for this margin varies with the size of the object/image itself—an evaluative exercise. The key, from a collections point of view, is consistency: using a standard *half-inch perimeter* will not only create a uniform visual rhythm for your matted objects but also provide the necessary aesthetic and functional buffer from the housing's window edge and the object/image area. The combined object and image dimension with this buffer will create the dimension for the window opening.

Step 4: Defining Your Margins

Configuring the window mat margins is a relatively easy calculation once the final size and window dimensions are determined. Simply subtracting the height and width of the window from the height and width of the final size will supply the remaining area that defines the margin space. Taking these results and dividing by two (to reflect a perimeter of mirrored margins surrounding the window) can result in an effective housing, depending on the dimensional orientation of the object and the desired aesthetic presentation. The object will always be the primary variable that directs these decisions: similar to how the initial evaluation dictates overall size and material determinations, the mat housing may have to be designed specifically to accommodate the relative visual needs or physical constraints of the work. If the object has a weighted margin (where one margin is wider than its corresponding sides), the housing will need to take this into account. This presentation format is a traditional layout for many historic and contemporary prints and photographs but will be relevant to any object.

   In the graph shown in figure 6.1, the overall size of the object sheet is 15 × 11 inches, and the image area is 11 × 8 inches, but there is also a signature and markings that the preparator wants to remain visible. Taking this into account, the determined window size is 14 × 9 in order to comfortably accommodate the image and markings and provide the visual buffer for presentation. To safely accommodate the full object and to fit into a standard frame, the final housing size has been determined to be 20 × 16 inches (height preceding width). Using these dimensions, the remaining margin space is 6 inches left to right and 7 inches top to bottom. The top, side, and bottom margins have been organized to create a traditional presentation with the top and side margins consistent at 3 inches and weighting the bottom margin at 4 inches. With the margins determined, the preparator can mark the mat board and cut the window.

Step 5: Marking the Mat

If cutting the window by hand, the preparator needs to create guides on the reverse side of the window mat to direct the cutting. These markings need only to define where the cut starts and stops, identifying where the resulting mitered corners of the cuts are made. This is best accomplished using a basic

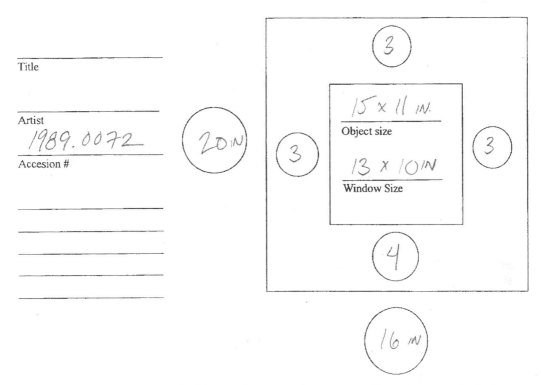

Title

Artist

1989.0072

Accesion #

(inside figure, circled numbers and handwritten measurements)

3

20 IN

3

15 x 11 IN.

Object size

13 x 10 IN

Window Size

3

4

16 IN

Figure 6.1. Matting Worksheet for Object and Housing Measurements. *Source*: Image credit: Andrew Saluti.

crosshair marking system: marking the margin as a distance from the outer edge of the finished size. Where those measurements intersect identifies where your cuts should begin and end. It is important to note that any marking made on archival matting should be minimal and removable: made with pencil only and with as little mark made as possible, only as much as needed to indicate the cut. Many times, preparators will go back and erase the remnants of these marks after the window has been cut. This is a pragmatic archival practice: when one considers the amount of time an object might be mounted in direct contact with the top window mat, the possibility for the offset of any marking that has been added onto the object surface is probable. Best practice is to make these marks as delicate and light as possible (while still being distinguishable and functional to the preparator).

A note on (or before) marking your board: While commercial grade acid-free mats will have a clear top and back side, archival board is consistent on both sides. Before measuring and marking the board, inspect the surface so you can see if there are any scratches, stains, or irregularities on or in the mat surface to ensure that your finished housing will be free and clear of any distractions or imperfections.

Step 6: Cutting the Window

With all calculations made and your guides marked, you are ready to cut the window. As stated previously, while it is prudent to make multiple passes when making a straight cut, cutting the beveled window is best accomplished by making a single pass with a sharp, fresh cutting blade. Regardless of the tools used, always check the condition of the cutting blade before cutting your windows, especially if using a shared or multiuse preparation space—mat cutting machines are often used to cut and trim a variety of materials, and a savvy preparator recognizes that archival board, much like all archival materials, is a premium expense. Dull or damaged blades will result in a ragged and imperfect cut, making the housing unpresentable and a distraction to the object it carries. A good rule of thumb is to always change the bevel cutting blade before starting any mat cutting project, especially if you are unaware of how long or for what material the existing blade has been used. Another keynote is to always use a piece of backing waste board under your mat when making precision cuts. This will give the blade the same resistance when cutting while also allowing the blade edge to cut into a sacrificial surface. For window cuts, never use a self-healing mat as a backing: the blade will want to find and track into previous cut grooves. If you use no backing when using a mat cutting machine or hand mat cutter, your finished bevel cut can look ragged and sloppy.

With the face (front) side of the window mat facing down, position the marked mat so the angle of the bevel will cut toward the outer edge of that margin. Line up the cut edge using the cross marks as parallel guides to the cutting device (if using a hand mat cutter, its best to insert the blade first so you can line up your straight edge at the appropriate variance from the actual marks). The blade should be inserted so the cut will begin at the point of intersection, or slightly before—the exact point of insertion will become known after a few corner cuts are successfully made and will depend on the specific idiosyncrasies of your cutting device. When making the cut, insert the blade fully before moving along the line of the cut: inserting while pulling/pushing the blade will result in a rounded corner. Stop the cut as the blade hits the second mark and release from the board. It's always prudent to make sure the cut has made its way fully through the material and has also intersected the previous cut before moving forward; however, never force the board to release. If the cut was too shallow or has not crossed with the perpendicular side to release the corner, do not continue to cut consecutive sides until resolving the incomplete cut. It is very difficult to try and complete these cuts by hand with a straight blade and make them look consistent; guiding the blade of the same tool used originally back into the problem cut to complete or continue the bevel will more often give better results.

When cutting your window mat, there are common discrepancies that can occur, including the aforementioned frayed cut edge due to a dull or damaged blade, rounded or imperfect corners, or marred beveled edged due to multiple, inconsistent passes with the blade. The most common issues that arise when cutting a window mat are what are known as overcuts and undercuts. These are terms associated with the intersecting cut at the corner of the window. The *undercut* refers to the visible torn or "popped" corner of the cut, where the blade did not adequately intersect the perpendicular cut and the board being removed (or the "dropout") was forced apart from the mat. This leaves a remnant of the uncut board in the corner, like a tail covering the miter. Skilled preparators can remove the undercut with a blade, but the blemish will rarely be invisible to the viewer. The *overcut*, as implied, is the opposite result, when the cut has surpassed the mark where the beveled edges meet and leave visible extensions of the cut at the corner. While the overcut ensures the complete cut of the window and frees the dropout, the remnants can still create a visible distraction from the object. Using a burnishing tool such as a bookbinder's bone folder can smooth the area to minimize the prominence of the errant cut. And while neither is ideal, the slight overcut is always preferable (and easier to minimize) to the undercut.

Step 7: Hinging the Mat

Now that the top window has been cut, the final step in creating the housing is to unite the backing board that will support the mounted object with the top mat. This is accomplished using archival tape to create a folio hinge that will fold the top mat over the backing board, not unlike the case of a book. To ensure the strongest binding, align the top mat (facing down) with the backing board (facing up) along the longest congruent edge. Add a strip of archival tape (linen tape gummed with methylcellulose is most common) along the entire seam—if possible, do not use separate or spaced pieces of tape—this will result in a weak hinge that may fail. Burnish the tape to ensure optimum adhesion, and then let the

Figure 6.2. Mat Window with an Overcut. *Source*: Image
credit: Andrew Saluti.

housing rest to allow the adhesive to cure. Once dry, carefully close the housing and lightly burnish
the hinged edge once again to create a tight bind that will lay flat. Note: it is best practice to allow any
water-activated adhesive to completely dry before introducing an object or trapping the housing in a
closed environment such as a glazed frame. The preparation management of creating mat housings
for multiple objects should consider an assembly-line–style approach: cutting all windows, hinging all
mats, and then introducing objects after an appropriate schedule for assembly.

Standard Mat Variations

Using this basic process is the base for an assortment of variations in mat housings. While the function of security and protection of the object must remain at the core of creating these devices, the
opportunity to create dynamic and versatile supports can easily be accomplished.

Previously discussed in this chapter, the selection of mat plies not only can affect the functionality
of how much safe distance the housing will provide the object but will also affect the presentation,
using a more dramatic depth that directs the viewer's attention to the central content. However,
these upgraded materials come at a premium cost, especially at the archival quality. An alternative
approach to the deeper ply is the double mat: a sequential window mat that provides added depth
and design to the basic mat housing. There is no unique process or method in creating a double mat
window; one simply measures and cuts an addition window mat that is added to the overall housing,
commonly enlarging the second window to create a cascading step effect. The common expanded
window offset in a double (or multiple) mat is between 3 × 16 inches and 3 × 8 inches, depending on
the finished size of the mat. This technique also invites the use of variation in mat color to enhance
the presentation or place to add focus on the object, though this approach is generally more common
in commercial framing.

Another common variation on the basic mat housing is a multi-window housing—a singular
hinged mat with multiple windows to accommodate more than one object mounted and presented

as one unit. This is often used when you have objects that are meant to be seen together (such as preliminary or process sketches, multipage documents, or variations of a final product) or are meant to be presented in a sequential order (such as unbound books, series, or illustrations). The approach to marking and cutting these multi-window housings is the same as any singular-window housing, made more complex by the plotting of margin space between windows. However, before moving forward, the evaluation of the objects is paramount to ensure that adequate space is accounted for when incorporating multiple overall object dimensions, especially relating to the part(s) of the object not visible, covered by the housing. Objects must be mounted independent from other objects and should never overlap or be in contact under a window mat. These restrictions, in addition to the added plotting of compound windows on a single sheet, can at times make these housings complex and cumbersome—but when executed properly, multi-window mat housings are an exceptionally effective tool when storing and presenting multiple or related flat objects.

MOUNTING THE OBJECTS

Once an archival housing has been created, the object must be fixed or mounted to the supporting backing. As previously stated, the preparator is not necessarily a trained conservator or paper specialist and should, when possible, concentrate on passive techniques that will not add or change the physical condition of the collection objects and always consult collections colleagues before attempting to make any permanent attachments to an object. When choosing a method for mounting objects within the housing, the first consideration should be a passive approach, using a corner mount rather than a fixed hinged method.

The corner mount is the most basic device for affixing flat objects: small triangular sleeves that cradle the object on the backing board and restrict movement but also allowing the object to be completely removed from the housing relatively easily and without specialized treatment or active conservation. This mounting system can be either achieved using commercial ready-made supplies or fabricated in-house with basic archival materials, making it the go-to for the preparator working with collections of works on paper.

The alternative to a corner mount is the hinge, a system of archival joints or tabs affixed to both the object and support backing. The hinge mount should always use an archival adhesive, such as a methylcellulose or a natural paste (such as a wheat paste). These glues will not only create a strong bond to the surface but also be able to be reversed or removed by a trained conservator. Because you are making a physical change to the object, this active (rather than passive) approach should be carefully considered and ideally performed by a conservator but, if done correctly, can be safely accomplished by the preparation staff.

The first consideration when deciding on which mount will be the best approach is the object evaluation: Will the object's media be safely held by corner mounts? If paper-based, are the corners of the sheet in good physical condition and stable enough to support the corner mount or a fixed hinge? (For example, thin and delicate papers may not have the adequate rigidity or structural stability to be captured by corner mounts.) If meant to be hidden, is there adequate overmat on the housing or margin of the object to accommodate the mounts? Consistent with any object preparation, this initial appraisal will guide the process and inform the preparator's decisions, actions, and timeline.

Corner Mounts

The methods for creating a corner mount for an object is easy and can be accomplished with some basic preparation lab materials. The fact that the mount can be "made to order" permits the preparator to customize according to object needs—size, shape, visibility, and so on. The material used should be an archival paper such as Permalife® bond or a cotton rag sheet or, if a clear mount is desired, an archival polyester sheet (commonly named Mylar® or Melinex®) can be used. The mounts are adhered to the backing using an acid-free tape or archival linen tape. A double-sided acid-free tape (such as a 3M ATG tape) can be used if the mount will be visible. Whichever tape or approach is used, it is vital that the adhesive is never in direct contact with the object.

Step 1: Selecting a Corner Size

The first step is to determine the size of the corner needed to maintain the object. It's important not to make these mounts so small that they will not secure the object within the housing and not so large that the object is overly challenged when inserting or removing from the mount. Another consideration may be presentation and what will be seen through the window when on view. While there is no general sizing chart (object evaluation will always drive the decision-making process), a good rule of thumb is to use a minimum of 1-inch mounts on objects as large as 16 × 20 inches, 2-inch mounts on objects as large as 20 × 30 inches, and at least 3-inch mounts for larger-sized works. Again, this all depends on the specific needs and conditions of the object, housing, and situation. Cut strips of the material to the desired mount size, noting that a singular mount will require a strip at least three times the width of the mount (this can be relevant when managing multiple preps).

Step 2: Folding the Corner

Once the material has been prepped, start by folding one end of the strip at a 45-degree angle with a small tail of material extending over the side. Next, match the fold on the opposite side, leaving the longer end of the strip exposed. Use a burnishing or folding tool over the folds to create crisp and tight folds. Cut the remaining material to match the end of the first tail fold. This extension of material is strategic: leaving a step of the material will help guide the object into place, especially when the object might be delicate, thin, or difficult to manipulate. Repeat these steps for as many corners are needed for the preparation.

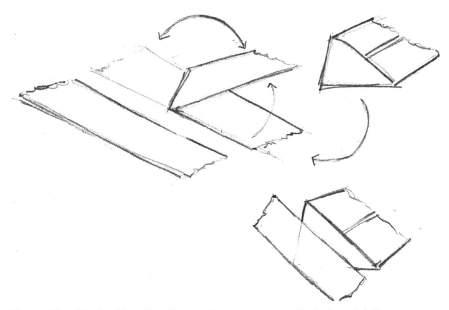

Figure 6.3. Making Mounting Corners. *Source*: Image credit: Andrew Saluti.

Variation: Creating a Dimensional Corner Mount

One of the major benefits to fabricating a corner mount is the ability to customize the shape and nature of how the object will rest in the sleeve. Areas of the corner mount can be cut away depending on the object they carry. If the object is not a flat sheet and has a dimensional girth, the corner mount can be manipulated to accommodate. Take, for example, a painting on illustration board. The board may have a depth of one-eighth of an inch, and the corner sleeve can be folded and constructed to accept a physical depth rather than a flat sheet, simply by adding the folds to capture that depth. It is important, however, that the object being mounted is not used as the model for the fabrication of the mount: a waste piece of material that matches the object's dimension should be used to score and fold the sleeve.

Step 3: Mounting the Corners

Now that the corner mounts have been made, the next step is to secure them in the precise position on the housing to accommodate the object. In order to handle the object as minimally as possible while still accomplishing an accurate placement, an effective approach is to start with the two bottom edge corners of the object, as these mounts will determine the position and carry the weight. Position the object on the backing of the housing in order to align proper placement with the top mat (if mounting in a window housing). With the extended tails on the backside of the object (in direct contact with the backing board), carefully slide the mount onto the corner of the object, leaving a small gap (1/16 inch) between the edge of the object and the sleeve. This will permit just enough space for any slight expansion or contraction of the object, depending on shifts in environment, without allowing the object to overly move in the housing. Do not force the corner into place or make the fitting too snug. With the corners in position on the object and now in contact with the backing, fix the mounts to the backing board by laying a strip of archival or acid-free tape across the mount and onto the support- ing board, making sure to leave a gap between the adhesive tape and the edge of the corner sleeve. Verify that the placement is correct by carefully closing the housing or inspecting the overall mount: this will be an opportunity to make changes in position if needed, and, if a change is required, only two corners might require adjustment or refashioning, rather than all four. To complete the mount, replicate the same placement of the corner sleeves on the upper corners of the object, remembering to leave a small buffer of space between the edges of the object within the sleeve. Repeat the process of mounting the corners with the archival tape to the backing board.

   For fabricated visible corners: Before positioning the corner sleeve over the object, using a piece of double-sided adhesive tape shorter than the distance of the corner, release one side of the adhesive strip backing, and position the tape on the back of the mount. Repeat this for all corner mount before positioning on the object. Placement of visible mounts may be easier if the preparator proceeds one corner at a time to ensure that there is no accidental contact with the adhesive on the back of the visible mount. Release the opposite backing for the double-sided tape and allow the corner to contact the backing. Do not burnish the corner with the object in the mount. Remove the object from the sleeve and burnish the corner mount to ensure greatest adhesion to the board. Repeat this process with each corner, being careful to remove the object before burnishing the mount. If the object is frail or brittle, this approach may not be suitable.

Prefabricated Corner Mounts

An alternative to assembling the corner mount is the option of using prefabricated archival corner mounts, sometimes called "photo corners." These clear mounting corners are available in a small variety of sizes, most commonly ranging in small (1/2 inch to 3/4 inch; 10–19 mm), medium (1¼ inch; 32 mm), and large (3 inch; 75 mm). These corners are constructed from polypropylene (a chemically

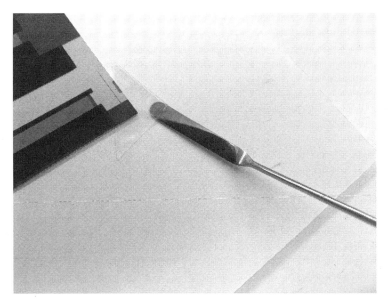

Figure 6.4. Placing the Prefabricated Corner w/ Microspatula. *Source:* Image credit: Andrew Saluti.

inert material) and come with an adhesive backing; no tape is needed to secure these mounts. The prefabricated corners also come in a "cut out" variation, with the outward facing part of the sleeve cut to expose as much of the object as possible while still securing the object—a very useful mount for objects with smaller margins. The drawbacks to using the prefabricated corner mounts are the inability to customize for size or shape of the sleeve—you are restricted by scale and object dimensionality. Placing these corners can also be slightly more problematic in terms of object handling because of the adhesive backing. A tip for applying these corners: use a microspatula tool to position the corners behind the object before burnishing to the backing. Trying to manipulate both the delicate placement of the adhesive corners and the position of the object by hand can pose a risk of mishandling or damage to the object—instead, lay the object in place on the housing, verify its position, and then adhere the mount just at the tip of the microspatula to allow placement of the corner behind the object where the two bottom sleeves need to be. Remove the object and burnish the mounts in place to achieve adhesion to the backing. For the upper mounts, follow the same procedure as with paper mounts: sliding the corner in place on the object to position, remembering to not burnish the mount with the object included. Note: even though many works on paper will allow for variance and flexibility in how the sheet is manipulated, the preparator should, whenever possible, try to avoid bending or flexing a flat object to fit into a mount. While these actions may not necessarily pose immediate risk depending on the condition of the sheet, mitigating the risk of possible tear, crease, or loss should take precedent over the ease of mounting.

Mountings Tabs

Even as corner mounts are the most common passive mounting system, there are additional prefabricated alternatives to creating hinges to flat objects. Mounting tabs and strips, similar to corners, can provide a secure mount without having to make physical additions to our objects. These mounts are constructed from a rigid Mylar tab with a self-adhesive band, allowing the tab to overhang the object to prevent movement. When mounted around the perimeter of a flat object, these tabs will safely maintain the object in position and are useful when the object is an organic shape with no corners to use the corner sleeve or when the condition of the object prevents the use of other such fasteners. Similar to that of prefabricated corners, and due to the nature of the mounts, the preparator can be limited by dimensionality of the object but can also employ these materials with other techniques, such as a sink mat or cavity housings, to adapt to the object need. There is also the expense, considering the use of mounting tabs will normally require multiple strips around the perimeter of the object.

ARCHIVAL HINGES

If all passive mounting strategies have been considered but deemed inappropriate or incompatible for the object, the preparator may consider creating a physical hinge to fix the object to a backing or housing. This work should be done in consultation with collections colleagues and, depending on the object evaluation, may need a conservator's involvement. However, if approached conservatively with minimal impact on the object, the mounting hinge can be the most effective method to safely securing an object.

An archival hinge can be created from a few different types of resources. A common material used by many collections is gummed linen tape—a staple of many preservation and preparation labs. This fabric tape is coated with a layer of methylcellulose that can be activated with distilled water, used for hinging archival mats and housings. Linen tape can ensure a strong and reversible mount but because of the girth and stiffness of the fabric tape will also be bulky and have visible dimension. Linen tape may be used for heavier papers and media, such as watercolors or cotton rag art papers, but for more delicate sheets, documents and photographs, the linen tape may not be suitable for a clean and effective mount and may even cause physical variation of the hinged area over long-term applications. For this reason, the ideal hinge for most works on paper and archival materials is a *fiber paper mount*. Usually comprising a mulberry or similar fiber, these hinges are not only thin and unobtrusive but also incredibly strong. These mounting tapes can be purchased pre-coated with an archival adhesive similar to linen tape or can be created by the preparator with the raw materials. The adhesive used should always be a natural archival adhesive that can be reversed, such as a methylcellulose or a starch paste. Avoid using any pressure-sensitive tapes, "acid-free" double-sided tapes, or other types of non-archival adhesives, such as white (jade) glue or spray adhesives—these should never be used for mounting objects. Other tools and materials needed for this process will be the microspatula (also used in corner mounts); a ceramic water wheel (ceramic tongue), a device that will distribute an even film of liquid to activate pre-coated materials; and blotting papers, absorbent sheets that will collect excess moisture away from other materials or papers.

Even though proper archival hinges are removable through conservation, adding a hinge to an object will make a permanent and physical change and needs to be done with care and strategy: being particular regarding the location of the hinges on the object, as well as the overall size and variation. Always use as few mounts as safely possible for the object and always hinge *only* on the top edge. This will minimize the physical impact of the mounting process and will not constrict any natural expansion and contraction of the object.

The most common hinge used for mounting flat objects may be the T hinge, a straightforward mount aptly named for the orientation of the two corresponding sections of hinge tape that create the system: a vertical tab that extends from the top edge of the object, overlapped by the crossing tab that adheres to the mounting board—quite literally like crossing a "T." This is an ideal mount for hinges that will be hidden behind a top mat or closing, only visible when the housing is opened, and is popular not only because of the ease of applying the mount but also because of the simplicity in releasing the object from the backing.

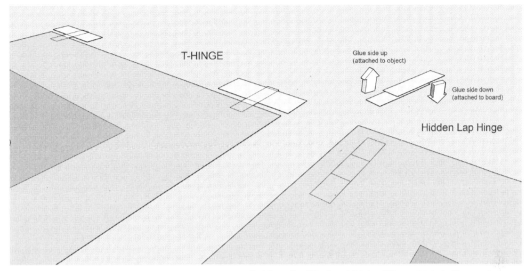

Glue side up
(attached to object)

Glue side down
(attached to board)

T-HINGE

Hidden Lap Hinge

Figure 6.5. Placement of a Common "T" Hinge (left) and a Blind or Hidden Hinge (right). *Source*: Image credit: Andrew Saluti.

Step 1: Evaluation

Like any other preparation task, the process of creating a T hinge mount starts with the object itself. An examination of the media, condition, and attributes will inform the materials used; the size, position, and frequency of the mounts; and any other variables that can dictate the process. How large is the sheet being mounted? Is the sheet a contemporary paper or does it show signs of age and wear? How frequently will it be handled?

Step 2: Prepping Materials

In preparing the hinge material, remember that the amount of material in contact with the object, as well as the number of tabs, should be as minimal as safely possible, that is, if your object is a vertical 10 × 8-inch photograph, the mounting tab does not need to be a full width (usually 1 inch) strip of mounting tape to secure the object. In this case, using a 1/2-inch strip of material will do the job. The length of this part of the mount is also variable and should be dictated by the object: for smaller objects, only a modest section of that hinge needs to be adhered to the top edge of the work (in the afore-mentioned example, only about a 1/4 inch of material). The total length of the object tab, or "stem," can be calculated from the contact length plus the width of the crossing tab, which is trimmed after the mount is complete. The corresponding crossing tab can be the full dimension of the tape, at least twice the width of the hinge stem in length. Considering the top edge of the object is only 8 inches wide, two T hinges will provide more than enough support inside the mat housing. *Tip: When using fiber paper mounts, it is ideal to tear the pieces to size rather than cutting. Depending on the material used, the cut edge can potentially tear, dent, or damage the object surface; the torn edge allows a soft, feathered transition from hinge material to object surface.* If using a pre-coated tape, be sure to use distilled water to activate the adhesive as minerals and substances from tap or well water may affect the object; using a ceramic tongue that can be cleaned regularly is best practice. If creating a handmade fiber paper tab with a natural starch paste or methylcellulose, prepare just enough of the adhesive needed to specifications (do not save leftover natural glues) and be sure to have a clean brush to apply the adhesive, as well as a scrap sheet of mylar or other polyester sheet to use as a surface to apply the paste.

Step 3: Attaching the Stems

Once all mounting materials are ready, place the object in its desired position on the backing board. Activate the pre-coated hinge using the ceramic tongue with distilled water or by brushing the hand-made fiber paper hinge with natural adhesive on the waste polyester sheet. The active hinge will glisten until the excess moisture has been absorbed. Do not introduce the hinge material to the object until the surface of the mount no longer shines—excess moisture from improper mounting can be extremely damaging to delicate or lightweight papers especially. Carefully place each stem on the upper perimeter of the backside of the object, glue side facing up, near but not on the outer edge corner—this can be a fragile area of a flat object. If additional hinges are required, add each hinge stem along the top edge sequentially along the perimeter. A microspatula can assist in guiding the hinge into place to facilitate contact with the object. Depending on the condition of the object, gentle pressure with a blotting paper will solidify the hinge connection. Allow the stems to dry and verify that the object has maintained its position on the mounting board before completing the mount.

Step 4: Crossing the T Hinge

Once the stems have cured and the object is in its appropriate position, the final step is to place the crossing material facedown onto the backing board, capturing the stem and securing the object. As with preparing the stem, activate or apply the adhesive on your mounting tab and carefully lay the cross laterally overlapping the stem with sufficient adhesion to the backing board. The placement of this crossing tab is important: not so close to the edge of the object that the strip may come in contact but not so far that the stem allows the object to swing or shift—this would be counter to the purpose of the mount. The ideal T hinge will allow just enough buffer, between 1/8 and 1/16 of an inch, between the object and the cross-mounting tab that can present the opportunity to cut the hinge if the object needed to be released. Burnish the cross-mounts down to the backing board with blotting paper, being careful not to harm the object.

Note: When releasing an object from a T hinge mount, use a blade to cut the T hinge should be approached with the utmost care and meticulous precision. When cutting the hinge, rather than cutting parallel to the edge of the object, slice the tab perpendicular, with the blade moving away from the work. This will not only be a safer action but also leave the stem intact: allowing the preparator to rehinge the object without adding any additional materials or mounts to the already hinged object.

Once the hinges have been applied, the mounts will require time to dry and cure completely and the object to adjust to the new housing. It is important to allow the mounted object to rest for an extended period (12 to 24 hours) before encasing the work within a frame, a storage device, drawer, or any other shift in environment.

Blind or Hidden Hinges

While the T hinge is ideal for visible mounts, concealed behind mats or other housings, there are common instances when the entirety of the object needs to be in full view. This evaluative decision may be due to markings, content, or relative attributes of the object that extend to the outer edge of the object, in which case an overmat would cover these elements. In these situations, the preparator may decide that the object would be best mounted in a float mat. The T hinge, while functional, would be visible and may deter from the intended presentation or interpretation of the object. The *V-hinge* allows a blind mount securing the object as if floating in the window or viewable area. Like its sibling mount, the V-hinge is named for the physical shape of the mount; the material is folded over in the form of a "V." Because this mount is hidden behind the object, the application and manipulation of this mount requires additional attention and a slightly more complex approach that that of the visible T hinge.

To initiate a blind hinge, the process begins as before: evaluation of the object to dictate practice. The materials needed will also be same; however, the preparation of the mounts will vary slightly. In this case, the tab materials (whether pre-coated or fabricated) should be at least 1-inch wide to allow for an adequate surface area for the mount, which will be folded over itself (half the total width of the material). The application of these mounts also varies from the visible hinge or corner mounts in that the object will need to be flipped face forward during the process and, depending on the media or condition, will require additional handling considerations for this process.

Step 1: Positioning the Object

Place the object in the housing to find the appropriate position in concert with the window. Using a hard graphite pencil, lightly (and as minimally as possible) mark the position near the two top corners of the object, so as to indicate both the lateral and vertical position for the work. Flip the object, face-down, so the same edge is in line with the marks, as if swung on a hinge.

Step 2: Attaching the Mounts

Activate or apply the adhesive as outlined in the previous method—paying attention to the sheen of the tabs before application (see T hinge process). Lay the first hinge near but not on the corner of the edge of the object so half the material rests on the board. Gently apply pressure and collect excess moisture with a blotting sheet—do not burnish. Repeat with the applicable number of mounts sequentially along the edge.

Step 3: Reinforcing the Mounts

To ensure that these mounts will carry the weight of the object, an additional cross-mount can be added to reinforce the V-hinge on the board. Tearing tabs long enough to overlap the hinge material attached to the object, activate or apply the adhesive and position over the part of the hinges that are on the mounting board—not to extend past the edges of the object. As with the cross-mounts on the T hinge, burnish with blotting paper to capture excess moisture and to ensure greatest adhesion. These mounts need to be fully dry and cure before continuing to the next step.

Step 4: Repositioning the Object

Once the hinges have dried, gently reposition the object by flipping it back to its front-facing orientation. Apply gentle pressure along the top edge of the object to crease the hinges in place. Close your mat housing.

Variations for Float

There may be instances where the object requires a float mount with a blind or hidden hinge, but the V-hinge is not applicable: if the object is a unique or organic shape or if the condition prohibits a secure hinge on the top edge. In these cases, the lap-hinge may be a solution. The lap-hinge is constructed similarly to the T hinge, using two corresponding tabs of pre-coated tape (this method is best achieved using a linen prefabricated mounting tape; fiber paper mounts can be difficult to manipulate as a lap-hinge) that overlap themselves in a parallel, corresponding direction, rather than crossing; this creates a long tab that has adhesive areas on the recto and verso of either side of the hinge. The assembly and application of the lap-hinge needs to be done in place, at the same time as activation/ application of the adhesives, making it a challenging operation to complete depending on the object being mounted. In addition to the challenges of applying the mount, depending on the length that the hinge is created, it will allow for a relatively broad range of motion, which can be antithetical to the objectives of mounting the object in place. Lap-hinges are useful in exceptional situations, where the placement of the hinge requires a discrete or narrow solution.

Another simple variation for float mounting is the use of tabs to hold the object in place around its perimeter. These can be affective when the object in question needs additional support beyond the corner sleeve due to condition or physical shape. A simple method for creating a basic tab is to cut a prefabricated corner mount in half, from the corner of the closed angle to the midpoint of the hypotenuse side, thus creating two "open-faced" triangular tabs that could be placed on any edge of an object. These tabs can safely secure the edge of the sheet without encapsulating a corner or adding to the stress of fitting the artifact into a sleeve for mounting. When using a tab mount, note that there will be a need to secure multiple sides to fully support the object in place. These can be very effective mounts for objects whose condition or structure won't allow the use of the corner sleeve mount as well as objects that are buckled or wavy or in general will not completely rest flat on the mounting surface.

Variations for Mounting

Sink (Cavity) Mat Housings

There are instances when the two-dimensional object may not be able to be safely or effectively mounted to the backing board in a mat housing: objects that do not have the surface stability or structure to maintain the attachment to the mount (this can stem from material characteristics or condition) or might be damaged by the introduction of a corner sleeve. Additionally, objects that are created on a more substantial backing than that of paper or other thin substrates, or exceed the dimension of the housing, may prevent the use of a standard hinged mat. In these cases, a *sink mat* (or cavity housing) can be created. The sink mat is a simple variation of the mat housing that creates a cavity for the object to rest in and allows the mat to close on the same plane as the surface of the object. When the cavity that the object rests in is engineered specifically to accommodate the dimension of the object, the need for additional security mounting can be diminished (but not always relieved) when properly enclosed under a mat window. Examples of objects for such housings include objects created on or mounted to a thick board or substrate, such as illustration board, hardboard, or any support that has a thickness or physicality that would prevent the standard mat housing to safely close and encapsulate the object.

The cavity is created by building up the margin sides of the housing to match the depth of the object. This can be accomplished in multiple ways: the cavity can be assembled from archival materials, like building blocks or layers, or the exact dimension/shape of the cavity can be cut out of a singular sheet that also matches the depth of the object. For the latter, starting from an acid-free foam core board or mat board can be used if the desired finished height is appropriate. In the case of a built cavity, which allows for a greater range of customizable dimension, use strips of archival mat board laminated on top of each other until the desired height is achieved. Using an acid-free two-sided gum tape to fix each layer to the backing board as well as to each corresponding piece, a stable and exact recess for the object to rest in can be created. The dimension of the cavity should exactly reflect the object being housed therein, allowing for marginal space for handling (depending on size and material, this dimension may range). The cavity should not be tight fitting or too snug on any aspect of the artifact, as this can lead to damage: the object should never be forced into the mount. However, there should not be too much space given around the object as this will create an opportunity for movement in transit or handling, posing additional risk of damage. Once in the cavity, the object should not shift or move but should comfortably and stably rest within the opening *and* be easily removed: this can be accomplished by adding points of access—cutting a small round or triangular recess or notch that doesn't affect the cavity's stability and support for the object (this can be added along a long edge of the margin) but allows for easy access to safely handle the work in place. The window mat can then be hinged to the top layer of the cavity wall and then rest on the surface of the object without force or disruption, encapsulating the artifact within the housing, stabilized for presentation or storage.

Archival Backing Mount

In addition to variations on window-based mat housing, artifacts and documents can also be presented independent of the window enclosure. In these cases, the archival mat board can be used as a backing support to stabilize the object while on view without any encapsulation or housing, that is, presented independent of any margin or physical structure. Common in archive display, the treatment allows the object to be installed within a case or controlled space free of any frame, allowing the viewer to engage with the entirety of the artifact or document. This approach presents a work on paper to be perceived as "object" rather than as "flat sheet." Creating this backing is relatively simple: the archival board needs to be trimmed to the size/shape of the document or sheet being supported, taking into consideration adequate space for whichever mounting procedure is to be employed. For example, a hand-scribed letter from a scientist's archive is to be shown in an exhibition of that person's research. The letter is five pages long and will be installed within a display case with other artifacts and specimen. Rather than mat each page of the letter or mount them all in one large multi-window mat, the preparator is choosing to display each page independently, with a simple easel mount to elevate them to an easily viewable angle for readability. To safely mount each page of the letter, the preparator is choosing to use corner sleeve mounts in order to not add any adhesive mount to the delicate sheets that might require active conservation to remove. Knowing that the corner mounts will require an additional .125 (1/8) inch of surface area beyond the original dimension of the document, the preparator trims 4-ply archival board to the specified size, adding a total of .25 inches to the measured size of the object. This gives the preparator the adequate margin to use the corner sleeves to mount the letter to the board, allowing a vertical standing installation of each page.

INTERLEAVING

Once the object has been successfully mounted in the archival housing, further protection must be included if the object is not immediately going into a frame or case to prevent damage to the visible surface. A sheet of interleaving is used as a loose protective barrier that rests on the mounted object, under the mat window. It is important that the interleaving material is, at minimum, the same size as the object it is protecting, so there is little opportunity for the edges of the sheet to slip and abrade the surface of the object. In addition, the interleaving sheet should not exceed the size of the housing, as it can easily catch and pull away from the object. There are a variety of accepted materials that can be used for interleaving, each having particular qualities that make them better or less suited for different object types or activities.

Glassine is a translucent, ultrasmooth, lightweight material that is unbuffered and pH neutral. Glassine is ideal for protecting prints, watercolors, and most types of works on paper, allowing visibility to the object surface. Because of its weight and strength, glassine is ideal for wrapping books and other objects but should not be used for paintings or varnished surfaces. Glassine is also not ideal for photographic negatives or other media that contain an emulsion layer, as this can adhere to the glassine surface in environments of variable humidity.

Archival tissue is also an ideal interleaving material for many types of works on paper, including photographs. Unbuffered tissues are great for use with textiles as interleaving as well as padding and packing.

Acid-free bond paper is a buffered, smooth sheet that is an excellent material for protecting photographic media, prints, and most works on paper. Acid-free bond is heavier than glassine or tissue and can also be used to create folios, sleeves, corner mounts, and other archival and document enclosures.

Polyethylene spun fiber sheeting (Tyvek®) is a nonwoven, inert, pH neutral sheet that has a smooth, soft finish that will not abrade objects. The material is waterproof and dust resistant but also remains breathable, allowing airflow for objects that are being protected. This material is highly durable—much stronger than other tissues, papers, and fabrics—but can easily be shaped and cut to size. There are specific grades of this material that do not have any coatings or finishes that commercial grade Tyvek includes for building construction.

Polyester sheet (Mylar®, Melinex®) is an optically clear film sheet that is chemically inert and ideal for interleaving when an uninterrupted view of the object is desired—especially in research presentation. Safe for most objects, with the exception of unfixed or fugitive media such as charcoal or pastel, as the surface can create a static charge that may pull media from the object surface.

FRAMES

A ubiquitous form of display furniture across collections, the frame is the basic support system for many wall-mounted objects. Frames are highly adaptable exhibition tools: they can encapsulate objects in a microenvironment that will secure an object in transit or installed in a gallery environment, or they can simply act as a secure mounting mechanism to relieve the object from the stress of installation or shipping. They can have an aesthetic function that reinforces an interpretive experience or be simplified to direct attention to the object being mounted. There are countless variations in the size, shape, and style, but similar to a mat housing, their functionality—from a collections point of view—is the primary purpose, with the style and aesthetic secondary.

Regardless of the type or style, the structure of any frame will be made up of two defining elements: the profile and rabbet.

The *profile* is the cross-section contour of the frame. Profiles can be elaborate and ornate or as simple as a 90° inverted "L"-shaped piece of material. The profile largely defines the aesthetic presentation of the frame but also impacts functionality in so far as how much dimension, weight, and structure the frame will add to the object (i.e., if the object requires stability in addition to a particular appropriate look, the profile will be the major determining factor). Contemporary frames will generally have a simple profile, while historic frames might include a more elaborate contour and finish. The face of the frame is the part of the profile that will be on the same plane as the viewable object. The face is an important aspect of the profile as it can determine how the frame will impact both the function as a protective and structural element and the object's aesthetic presentation from the viewer's perspective.

The *rabbet* of the frame is the interior depth dimension of the part of the frame that will hold the object and framing materials inside the structure. Identifying this measurement is critical for the preparator when deciding on a frame, as it dictates whether the frame will be an adequate size for the object at hand. This measurement is far more significant and takes precedence over any profile determination, as the function of the frame will always trump the form.

There are two significant variations of frame moldings (lengths of framing material): wood frames and metal sectional frames. Each kind of frame has pros and cons for use, and both are commonly used in museum collections practice.

Wood frames are, as implied, composed of wooden molding that is cut to a specific size and joined to create the final frame. The wood frame is a fixed size and can be easily reused to house objects to that predetermined size or matted to the finished interior dimension (see list of standard sizes). Wood frames come in a wide variety of profiles and can have a broad range in size. Museum-quality wood frames will also incorporate an interior support structure—called a strainer—quite liter-

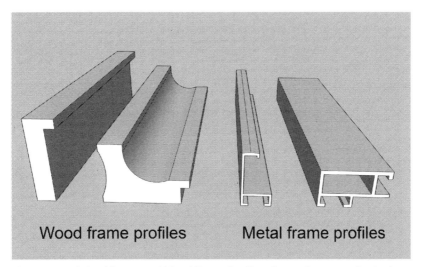

Figure 6.6. Wood Frame and Metal Frame Profiles. *Source*: Image credit: Andrew Saluti.

ally a frame within a frame. This allows the wooden frame to carry a large load and better support a hanging mechanism, taking the pressure off the outer rails of the frame.

Metal sectional frames are constructed from aluminum molding that is shaped to create a range of contemporary profiles that can be assembled using special compression bracket hardware and then disassembled once not in use or when the object needs to be removed or changed. Metal sectional frames are quite versatile in that common profiles can be put together in various configurations depending on the size needed: a 16 × 20-inch frame can be disassembled to use the separate 16- and 20-inch sections with other sizes. This also allows metal sectional frame stock to be easily stored when not in use.

When deciding on whether to use a wood frame or a metal section frame, consider the following comparisons:

Wood frame pros:

- Wood frames profiles are often more suited for a broader range of objects.
- Wood frames can carry a larger load and support larger objects than metal frames.
- Wood frames can have a greater range in rabbet depth and stability.

Wood frame cons:

- Wood frames are a fixed size.
- Wood frames often require greater storage needs.

Metal sectional frame pros:

- Metal frames are more versatile as they can be assembled in different configurations according to size.
- Metal frames can be disassembled and stored easily.

Metal sectional frame cons:

- Profiles are generally contemporary and not necessarily appropriate for pre-twentieth-century objects.
- Metal frames cannot easily accommodate larger objects or heavier objects.

Like so many decisions in preparation work, the decision to utilize wood frames or metal frames primarily centered around object evaluation: What is both functionally and aesthetically appropriate for that object? Another consideration is use: Will there be a need for frequent installation of framed objects, and what are the sizes that will need to be accommodated? Does your institution have adequate storage for a selection of frames? Will objects be stored in their frames or will they be unframed and stored flat, allowing for reuse of the frame (as well as the aforementioned storage burden)?

When dissecting how the frame creates a stable support for flat or matted objects, the following elements are included in the closed frame package.

Glazing—the clear acrylic or glass protective barrier. Museum-quality glazing is enhanced to filter out UV to protect the object on view. It is best practice to use acrylic rather than glass, as it won't shatter or crack as easily and is lighter weight. However, the surface of acrylic glazing will often build a static charge that can create a pull on the object surface. Certain fugitive media, such as charcoal or pastel, should not use acrylic glazing without an antistatic coating and proper distance from the object surface.

Spacer (optional)—a spacer can be added to create a larger space between the glazing and the object. The spacer is fabricated to fit in the rabbet and hidden under the face, creating a consistent, flush presentation between the glazing and object. Some wood and metal moldings can include a spacer in their profile.

Matted or mounted object—the object rests below the protective glazing layer, separated from direct contact with the glazing by a mat housing or mounted to an archival backing with spacers between the backing and the glazing.

Moisture stabilizer (optional)—silica gel sheet that will stabilize a consistent relative humidity within the enclosed microclimate of the frame. It is suggested that a moisture stabilizer be used whenever an object is traveling outside its institutional environment or will be on view for an extended time frame. Consult a paper conservator for guidance.

Backing board—rigid protective layer that will withstand puncture or damage, as well as provide a vapor barrier. Best practice suggests using a corrugated plastic board rather than a foam board or other paper-based material.

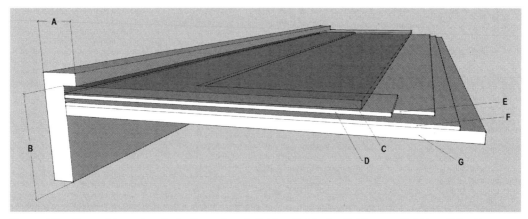

Figure 6.7. Frame Dissection: A. Profile or face B. Rabbet C. Glazing D. Top mat E. Object F. Backing mat G. Backing board. *Source*: Image credit: Andrew Saluti.

Strainer—the rigid support that encloses the object package inside the frame, as well as providing a stable structure to attach hanging hardware for installation.

If the frame will be traveling outside a stable environment, it is good practice to seal the perimeter of the package (glazing, object, moisture stabilizer, and backing board) with an archival sealing tape. This will create an impenetrable barrier from dramatic fluctuations in the environment, pests, and dust infiltration and will also make the assembly of the frame easier. Tip: If the object has been previously matted and is being framed for a temporary installation, place the interleaving sheet between the mat housing and the backing board. Once the object is removed from the frame, the interleaving sheet can be immediately replaced.

Variations of Frames

In addition to the standard wood and metal classifications, there are additional styles of frames that serve particular functions. These include profiles for floating canvases, deep shadowbox-style spacers, and the use of the frame as stabilizing support for travel.

A *canvas floater frame* is a profile that not only allows for a non-glazed presentation of an object, usually for a painting on canvas, but can also be used for any flat object where glazing is not necessary and the entirety of the object (perimeter edge) is to be viewed. The canvas float resembles an inverted basic frame. Where the face of the frame would normally come over the top of the glazed surface, the floater frame creates a stepped bracket that sits behind the object, allowing for special hardware to secure the object from the verso. This allows the object to appear as "floating" inside the frame rabbet. When selecting a floater frame profile, the rabbet depth is still an important dimension to consider: even though there is no glazing to hold, the frame will still give protection to the object if the profile is taller than the object depth. If the floater frame profile is shallower than the object surface, the framed artifact will be more susceptible to potential contact and damage.

Shadowbox-style frames create a large, enclosed cavity to present objects of varying size within a wall-mounted frame. This style of frame is often used in commercial or residential situations to show-

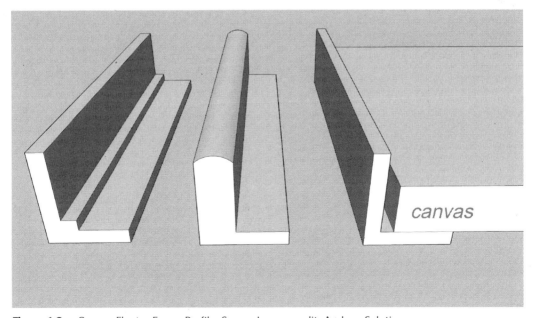

Figure 6.8. Canvas Floater Frame Profile. *Source*: Image credit: Andrew Saluti.

case objects that may not easily be displayed, such as textiles, flags, garments, or small dimensional objects. The shadowbox is a versatile option for presenting low-profile (but not flat) objects in secure presentation furniture. These frames can be fabricated by adding spacers to a deep rabbet profile or be fabricated with the spacer depth and glazing channel incorporated into the profile design. Note: shadowbox frames allow space for movement within the frame and may not be an ideal choice for objects in transit.

 Travel frames are any non-presentation frame that is used to secure an object for handling, shipping, or storage. These frame structures are generally built as simple, functional enclosures rather than finished or stylized frames for exhibition. Travel frames may be constructed for specific crate or packing needs but are sometimes used as an object's long-term storage solution. Unframed canvases or other independent flat objects utilize a travel frame for the same security the frame provides other objects, such as the extended rabbet profile depth for canvas or a safe and fixed surface for handling.

PAINTINGS/CANVAS PREPARATION

Another ecumenical practice the preparator will routinely engage with flat objects is the proper preparation of stretched canvases. This is essential for the object if it is being installed in an exhibition but is equally important for the general preservation of the painting. The stretched canvas is particularly vulnerable to risk if the painting support (canvas) is open to the environment. Like matting a work on paper, the preparator can take action to protect the object from the hazards of transit, installation, and environmental risk. This includes backing the auxiliary support (stretcher frame) to shield the verso of the main support surface, creating a cushion within the rabbet of the frame, and using specialized hardware to mount independent canvases within a frame.

Backing a Canvas

It is common to find unbacked canvases in collections, where the stretched canvas is completely open and unprotected whether it is housed in a frame or independent. The potential for damage in these situations is exponentially enhanced from multiple points of view. The open canvas is at greater risk of puncture or physical damage from the back. The object is open to environmental risks, such as sudden changes in humidity and temperature that might strain the painted surface. The bare canvas can be a harbor for pests, dirt, and debris, which can fall in the sensitive space between the canvas and the stretcher frame. Adding a rigid barrier behind the canvas can alleviate these risks, as well as assist in stabilizing the painting from shock and vibration during transition. Note: It is important to carefully evaluate the recto of the canvas to verify that the object condition is stable enough for the action of applying the backing. If the canvas is sagging, has incurred loss or deformation, or seems particularly fragile, consult a paintings conservator before taking action. If the object is already housed within a frame, leave the canvas in place. The frame will act as a perimeter support system during the backing process. If the canvas is unframed, a cushioned support or surface may be needed to safely attach the backing, so as to not damage the painting surface while working on the reverse side.

Backing Materials

Selecting the right kind of backing materials and hardware is key. For the protective layer, use a rigid board that won't deteriorate or fail in variable environments and one that will withstand and absorb the possibility of significant physical dangers such as puncture or strikes. Foam boards and archival cardboards have been used in the past, but these materials won't necessarily withstand shifts in humidity or infestation. Hardboards, such as Masonite®, can withstand a large range of physical attack but will add significant weight to the object, possibly straining the auxiliary support it is attached to.

The ideal material to use is a corrugated polyethylene sheet: chemically inert, able to withstand shifts in the environment and repel pests, and extremely lightweight and durable. If there are markings on the verso of the canvas that is set to be covered, an acrylic sheet can also be used. The sheet should be trimmed to an inset size of the auxiliary support, leaving enough perimeter that the new backing will not cover any part of the primary support material (canvas). Tip: if using corrugated plastic board, trim the corners to an angled edge to remove the sharp point of the plastic sheet before fastening the backing.

The hardware used to fasten the board to the backing should be corrosion-resistant screws and cup washers to protect the backing surface and secure the mount. Brass or stainless steel screws are recommended. The size of the screw will depend on the girth of the stretcher material but consider using as conservatively shallow a screw as possible (such as a #5 or #6 screw), so as to not unintentionally split or puncture the stretcher (and potentially the canvas). Additionally, in order to create an airtight seal between the backing and the object, it is sometimes recommended to use a closed-cell foam strip around the inside perimeter of the backing board. Self-adhesive foam weather stripping works well for this gasketing application. When positioning the hardware, be sure to avoid the movable interlocking corners of the painting stretcher, so as to not disturb the natural expansion of the support system. Also, avoid placing the hardware too close to the interior edge of the stretcher, as this may lead to splitting or cracking the material and cause the backing or the support to fail. Place screw position evenly around the backing, approximately 8 inches apart. Never drill into the backing board as it sits on the stretcher: use an awl to puncture placement holes, and, whenever possible, tighten screws by hand into the support. Do not overtighten to the point that the board compresses: hand-tighten to the point where the foam gasketing layer just slightly compacts. This will create a stable, reinforced, and impermeable protective layer for the painting. This new backing layer can also be marked with pertinent collection information or carry an archival sleeve for related documents or information.

When adding the appropriate hanging hardware, such as D-rings or other corresponding mechanisms (see chapter 11), it is important to avoid placing these devices on the surface of the backing board. If housed in a frame, the hardware should always be fastened to the frame structure rather than the object. If the backed canvas or object is not intended to be framed, be sure to either leave adequate margin for the hanging mechanisms to be added or notch sections of the backing to allow for the hanging mechanisms to rest directly on the stretcher surface, rather than sandwiching the backing material to the support. This will create a more secure hanging structure for the object, as well as save the backing material from stress or wear that may expedite a failure in the surface.

Prepping a Frame for Canvas

Once the canvas has been properly backed, it may be appropriate to mount within a frame for added support. Or, the preparator may need to remove a painting from its current housing to augment the existing frame to a more secure housing for the canvas. There are two procedures that should be considered: shielding the canvas surface from the potentially acidic or unsealed surface of the frame molding and to cushion the point of direct contact with the canvas surface. To seal the interior of the frame rabbet, use a vapor barrier material such as Marvelseal®, an aluminized polyethylene and nylon barrier film, to prevent any transmission of off-gassing chemicals or other hazards from coming into direct contact with the object. The uppermost surface of the rabbet can then be cushioned, where the canvas is in direct, compressed contact with the frame. This will prevent what is known as "rabbet rub," the gradual abrasion of the painted surface against the inner cavity of the frame, which often leads to areas of loss and damage. The cushion material should be an inert material such as acrylic felt or polyethylene foam sheeting. Adhesive-backed acrylic felts can be purchased in a variety of lengths and thicknesses to accommodate a wide array of frame sizes. When installing the lining material, be careful not to allow the felt or padding to appear too close to the rabbet edge, allowing the viewer to see the material. Run the cushion along the entire perimeter of the interior frame, wherever there is direct contact with the object. Once in place, the frame is now properly prepped to accept and support the painted surface.

Mounting the Canvas

With a properly backed canvas and a prepped frame housing sealed and cushioned, the final step is to secure the canvas in place. There is a specific type of mounting bracket that should be used for this procedure: the offset clip (commonly referred to as the Z bracket). This step-shaped piece of hardware is designed specifically to hold a canvas stretcher in place, whether inside the rabbet of a frame or resting in a floater frame. These brackets can be purchased in variable heights to accommodate different object depths as they rest in a housing. They will normally have a hardware hole on one or both ends of the bracket, though the clips should only be fastened to the frame or housing surface—never to the object support. This will allow the object to expand and contract freely in the frame while still being securely held in place. Similar to the guidance in positioning the hardware for the backing material, place each appropriately sized bracket along the perimeter of the frame so each stepped fastener is just resting on the object surface (if the depth needed falls in between the given heights of the bracket, an inert material, such as the rabbet liner or archival mat board, can be added to the underside of the part of the bracket that is in contact with the canvas to fill the gap). Place a step evenly around the object, avoiding the corners of the support and spacing approximately every 8 inches. Once plotted, begin to fasten the brackets into the frame, screwing in opposing sides of the object each time. Once completely fastened, the bracket should just make contact with the object: if the canvas compresses or contorts, the brackets are not the correct height and should be removed immediately. After securing all brackets in place, the painting is now ready for installation.

Figure 6.9. Canvas Z Brackets. *Source*: Image credit: Andrew Saluti.

NOTE

1. Based on informal collection surveys conducted in 2019 from the online collection databases of the Metropolitan Museum of Art, the British Museum, and the Museum of Fine Arts, Boston.

REFERENCES

Clements, Gayle F. "Guidelines for Framing Canvas Paintings in Traditional Frames without Glazing, Part I." *Oklahoma Field Advisory Service: Technical Bulletin*. MuseNews 24:1 January, 1994. https://www.okmuseums.org/sites/oma2/uploads/documents/Technical_Bulletins/Technical_Bulletin_19_-_Guidelines_for_Framing_Part_I.pdf.

Hamel, Annajean. *Matting and Framing for Works on Paper and Photographs*. NEDCC website. Andover, MA. (2019). https://www.nedcc.org/free-resources/preservation-leaflets/4.-storage-and-handling/4.10-matting-and-framing-for-works-on-paper-and-photographs. Accessed March 2021.

Hartin, Debra Daly. *Backing Boards for Paintings on Canvas*. Canadian Conservation Institute (CCI). Notes 10/10, (1993, revised 2016). https://www.canada.ca/en/conservation-institute/services/conservation-preservation-publications/canadian-conservation-institute-notes/backing-boards-paintings.html.

Munroe, Susan Nash. "Making Mounting Corners for Photographs and Paper Objects." *Conserve O Gram*, July 1993 Number 14/1. National Parks Service, Curatorial Services Division, Harpers Ferry, WV.

Pasiuk, Janet. "Safe Plastics and Fabrics for Exhibit and Storage." *Conserve O Gram*, August 2004 Number 18/2. National Parks Service, Curatorial Services Division, Harpers Ferry, WV. https://www.nps.gov/museum/publications/conserveogram/18-02.pdf.

Phibbs, Hugh. "Preservation Matting for Works of Art on Paper." Supplement to *Picture Framing Magazine*, Feb. 1997.

Smith, Merrily A., Margaret R. Brown, and Library of Congress. National Preservation Program Office. *Matting and Hinging of Works of Art on Paper*. Washington: Preservation Office, Research Services, Library of Congress (1981).

Why is Tyvek So Good in Conservation Applications? Preservation Equipment Limited blog. https://www.preservationequipment.com/Blog/Blog-Posts/Tyvek-for-Conservation.

7

Preparation in Action

MOUNTING SCROLLS FOR EXHIBITION

Donia Conn, Assistant Professor of Practice, School of Library
and Information Science, Simmons University

Scrolls can add interest to an exhibition due to their often colorful and intriguing content and can add a sense of mystery to any exhibit case. However, safely mounting them to the precise location you want without damaging the object is less straightforward. Scrolls are tightly curled and range from very large to very small, so they do not fit into a simple cradle or matting that most of our paper-based collections do. This case study will explore the options for safely mounting scrolls for exhibition.

The scroll is one of the earliest formats used for literary texts; references can be found dating back to ancient Egypt in 4000 BCE. A scroll is a roll of material made up of multiple sheets. These sheets are glued or sewn together to form a single long strip. These long strips are frequently, but not always, attached to a central rod (or two rods) which is fitted with a handle to facilitate their use. Most scrolls are written on one side of the material and oriented either horizontally (in antiquity) or vertically (Medieval and beyond). The type of orientation used will significantly impact how a scroll can be mounted, as will the material used.

The earliest examples of scrolls were made with papyrus, an abundant plant material found along the shores of the Nile. Papyrus sheets were made by layering strips cut from the stem of the plant and pounding each layer to release the mucilage that holds the sheet together. Papyrus is strong and stable but does not fold without breaking, so creating the scroll was the only means of joining multiple sheets in one container. Papyrus scrolls were the primary form for written texts through the sixth-century CE when they were superseded by the codex, our modern book form. Very few papyrus scrolls exist as complete scrolls today. The best examples we have are those scrolls found during archaeological digs at Herculaneum. Unfortunately, they cannot be unrolled, but digital technology is helping us by recreating them through advanced imaging techniques.

The scroll continued to be used throughout Medieval Europe, although parchment supplanted the ancient papyrus. While parchment could be and was folded and bound into the codex form, certain types of information gathering lent themselves to the scroll format rather than the codex. According to the *Medieval Scrolls Digital Archive* hosted by Harvard University, the information can be broken down into four categories: small amulets, prayers, and charms that could be worn just as many wear the St. Christopher medal today; heraldic or genealogical information; liturgical scrolls such as the Torah, which is still used in scroll format; and records whose length is not known at the start of recording. This final example is the type of scroll that is the focus of this case study.

In early 2003, I was an advanced conservation intern (a three-month early-mid–career opportunity for conservators from around the world) at the Folger Shakespeare Library's (hereafter simply the Folger) conservation lab. In addition to the book and paper conservation work that was the focus of the internship, my time also coincided with the installation of the exhibit *Elizabeth I: Then and Now*. The whole conservation lab was busy treating and mounting objects for the show. The majority of the items going on exhibit were straightforward to mount, but two objects needed special attention. One was a modern replica of the dress that Queen Elizabeth I wore in George Gower's 1588 Armada Portrait. The other was a New Year's Gift Roll from 1585.

The 1585 Gift Roll documents the long-standing custom of courtiers presenting the monarch with gifts on New Year's Day. The ritual was a lavish public ceremony, and gifts, both given and received, were recorded on rolls and stored in the Jewel House. The 1585 roll going on exhibit is made of five sheets of parchment glued together to form a single roll approximately 16 inches wide and 11.5 feet long. The scroll was signed by Queen Elizabeth I at the top and the bottom of each side of the roll; gifts received in order of rank were on one side and those given in return on the other.

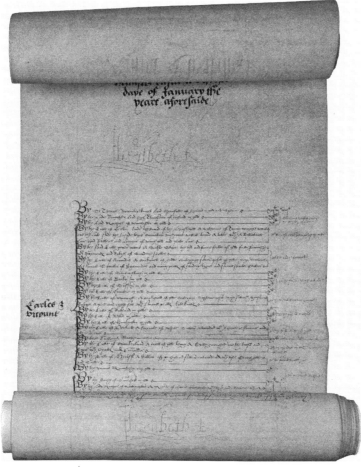

Figure 7.1. New Year's Gift Roll of Elizabeth I, Queen of England (manuscript), 1584/1585 January 1, Source Call Number Z.d.16. *Source*: Used by permission of the Folger Shakespeare Library.

The plan for this object was to display it vertically in one of the large wall-mounted cases in the exhibit hall. This meant that the simple method of mounting the scroll to a flat board with polyethylene strapping holding the rolled ends of the scroll in place and placing flat in a case (the perfect option for small scrolls) was not going to work.

The conservation lab at the Folger is a well-equipped and well-funded facility that has always taken the opportunity to expand the knowledge and use of new technologies and materials for the field. One of the materials being experimented with in early 2003 for exhibition mounts and protective enclosures was the PETG plastic sold under the brand name VIVAK®. VIVAK® is a clear, thermoplastic, rigid sheet of polyester that is easily cut and creased to create book cradles. The use of VIVAK® made creating clear custom book cradles easy and inexpensive when compared to Plexiglas cradles that required specialized equipment to shape or a large budget to purchase premade cradles.

It was decided that the mount for the Gift Roll would be made with VIVAK®. Having made several book cradles out of the plastic and knowing the rigid yet thermoplastic nature of the material, it became the ideal choice. In order to highlight Elizabeth I's signatures in the best way while still protecting the scroll itself, we designed a mount with a simple curve on the bottom and an almost closed roll at the top (see figure 7.2).

In order to create the mount, we needed to find something that would heat the VIVAK® in a larger area than a simple heat strip or heat gun could. Luckily, the lab had a vintage electric buffet warming tray that was used in the lab for paper splitting and keeping animal hide glue and gelatin warm during treatments. The pebbled glass top provided a gentle, even heat across its width that was the perfect size for the mount we needed to make. We also had a used shipping tube with the right size diameter that we decided to use as the curves' template.

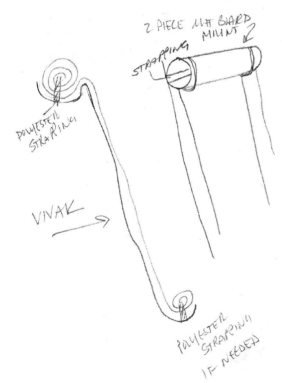

Figure 7.2. Diagram for the scroll mount using Vivak and a mat board tube. *Source*: Courtesy of Donia Conn.

While making the mount out of VIVAK® was good in theory, it proved more complicated in practice than we had anticipated. We experimented with some scraps and found that the warming tray worked great in heating the VIVAK® to pliability. The drawback was that to create the shape quickly enough before cooling and stiffening, it was not possible to do with only one person. In the end, we needed to work quickly as a team and utilize a piece of fabric to help guide the VIVAK® around the tube in a series of steps to make both curves. This was not easy since the piece of VIVAK® itself was long and awkward to handle. In the end, however, the Gift Roll fit into the top support perfectly, and the bottom nestled comfortably in its bowl, and the crystal clear quality of the plastic meant that nothing was obscured when on exhibit.

As great as the VIVAK® looked on exhibit, I think I would go back to a more traditional material and approach if I were to do it again. There is a wide range of shades of white and cream in museum-quality mat board these days. Given a choice, I would use a 2-ply mat board of a sympathetic color to the scroll I was mounting to create a tube in the diameter I needed for both top and bottom. Both ends of the scroll would be wrapped around the tube, and the tube and scroll mounted to a piece of 4- or 8-ply mat board of the same shade using polyester strapping. Polyester strapping is preferred here due to its more rigid nature, which would hold better than the softer polyethylene strapping used more frequently. I would then make sure that the mounting hardware in the case was robust enough to hold everything in place without slipping.

Although it takes a little more effort to create mounts for scrolls, they can add great dimension to an exhibit and don't need to be overly complicated.

8

Three-Dimensional Object Preparation

Much like two-dimensional works mounted to the wall or placed in archival casework, three-dimensional objects will mandate a particular array of considerations and procedures when being prepped for installation. The special considerations that these objects present can be both similar to and diametrically different than that of their two-dimensional counterparts. Holistically, the approach to the preparation process for these objects is not dissimilar, including an evaluation of the object and environment, followed by the construction and implementation of a stable and secure method for display. There are, however, obvious and significant differences between "flat" objects and "dimensional" objects when addressing installation needs—primarily in the physicality of both the object and in particular regard to environmental interaction and interpretation.[1] Objects that exist within a space, meant or intended to be seen in the round, examined from all sides, these objects and artifacts require added evaluative considerations and attention as to how they will safely be mounted and presented. In the approach to preparing flat or wall-mounted objects for installation and display, there are general practices and procedures that act as an umbrella approach and will accommodate an array of different kinds of objects and media: the kinds of furniture, frames, or mounting hardware used; the methodologies of calculating the installation position on the mounting surface; and standard practice on how to prepare objects for display. While there are certainly variations depending on the specific needs of each object, the overall techniques are largely consistent. For dimensional objects, this is not necessarily the case. The approach to preparing for installation can vary greatly depending on media, physicality, scale, and the context of the object in its presentation, all of which must be informed by the details of the installed setting (e.g., whether the object will be enclosed within casework or open to the environment; freestanding or secured to a base, mount, or pedestal). Any dimensional object or artifact, depending on what it is and how it will be installed, will certainly demand an explicit and tailored set of considerations, needs, and activities—these are often dictated by specifically outlined institutional practice and procedure. There are, however, some general principals, standards, and fundamental practice that transcend many of the unique circumstances and individual needs associated with the wide array of attributes that dimensional objects present. These include an assortment of standard tools, a basic knowledge of artifact cleaning (especially important when objects and artifacts will not be enclosed), different solutions for mountmaking, and the importance of and approach to creating templates for installation. It is once again important to note the importance of communication and research: always consult your collections colleagues, curators, and conservators before implementing any physical mounting or installation techniques.

GENERAL APPROACHES AND TECHNIQUES FOR CLEANING

Part of the prepatory routine when dealing with dimensional objects and artifacts, especially when preparing for installation and display, is the potential need for surface cleaning. Performing proper cleaning and surface care for the object is an important aspect of the preparator's process: not just in preparation for the installation and exhibition but also for the ongoing preservation of the collection. This procedure, however, must be carried out with extreme care with informed action—in many cases this activity may require the intervention or oversight of a trained conservator, who may need to employ a more aggressive approach depending on the condition of the artifact. In addition, the specific type or genre of object/artifact will mandate varying approaches to general surface cleaning. For example, direct surface cleaning of many archaeological artifacts is always kept to an extreme physical minimum in order to preserve any interpretative elements or residue that resides on the surface and may inform historical research, whereas the cleaning of bronze sculpture, depending on various condition and installation factors, could potentially be slightly more vigorous by the collections team. The level of scrutiny in determining what actions can or should be taken on by the preparator or collections professional versus what would be deemed as intervention by a conservator is, consistent with any object preparation, an important part of the evaluative and communicative processes (see chapter 2) as the essential difference between active and passive activity. For the preparator, a planned cleaning routine should be employed, especially in circumstances of long-term and permanent display. The careful but consistent removal of loose surface dust and particulate, which when performed correctly, is essential not only for exhibition and interpretation but also as a preservation technique and one that the collections professional must safely carry out. Again, while it is always important to consult a conservation professional that specializes in the media in question before engaging in physical action, a restrained and conservative approach to cleaning will generally be an appropriate step in preparing the object for installation.

Tools for Cleaning

Using the appropriate tools for object surface cleaning is essential. Preparators should avoid any cleaning tools or materials that may potentially abrade or get caught on the surface of any kind of object, such as stiff scrubbing brushes or sponges. Paper towels or microfiber cloths may not be the ideal approach to wipe or run across a surface, as the fibers can easily be caught and cause unintended damage by catching and pulling on areas where the finish or glazing may be broken or chipped or the potential to tear and leave additional material on the physical media surface. This can be especially true for unfinished/unvarnished wood surfaces and painted metal surfaces—and this is why a thorough evaluative process becomes once again essential to the preparator's process. Compressed air should also be avoided, as the flow may be too aggressive and can cause a potential risk of moisture or freezing shock and damage. Overall surface cleaning of dimensional materials will generally consist of a combination of gentle brushing and suction using appropriate tools.

Natural hair brushes: Using a soft natural hair brush, such as extremely soft goat or sheep hair, can ensure nonabrasive treatment of the surface and will remove surface particulate that collects in crevices of the object surface. Protecting the object surface from a metal ferrule (ring that captures and attaches the bristles to the handle) can be accomplished by wrapping a cloth tape around the metal edge. Brushes should always be cleaned before use and will many times be isolated for specific collection media (e.g., using a singular brush for cleaning all cast bronze surfaces, one for wooden surfaces, and one for taxidermy). Therefore, these brushes should be replaced frequently, as certain materials or media may break down the natural fibers. This also may inform the cost or quality of brush used by the preparation team: while unnecessary to purchase artist's quality brushes, the Hake-style brush (wide and flat natural hair brush with bamboo or wooden handle and no metal ferrule) is an

Figure 8.1. Collection Object and Artifact Cleaning Tools. *Source*: Image credit: Andrew Saluti.

inexpensive favorite for many collections professionals. The dry brush cleaning technique is often used in conjunction with a low-suction vacuum to collect the loose materials removed from the surface.

Bulb air blower: The use of compressed or pneumatic air is strongly discouraged by conservators when performing surface cleaning on collection material due to a lack of control of airflow and the potential for spitting and freezing of water vapor on the object surface. The bulb air blower is an important tool that will assist in the removal of dust and particles from areas that the brush or vacuum cannot access, providing a gentle yet focused burst of air (or suction) with the accuracy of the bulb nozzle. Some bulb blowers can include a High Efficiency Particulate Air (HEPA) filtration device to mitigate the blower exhausting debris back into the environment.

Low-suction vacuum: Vacuums are an essential tool for object preparation and collections maintenance. When selecting a vacuum that will be used directly with collection objects, certain specifications should be considered, including filtration, suction control, and available attachments. Vacuums must be effective in controlling the amount of dust and particulate that is captured versus what is projected back into the environment—the HEPA filtration system is ideal for most collection spaces and uses. For specialized projects or environments that demand high levels of filtration, ULPA (Ultra Low Penetration Air) vacuum systems should be considered. Depending on the nature of the object being cleaned, the preparator's ability to control suction is also essential: the intensity of suction when cleaning a textile compared to a stone or metal surface, for example, can be controlled by dial adjustment on many museum-quality vacuums. Attachments, such as micro-tool adapters, nozzles, and brushes, will also add to the control of use and effectiveness of the vacuum. Machines isolated for object cleaning should not be used for general maintenance or housekeeping. Filters should be cleaned or replaced frequently depending on use.

PASSIVE METHODS: DRY-CLEANING TECHNIQUES

Why is dust a danger to objects? Considering the multitude of different surface conditions and finishes, one might assume that a little dust build up is not an urgent preservation issue. Dust is made up of a variety of solid particles, including plant pollen, natural fibers, and minerals from soil and dirt, as well as human and animal hair, skin cells, and insect remains. As dust settles on the surface and in crevices of objects it creates varying degrees of risk in collections. Dust is unsightly: it can deter from the intended interpretation of the object, distracting the viewer from the functional, historical, or conceptual context that was the rationale for the display. Dust is *hygroscopic*: it can attract and hold moisture from the environment and collect on the object surface. Certain dusts may also be acidic and, if left unmaintained, will cause etching, scaring, or discoloration on patinated, finished, and unfinished surfaces. Organic dusts can attract pests and biological growth, such as mold. For all these potential hazards, a cleaning routine for all objects (on public view or in storage) should be employed by collections staff. Consistent dry-cleaning methods can prevent the majority of long-term damage for most objects; however, if dry brush or vacuum techniques prove to be inadequate for the level of buildup, more active and techniques—such as the introduction of solvents or detergents or a more aggressive physical scrubbing or abrasion—may be required under the supervision, consultation, or direct engagement of a trained conservator.

Step One: Evaluation

The first step in any dimensional object preparation, as with all collection objects and regardless of the media, genre, or type, is a comprehensive evaluation—collecting information about physical attributes, identifying overall condition, researching media-specific needs and/or areas of concern for the intended installation; isolating any known or possible losses or damage, repairs, or previous areas of conservation; and consultation with curators, conservators, and collections colleagues about special considerations before handling, prepping, and installing the work. Can the object be safely presented in its current state, and if not, can the object be prepped using passive methods? What is needed to create a secure environment for display? Are there special furniture or mounts required, do they already exist, or will they require special fabrication? When considering surface cleaning for an object in preparation for display, the preparator's best course of action is to employ a cautious and conservative approach, engaging in dry-cleaning methods only: the use of brushes and/or a low-suction vacuum to remove the buildup of dust or particulate that has settled on the surface of the object.

Step 2: Preparing the Workspace

A routine cleaning will generally be performed in the location of installation or storage environment, whereas cleaning for object installation preparation should be done in the controlled environment of the preparator's lab or workspace. When engaging in a coordinated routine exhibition or installation cleaning, care should be taken to protect surrounding display elements: create a poly sheeting (4 to 6 mil for durability) bib or barrier between the object base or mount and the display furniture: using low tack tapes such as painter's tape to secure poly sheeting around the object (never placing any adhesive tapes directly on the object surface) will protect the surrounding elements and facilitate containment of all dust particulate being removed (much like the apron used to collect hair in a barber's shop or salon). All identified cleaning tools needed should be assembled and easily transported; mechanical devices should be charged or a power source should be identified and accessible without creating a hazard while working. In preparation spaces, a similar approach will ensure easy cleanup and containment. Select a workspace that will enable the preparator to easily access the entirety of the object from multiple angles and vantage points without the need to move or shift the object (overhandling will create the potential for risk and damage). Before moving the object into position for cleaning, remove any materials not actively being prepped or directly engaged with from the workspace. A layer of poly sheeting should be preemptively placed around the working footprint and secured to the workspace with low tack tapes. Like the bib analogy previously mentioned, this will not only capture any debris that is removed from the object surface but also protect the workspace during the preparation and mitigate the need to repair the workspace post-preparation. It is also important not to use a woven fabric, blanket, carpet, or soft drop clothes for this protective barrier, as particulate that escapes the cleaning process will be easily captured by these surfaces and can be reintroduced into the environment or object post-preparation. The use of poly sheeting ensures all debris and particulate removed during the process can be encapsulated and removed from the preparation environment. All tools should be accessible during cleaning: appropriate brushes for the media at hand are cleaned or purchased, mechanical devices (vacuum) and attachments organized, power sources identified, and extension cords out of direct paths or near work surfaces. With the workspace prepared and tools identified and assembled the object can be introduced into the workspace.

Step 3: Passive Surface Cleaning

The methodical approach to surface cleaning is the preparator's best strategy to a safe, effective, and passive object surface cleaning. As previously stated, the use of a cloth rag, microfiber, or paper duster should be carefully considered after thorough evaluation that the object surface has a finish, glaze, or protective layer that is unbroken and only introduced if the surface of the object has been deemed stable enough for this direct action. A safer procedure consists of the combination of brushing the surface to agitate dust and particulate to then be collected by a focused low-suction vacuum. In any case, starting at one physical point or quadrant and gradually progressing across the surface, rather than attempting to take on the process in general areas or by identified buildup, will ensure that the entire object surface areas have been addressed rather than a less systematic approach. Always start at the highest point of the object, moving across the object surface laterally, letting gravity assist in the cleaning process as debris and dust that is agitated and not collected by the vacuum can fall to a yet-to-be-cleaned portion of the work rather than a previously completed section. This generalized approach will accommodate a vast inventory of object types: also including frames (though never used on the surface of a painting), furniture, unglazed textiles, and more. Well-informed research and communication with collections colleagues should guide the preparator's process before engaging in this or any direct object.

MAKING MOUNTS AND THE IMPORTANCE OF TEMPLATES

As previously discussed, there is a wide variety of specific needs and approaches that dimensional media, objects, and artifacts mandate—a far less uniform approach to preparation than that of flat or traditionally wall-mounted media. When trying to define an umbrella methodology to preparation techniques for installation, another consistent exercise is the need for support structures, including mounts, cradles, pedestals, and casework. Mountmaking is specialized fabrication, one that can take years of unique training and dedicated research. There are, however, basic structures, templates, and tools easily created and utilized that will allow the preparator to safely mount a wide variety of dimensional objects.

Tools and Materials

Soft or flexible measuring tape: Gathering accurate measurements of your object is essential in the preparation process. When one considers the variable surface, shape, and articulation of many dimensional works, acquiring precise dimensions can be challenging. And, attempting to do so with the wrong tool—a rigid measurement device such as a retractable measuring tape or metal ruler—will create a potential risk to the object. A soft or cloth measuring tape is an effective tool to capture nonlinear and radial distances. The soft measuring tape will also promote safer direct handling and contact with the object throughout the process.

Calipers: A caliper is any measuring device that consists of adjustable fingers or extensions used to identify distances and measure spaces of irregular or organically shaped objects or artifacts, specifically for dimensional areas where a rigid ruler or measuring tape would be ineffective or inaccessible.

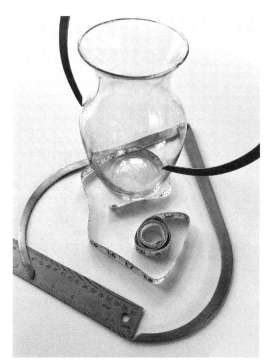

Calipers are available in a variety of styles for various applications: the most common (and versatile) being a basic single post hinge regularly used in machine shops and fabrication to quickly gauge the accuracy of a physical distance or area. In mountmaking, the caliper is instrumental for creating fixed measurements without directly handling the object.

Contour or profile gauge (see figure 8.3): This measuring device is indispensable in the templating of form fitting mounts, cavities, and stands for objects with irregular or organic shapes. The profile gauge is a simple device that consists of a linear series of pins that will move to conform to the shape of a surface. This realized contour can then be traced for a template or a guide for cutting out exact forms to fit to an object's surface. Like the calipers, this instrument allows the preparator to capture accurate references to dimension and form without having to overly manipulate or mishandle the artifact.

Vivak/acrylic sheeting: Acrylic sheeting, commonly known as "plexiglass," is a backbone of mountmaking for its rigid stability and easy manipulation, while being visually discrete. Acrylic (or plastic) fabrication requires experience with

Figure 8.2. Measuring devices used in template making: calipers, flexible measuring tape. *Source:* Image credit: Andrew Saluti.

and access to fabrication materials and bending tools. Vivak is a polyester sheet that has the rigidity of other acrylic sheeting but can be forged, bent, and manipulated without the need of specialty tools, heat, or molding. This approach can make the mountmaking process accessible for preparation teams without outfitted workshops or elaborate mountmaking facilities.

Mat board or cardboard: The previously discussed importance of templating any device meant to support an object underscores the value of basic construction materials that are already common to the preparator's inventory: mat boards and corrugated boards. The creation of templates and guides must be easily constructed and manipulated in order to adequately define the best and safest solution (not necessarily requiring special fabrication tools or facility) as well as to allow for trial, error, and adjustment (using inexpensive and disposable materials). Basic acid-free materials such as these, in addition to tapes and polyethylene foam, help model and problem-solve the intended mount without introducing additional risk during the process.[2]

Polyethylene foam: Already identified as an essential tool used in handling, cushioning, and securing objects and artifacts in transit, the inherent qualities of polyethylene foam make it an ideal material for cushions and cradles in many display scenarios. Inert and easily shaped, polyethylene foam can be wrapped to match display environments or hidden to provide support without extensive fabrication.

Polyethylene strap: Largely used in the display of books that are required to lay open at a particular page, polyethylene strap provides gentle, forgiving pressure to any mounting situation that requires a secure band, tie, or restraint. Poly strapping is not only flexible but transparent, permitting an unfettered yet reinforced presentation of the object.

Hygienic or crystalline wax: Another standard material in dimensional object preparation is the conservative use of small beads of wax to stabilize and secure.

3D scanning, modeling, and printing: As collection practice advances, new technologies offer opportunity to further mitigate risk and heighten the specificity and accuracy of the mounts produced for objects and artifacts. The archival quality of 3D scanning, that is, the detail of object surfaces that can be accurately captured, can now allow for digital design and fabrication of object mounts, support structures, and even surrogate elements and duplicates. Research and practice are continuing to develop, and these digital approaches to object preparation and presentation have the potential to become standard approaches alongside traditional analog and physical techniques.

Basic Approaches to Mountmaking

The practice of designing and fabricating object mounts is a fine craft: one that depends on years of experience and extensive knowledge of both sculptural construction and object materiality. This specialty skill set often materializes within museums as a valued, unique member of the collections or exhibitions team, sometimes for expertise with a discrete type of object, artifact, or mountmaking skill. Similar to many institutional needs when it comes to hiring a conservator as contractor rather than full-time staff, mountmakers can be hired on as-needed basis, when the objects selected for exhibition require a bespoke apparatus for display. The object's condition and needs will ultimately dictate the necessity of engaging with an external mountmaker. Just as often, however, and quite possibly more commonplace, the preparator is assigned the task of fabricating, fitting, and installing these mounts. And, while having expertise in fashioning mounts is not necessarily a prerequisite for the preparation staff, some basic knowledge of the principles and methodologies of mountmaking is indispensable.

Before discussing the general principles that guide the mountmaking process, it is prudent to first define the various types of mounts that support our objects while on display. It is relevant to note that a mount is ideally crafted or customized to meet the specific physical need of the object being presented. However, a generalized overview of these devices can be broadly categorized into three main types: armatures, cradles, and brackets. An *armature* is a mount that holds an object in a desired position, usually designed to reinforce that object/artifact's original intent or natural state. Armatures allow for the presentation of the object in a freestanding, unobstructed manner: many times through the use of strategically positioned supportive mechanisms mounted to the base to rest. The armature must capture and support the object in a desired position without adding physical strain or pressure to the surface or composition. A *cradle* is a mount created to allow the object to rest, free of any grasp or constraint, in a desired position. The most common employment of cradles is for the presentation of volumes and books, constructed to present the object opened to a specific page or spread while supporting the binding at a designated viewable position. A *bracket* is a type of mount created as the intermediary between the object and a fixed presentation surface like a gallery wall, freestanding pedestal, or case interior. The bracket safely and securely affixes the object for display, unencumbered from a stand or base, and is commonly employed for wall-based installations. There are, of course, numerous variations and combinations of these basic principal styles; these defined classifications simply identify a specific function: An armature holds a position, a cradle allows rest, and a bracket connects to a surface. An armature can make use of a bracket, a cradle can connect to an armature, and so on.

When navigating the process of designing and constructing a mount for an object on display, one should consider the fundamental principles and methodologies of effective mountmaking.

The mount should never put stress on the object. This may be the single most important thing to consider when developing the mount, as faulty or ill-conceived designs can cause not only immediate damage and risk but also add potential long-term issues that may not be immediately seen. The object should neither be forced to fit into the mount nor should the mount be constructed in a way that positions the object in an unnatural position: from a preservation standpoint, the mount should support and present the object in its *natural state of rest*. This will help to ensure that a minimum level of stress is exerted on the object for the duration of the installation.

The mount is made from stable materials. Considering that any device created to support the object will have long-term and continuous contact and that these mounts are often enclosed within micro-environments (often with other objects), neither the materials and techniques used in the fabrication of mounts should introduce adverse chemical or physical materials nor should you utilize resources that may present damaging elements through decomposition or off-gassing that will contribute to immediate or long-term degradation of the mounted artifact.

As outlined in the 1998 guide *Mount-Making for Museum Objects*, it is suggested that only materials that have been vetted as stable should be introduced and new or undocumented materials should be avoided until their stability can be properly determined by a conservator or conservation organization. These materials are often readily found in preparation workshops and archival labs. Approved structural materials include acrylic and polyester sheet, polyethylene foam plank and sheet, archival mat boards, corrugated plastic boards (polyethylene or polypropylene), foam boards (archival quality preferred), and metals such as stainless steel or brass strip, rod, or tubing. For padding and support, additional materials include polyester quilt batting, and synthetic felts, and fabrics such as cotton, silk, and unbleached linens are recommended. Adhesives such as hot-melt glues (clear or white), adhesive transfer tapes (acid-free), and other water-activated archival gummed tapes, such as linen or holland tape, can be used for assembly but should not be used to carry load.

The mount is inobtrusive to the object. While security and support are always primary considerations, the mount should also not be constructed or installed in a way that interferes with the presentation or interpretation of the object. The most effective mounts are those that secure the object while on display while remaining out of sight—as invisible to the viewer as possible—so the object can be exhibited as close to its natural and inherent function/position/context. If the mount is so visually or physically commanding (or overbearing) that it becomes an object in and of itself, in concert with the intended presentation, it will be easily misconstrued in the installation or diminish the intended purpose or contexts created by the installed object.

Following these principles will be central to the preparator's process in the development of these essential mechanisms for proper display of collection material. In addition to the preceding core values, additional considerations that the preparator must bear in mind include the following.

Padding points of contact: When creating support systems that utilize any type of closed or snug clasp, bracket, or armature that will have direct and continuous contact with an object, the surface of those mechanisms should be padded or covered with an intermediary material that will facilitate nonabrasive contact. Examples include the use of polyethylene foam pads to cushion the base of an object sitting in a cradle or silicon tubing around metal wire armatures or monofilaments to prevent unintended damage, scuffing, or puncture. This method should also be applied to other exhibition furnitures such as pedestals and frames: use synthetic felt lining within the rabbet of a frame as protection for the canvas or panel housed.

Position and orientation: The determination of how an object shall be displayed is a collaborative decision by way of curatorial and conservational input. As previously stated, the ideal situation is to create a mount that supports an object in its natural state of rest, but what if that object or artifact is, by nature, one of utility, function, or part of a larger structure? The decisions made in how the object is physically presented have enormous implications on how they might be, or are intended to be, interpreted—thus enhancing the curatorial narrative or context. A common example for this is the implied use and/or activity created by the positioning of hand tools: once accessioned and included in a preserved collection, the object ceases to be a functional tool and becomes a preserved artifact, but, when on display, does the tool's position at rest (perhaps laying on a display surface) adequately convey the meaning, the history, or the function? Whereas, when the tool is elevated, positioned, or otherwise presented in a way that replicates use from the viewer's point of view, the history and meaning are reinforced. As with any preparation exercise, these decisions are driven by the object—informed by condition evaluation in consultation with curatorial and conservation colleagues.

Additional guidelines to consider in the fabrication of a mount for an object or artifact from the National Park Service's 2019 publication *Exhibit Planning, Design, and Fabrication Specifications*:[3]

- No object can be altered or repaired to accommodate exhibit mounting.
- Mounts should provide adequate support to prevent physical stress or unbalanced weight distribution on the object. The object's center of gravity or original intended attitude should be considered.
- No mount should be permanently attached to any object and easy access to the object should be afforded for curatorial maintenance and emergency removal.
- The fastening system must be based on a mechanical design and not adhesives or sticky substance.
- Mounts must anticipate in their design the tendency for organic materials to droop, sag, or experience dimensional changes.
- Vibration and abrasion should be minimized by the nature of mount's design and material selected for construction.
- Susceptible objects should not be subjected to creasing and folding or deformation by the placement of heavy objects directly on top of them.
- Fragile objects, including all textiles, should be supported over as great an area as practical.
- The mount must secure objects that are displayed in the open to be reasonably safe from theft.

CREATING A TEMPLATE

An essential part of the process in creating any specially designed mount, stand, or piece of exhibition furniture to present and support an object or artifact is to create a *template*: a model or mock-up of what the final mechanism will be. Starting with a template, the preparator can problem-solve challenges to the final design, working out careful forms and contours of irregularly shaped object surfaces, and create a model to inform the fabrication process. Templates can (and should) be constructed from inexpensive materials, allowing for the easy alteration or the creation of multiple variations to test against the object needs. Paper, cardboard, scraps from archival materials, and polyethylene foam are all excellent options the preparator might use in the templating process. Once a template has been satisfactorily completed according to the exact specifications of how the object will rest or be positioned, the template can then act as a direct, measurable guide in the fabrication of the final mount.

As an intermediary step in the creation of the final object support system, why is creating a template such a valuable and necessary part of the preparation process? From a procedural and sustainable point of view, the template allows the preparator the opportunity to identify and navigate any unique challenges that the object may present to creating a stable mount, working through the trial-and-error phase before moving on to a finished construction, easily making alterations, adjustments, or even starting over as needed—with little investment in both time and resources.

The template is ultimately disposable—not necessarily in that the final version can't be reused or saved for multiple mounts, or that the template must be destroyed, but rather that there is a non-precious, "working" mentality in the templating process that allows the preparator flexibility and space to experiment and test various approaches before moving on to a final version with refined, permanent materials.

Another valuable rationale pertains directly to care: using easily manipulated and non-precious materials to troubleshoot and experiment the final design, the preparation team can limit overhandling and mitigate risk or damage to the object in the design stage of the mountmaking process. The created mock-up will ultimately define how the device will interact with the object—clearly identifying points of contact, outlining locations for hardware or posts, and ensuring the object will rest as intended. Any adjustment can be much more easily fashioned in the template phase, rather than having to tweak and modify what is intended to be the final mount. Not implementing the use of a template or model can often result in excess handling and manipulation, trying to modify rigid and refined materials with the object—greatly expanding the potential for damage or faulty mounts.

Starting with basic sketches and accurate measurements are essential to this process. Using tools such as calipers and soft measuring tapes to document the physical details of the object, especially where direct contact or molded support will be needed, is a primary step—especially when precise dimensional references are required. Often, dimensional objects and artifacts will have physical characteristics that pose a particular challenge to obtaining this exact documentation, due to an irregular shape, surface structure, or the fragile or sensitive condition of the item in question. A contour or profile gauge can be implemented only when the object is stable enough for direct contact: an excellent tool for a highly accurate representation of the exact silhouette captured through a series of positionable pins. However, the contour gauge is limited to whatever depth of form the pins can reflect (usually between 2 to 3 inches or 5 to 8 centimeters deep), as well as the length of the tool itself (commonly as long a span of 10 to 12 inches or 25 to 30 centimeters). Additionally, if the surface of the artifact is sensitive to any direct contact, capturing the form through the use of such tools that require direct contact would not be appropriate. In these cases, the simple reflection of a profile constructed from easily cut materials (such as 2-ply mat board or stiff papers) can be achieved by fabricating multiple shapes and contours, cut to reflect specific sections of the object surface, then assembled with a repositionable tape (such as artist's tape or painter's tape) to mimic the entire form, and can provide an accurate

Figure 8.3 Using a Contour Gauge. *Source*: Image credit: Andrew Saluti.

contour to model the mount from. This method allows one to create a contour of any size, as well as the ability to adjust and mold the shape without necessarily having direct contact with the surface of the artifact. Once the final profile is achieved, this assembled template can be traced, scanned, or used as a model to inform, measure, and test the mount during fabrication, before the artifact is introduced.

Another template that is essential in the dimensional preparation process is the reflection of a footprint or base. This template can be employed in multiple scenarios: used to guide the creation of an archival barrier between object and display surface (especially when that surface has been painted, such as a pedestal or shelf), to trace the perimeter of the stable seat for the layout and padding of storage devices, and to identify any security, pins, or connection points that are unseen, underneath the object, hidden, or otherwise not accessible when the object is installed. Tracing the footprint of an object should be done with great care so as to not impact its surface—such as following the shape by dragging a marking utensil against the base while resting on a piece of paper or other templating material   this action can result in transferring as much mark onto the object as to the templating material. To start, these actions should always be performed using pencil or nonpermanent marking materials rather than any ink-based marker or pen—if there is accidental contact, the graphite will be easier to remedy than ink. The preparator should consider a barrier between the object and marking tool—such as a buffer of thin polyethylene foam attached to the tool to shield and separate the mark from the object surface. After the contour has been accurately transferred to the template material, remember to reflect the added area created by the buffered mark, so as to accurately define the object footprint. The active use of the footprint template will dictate what materials should be used: for a barrier between object and surface, a piece of Mylar or thin polyester sheet is ideal. For templates that are intended to be used to mark hidden posts, brackets, or security hardware, a rigid material, such as 1/4-inch plywood or other hardboards, will prove best, as they can be reused, stored, and kept as documentation of the object's installation need (this is especially relevant to outdoor sculptures with hard connections to bases).

Figure 8.4.   Footprint Template for Bronze Sculpture. *Source*: Image credit: Syracuse University Art Museum.

Basic Template: Book Cradle

The display of books and bound volumes is common in many object displays, especially in exhibitions of an archival or historical nature. To properly support the often-fragile structures, these objects are paramount to their preservation. Depending on how the book was bound, the overall condition of that binding, the age of the text, and the desired page to display, these are all factors that warrant and inform the creation of a common mount for the display of such material: the book cradle. And, while there are a multitude of object-specific and display-specific customizations and variations that can be considered, the basic construction can be achieved through a uniform template.

As with any mountmaking or installation process, the first step in creating a book cradle is evaluative; however, before addressing the needs of the book to be displayed, the preparation team should first consider and document the intended display environment: especially if the book in question will be installed inside casework or under a vitrine; a common mistake when creating a cradle for a book, especially larger-sized volumes, is that the final mounted object exceeds the physical space of the interior of the intended display environment. Exact interior dimensions of the exhibited location of the book must first be documented to inform cradle production and to ensure the object will in fact be able to be safely displayed as designed. Once this information is in hand, the following steps can be followed to create the cradle.

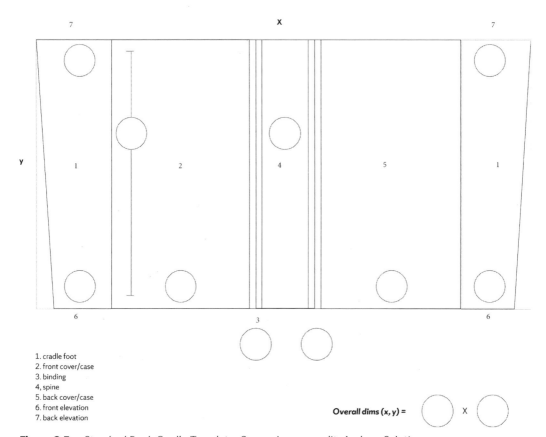

1. cradle foot
2. front cover/case
3. binding
4. spine
5. back cover/case
6. front elevation
7. back elevation

Overall dims (x, y) = ◯ X ◯

Figure 8.5. Standard Book Cradle Template. *Source*: Image credit: Andrew Saluti.

Step 1: Identify Desired Page and Position

Identifying the exact page to be on display is paramount in the construction of the cradle, as it determines multiple factors in the production of the mount: the overall shape of the base to support the contour of the binding, the angle at which the book must be supported, and the height at which the book needs to be presented. While some volumes will lay comfortably open without extraordinary support, others will demand a more complex design to properly support and present the selected spread.

Step 2: Mock the Final Presentation

Propping the book at the proposed angle and height for presentation will allow for accurate measurements to create a working template. Use polyethylene foam blocks and wedges to safely replicate the final intended position of the book. Note: in general, the narrower the book is opened and mounted for display, the less strain will be placed on the binding. While an extremely narrow opening will not necessarily present an optimal viewing experience, a forcibly wide book opening may place excessive strain and potential damage to the volume—finding the "sweet spot" of how far the book can safely and naturally be opened, and at what angle it will comfortably rest, is an essential first step to the templating process, and may require consultation from curators and conservators.

Step 3: Measure All Aspects of Presentation

Using the template guide (figure 8.5), carefully measure the identified elements of the cradle: the back and front heights of the support foot (this can vary depending on the angle of interpretive elevation for the book, as well as the scale of the overall object), the height and width of the front cover case, the dimensions (and shape) of the binding and spine, the height and width of the back cover case, and, if at a different angle or height from the front cover, the front and back elevations of the corresponding back cover cradle foot.

Step 4: Create a Template for Cradle Measurements

Once all pertinent dimensions have been collected from the mocked setup, the overall size and shape of the cradle can be determined. Using the template guide, calculate the x and y by adding the corresponding measurements. This will not only illustrate the full size of the mount (and the material needed) before bending/folding but also reveal the physical angle and elevation of the presentation—which should be again verified against the actual interior allowance of the intended case or display.

Step 5: Create a Template for Cradle Modeling

Before transferring to the final mount material, create a working template to verify the design that will accommodate the object and to allow for adjustments and tweaks before final fabrication. For book cradles, heavier-duty materials such as foam core, corrugated plastic board, or cardboard work well; select a material that will hold the folded shape as well as carry the load of the object but that can also be ultimately disposable in the testing and fabrication process. Once the shape has been accurately transferred to the template material, cut and trim to the outer shape and score (or mark) the designated folds with a bone folder or burnishing device for precise folds. Note: precision even in this preliminary phase is key, as this template will verify how well the finished cradle will perform.

Step 6: Use the Finalized Template as Guide for Construction

With the overall shape of the cradle now trimmed, scored, and ready for bending and folding, manipulate the template into the form of the designed cradle. In some cases, taping the feet down to a work surface for added stability will help in testing the template's accuracy and success (template material may not hold as firmly as final acrylic or cradle material). Allow the object to rest in place, and make note of any corrections or alterations that may need to happen: Is the book naturally sitting in place at the desired page? Is the spine and binding being adequately supported or is the book forced into position? Make any necessary alterations to the template and continue to test until the desired mount is realized. Some additional considerations for the cradle may be the inclusion of an added foot bracket to stop the book from sliding forward (accomplished by fashioning a simple right-angle bracket at the forward edge of the cradle), as well as the use of polyethylene straps to hold the desired spread in place (as previously mentioned in tools and materials but can also be cut from clear and clean poly sheeting). The strap should comfortably fit round the entire book: not loose enough to allow for the pages to move on their own but not so tight as to pull and/or tear the pages. Once all alterations or additions have been tested, the template can be used as the guide for final fabrication of the cradle.

While the preceding step-by-step process outlines the specific process for templating mounts for book objects, a similar approach can be employed with any object: beginning by safely mocking the desired installation; gathering dimensions and data; designing, fabricating, and testing the template; and followed by fabrication of the finished mount.

PREFABRICATED (READY TO USE) MOUNTS

Although templating and mountmaking processes are valuable skills for any preparator, not all members of a collections team may be experienced in specialized fabrication techniques or have access to the appropriate and needed equipment or facilities to create the desired mount. In these cases, investigating the availability and viability of prefabricated mounts and furniture may adequately deliver the support and structure the object needs to be safely installed for display. A ready-made or commercially available option may not be appropriate or functional for very specific or unique objects and object needs where a custom mount is required—if the preparator does not have the experience or option to fabricate, this is where the services of a professional mountmaker should be contracted. However, depending on the details of the object and installation scenario, investigating a mount, armature, cradle, or other exhibition furniture that can be purchased and adapted to the object can be a prudent alternative.

There are a variety of prefabricated mounts available for a host of objects and installation needs; reference the "Preparator's Resources" chapter of this book to find suppliers.

Spider mounts are a prefabricated and customizable armature consisting of four extended and bendable metal rods attached to a presentation stem that is mounted to a stable base, usually acrylic. The arms can be fashioned to conform to any contour of the object that requires direct support and can also be repurposed for different objects. They come in a variety of heights and base colors and are a common solution for dimensional objects with irregular or organic shapes and surfaces.

T-arm mounts are ideal for small to midsized upright standing objects that require armature support to be displayed in their intended position. Like spider mounts, the crossing supporting armature rods can be bent to conform to the object shape or need, and the mount can be purchased in multiple heights as needed. A wall-mounted variation of these bendable armatures is also an option, depending on the installation plan. Note: when utilizing prefabricated T-arm or spider mount armatures, it may be necessary to pad any part of the mount that comes in direct contact with the object with poly tubing or other inert material.

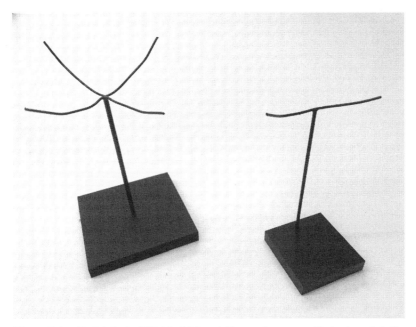

Figure 8.6. Prefabricated "Spider" Mount. *Source*: Image credit: Andrew Saluti.

Polyethylene foam book cradle sets are a common solution in library, archival, and special collection study rooms for the temporary presentation of books and volumes. These kits include support blocks made from an inert and archival rigid, yet cushioned, material that are shaped into a system of wedges, planks, and rods that can be reconfigured into multiple variations depending on the scale of the book and where the support is needed. These ready-made kits also come in a black foam that can be less obtrusive while on view. These sets are not as discreet or specifically supportive as customized cradles but will safely support a large array of books and will be easily reused as needed.

Benchmarkä Butterfly book mounts illustrate a unique cradle approach that allows the collection staff to easily modify a ready-made system, providing ultimate versatility and flexibility in use (and reuse) for multiple installations. What makes these mounts unique from other cradle designs is the hinged brass fittings supporting the main plates of the cradle. The mechanism is designed with the ability to alter the height and angle of each side of the cradle, creating a mount that can be customized to accommodate most any book at any presentation perspective with any opening. The mounts come in mini, standard, intermediate, and folio sizes. The upfront cost of a

Figure 8.7. Polyethylene Book Cradle Kit. *Source*: Image credit: Andrew Saluti.

Butterfly mount may be more than a traditional book cradle's; this must be weighed against the opportunity for customizable reuse and flexibility in design.

Acrylic cradles are a standard ready-made mount that use a nonspecific "M"-style base for open book presentation. They can come in variations that include a range of sizes, lipped edges, and elevated viewing angles. These generic cradles can safely accommodate books and folios that do not require any specialized support structure or variable shaped mounts for the casework or spine of the book.

Easels, stands, and object-specific mounts can be found in a large selection of different sizes, styles, and finishes. Basic acrylic easels and stands will provide basic propping and support in broad applications. Plate stands and easels can be found to present many flat objects in a vertical orientation with nonspecific support provided to the object (use of these general display mounts should be carefully tested and monitored in long-term presentation situations to verify that any points of contact will not cause damage). Mounts for discrete object types such as guns, swords, dolls, handheld fans, athletic balls and equipment, and so on, can also be found as prefabricated display furniture from archival and display suppliers.

TEXTILE PREPARATION

The installation of textiles often poses a particular and unique set of challenges in the preparation for installation, as these objects generally require a greater range of support and structure to be installed and viewed effectively and with the artifact's original intent. Some standard approaches to prepping textiles can be employed by the collections and preparation team; however, invasive or potentially structural altering techniques should only be performed by a trained textile conservator.

The most basic approach to preparing textiles for installation is a passive technique, where the object is allowed to naturally rest on a mount without any attachment or mechanism, aiming to create little to no point of stress on the textile. This is commonly achieved with dowel systems hung from a bracket or suspended from a stable point. Any dowel of tubing that carries a textile should have a padded or protective archival barrier between the artifact and the mount. Wooden dowels can be encapsulated with an archival foil film (such as Marvelseal®) before inert padding is added to cushion the object in place.

For garments, polyethylene archival dress forms can be customized to support the specific contours and construction of the artifact. These specialized foam mounts encapsulated in a polyester fabric are shapable and pinnable, allowing the garment to rest in the original intended manner. Garments should never be stressed or forced onto forms and mounts—if extra space is required to set the garment in place, additional polyester batting or padding can be added after the object has been carefully placed over the form.

The following active techniques may require the consult or contract of a trained conservator. Flat textiles that are not meant to hang draped are often presented in one of two basic ways; both require simple stitching methods. These characterize objects such a rugs, blankets, and quilts. One approach incorporates a Velcro perimeter to secure the textile on a desired surface; a corresponding strip of Velcro is temporarily hand sewn on the verso of the textile. Another stitching method incorporates a sleeve that is added to the verso of the textile, allowing a rod or bracket to pass through and carry the object in place. Both these approaches require a primary evaluation of the textile—it is not suitable for objects that cannot carry their own weight to be installed in this manner.

Textiles that require a frame to enclose and protect the object can be sewn to an archival backing, such as a museum-grade mat board or an archival board covered with a cotton barrier. The points of sewn stabilization should be carefully considered, so as to not stress or pull the object into a desired position.

NOTES

1. Acknowledging that all objects have dimension, regardless of whether they are a flat work on paper or a sculptural wood carving or natural specimen, for the sake of this chapter any object that would not fall under the blanket description of "flat" or wall-mounted will be considered as "dimensional."
2. Considering that these templated forms will need to come into direct contact with objects and artifacts, the use of acid-free materials should be considered, acknowledging that these templates will not necessarily be used for permanent or long-term periods and that the cost of these materials may be greater than using lower quality supplies.
3. *Exhibit Planning, Design, and Fabrication Specifications*, National Park Service. 2019. https://www.nps .gov/subjects/hfc/upload/NPS-Exhibit-Planning Design-and-Fabrication-Specifications-2019.pdf.

REFERENCES

Barclay, Robert, André Bergeron, Carole Dignard. *Mount Making for Museum Objects*. Canadian Conservation Institute, Ottowa, Canada, 1998.

"Benchmark Butterfly Bookmounts." Benchmark Catalog. Accessed December 2021. https://www .benchmarkcatalog.com/collections/benchmark-butterfly-bookmounts.

British Columbia Museums Association. *Your Museum Coach: Cleaning an Artifact*. Video, 2014. Accessed June 8, 2020. https://www.youtube.com/watch?v=EuHolpj20nE.

Conservation Center for Art & History Artifacts. *Collection Housekeeping Guide*. PDF. www.ccaha.org. Philadelphia, PA, 2020. Accessed June 2021. https://ccaha.org/resources/collection-housekeep ing-guide.

"Displaying Textiles." The George Washington Museum, The Textile Museum website. Accessed December 2021. https://museum.gwu.edu/displaying-textiles.

Johnson, Jessica S. and Steven P. Floray. "Choosing a Museum Vacuum Cleaner." *Conserve O Gram*, June 2003, Number 1/6. National Park Service. Washington, D.C.: National Park Service, 2003. https://www.nps.gov/museum/publications/conserveogram/01-06.pdf.

"Mounts." Northern States Conservation Center website. Accessed September 2021. https://www .collectioncare.org/mounts.

Museum Textile Services. *Vacuuming Textiles*. Museumtextiles.com. Accessed July, 2021. http://www .museumtextiles.com/uploads/7/8/9/0/7890082/vacuuming_textiles.pdf.

National Park Service. *Museum Handbook: Part I, Museum Collections*. Washington, D.C.: National Park Service, Museum Management Program, 1990.

Plowden and Smith. *Why is Dust Such a Risk for Museums in Lockdown?* May 2020. Plowden-smith.com. Accessed July 2021. https://plowden-smith.com/why-is-dust-such-a-risk-for-museums/.

9

Preparation in Action

SIMPLE FOSSHAPE SUPPORTS FOR TEXTILES

Kirsten Schoonmaker, Textile Conservator

Floppy, familiar, and surprisingly fragile, historic textiles and garments present an array of challenges to collections professionals. How textiles are displayed has a considerable impact on the public's understanding and respect for textiles. Flat or drooping textiles can read as tired, old, and uninspiring, unworthy of careful examination. Garments, in storage and on display, can be incredibly challenging to interpret with the absence of the body. Preparing costumes for exhibition can be time-consuming and labor-intensive, but there are simple and affordable interventions that add needed support for textiles on display, adding life and volume to make the object understood. Fosshape, a malleable and versatile thermoplastic polyester nonwoven material, can be used to efficiently fabricate lightweight body-shaped supports for garments. Given its low cost and ease of fabrication, Fosshape is a valuable addition to a preparator's material options.

Invisible mounts for garments and textiles can be made from a number of materials, including Ethafoam, dismantled mannequins, and soft-padded cushions, but the felt-like thermoplastic Fosshape is an increasingly popular material for dynamic textile mounts. Fosshape, developed and sold by Wonderflex World (and now University Products), is composed of a proprietary blend of polyester polymers (polyethylene terephthalate). The Fosshape fiber has an inner core with one melting point and an outer layer with a lower melting point. When heat is applied, the outer polyester with the lower melting point softens and contracts, shrinking by up to 30 percent. As it cools, Fosshape hardens in its new conformation. The nonwoven felt can be cut and sewn to create a soft form, but when heat is applied using a steamer, the material becomes rigid, permanently taking the desired shape. Fosshape can be set into shape using an existing dress form or mannequin or a customized mold can be developed.

Fosshape has been subjected to an Oddy test and tested for harmful additives. The results indicate that Fosshape is safe to use near and in direct contact with objects. Ongoing research continues to evaluate how hardened Fosshape may perform over time, but the material is now widely accepted in costume conservation labs and mount-making studios. Working with Fosshape requires no special tools or safety equipment, making it ideal for a partnership with an intern or volunteer with some fabric know-how. With a sewing machine, an industrial steamer, and some basic sewing skills, a wide range of mounts can be fabricated.

SUBTLE SUPPORT

A simple Fosshape mount was designed and fabricated for *Grandma Moses: American Modern*, exhibited at the Shelburne Museum in 2016. The exhibition primarily featured paintings by Anna Mary Robertson Moses, better known as Grandma Moses, presenting her work in conversation with fellow "folk" and modernist contemporaries. In addition to the wall-hung paintings, a variety of three-dimensional objects and ephemera were used to enliven the installation. Among these objects was an apron worn by Grandma Moses. This 1950s apron, made of soft printed plain weave cotton and speckled with a few dashes of paint, was in good condition. The cloth was flexible and no areas of strain or weakness were noted. No style of display was precluded by the condition of the textile. However, early in exhibition meetings, it was determined that a mannequin would not be desired for the display of the apron. Rather, it was proposed that the apron be laid flat in a case, carefully arranged to spark connection with Miriam Schapiro's *Patience*. However, a soft cotton apron laid flat on a deck can look, for lack of any better word, lifeless. In order to make the installation of the apron a bit more lively, and prevent any creases from forming in the shoulders, it was decided that an invisible mount would be developed. Given the tools, time, and skills of the team, Fosshape was selected as a promising material with which to work.

As Grandma Moses's apron would be loaned by a co-organizing institution, a mock-up of the apron was made to develop the mount prior to the arrival of the object. Ebay searches turned up a 1950s commercial sewing pattern that captured some of the key construction seams of the original apron.

The mock-up was cut and sewn in cotton muslin so that the amount of support and final shape of the support could be determined without handling the object. The final design was for a mount that provided support to the shoulders, a subtle rise and support to the bust area of the apron, then tapered away to zero at the waist. The mock-up pattern was adjusted for the mount, and the center front and side front panels were cut from Fosshape. These panels were butted together in order to reduce bulk and seamed with a zigzag stitch on a domestic sewing machine. The Fosshape, still flexible in its felt form, was arranged over sandbags and rolled towels that created the desired volume of the finished mount.

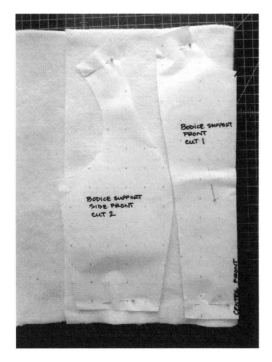

Figure 9.1. Cutting Fosshape Utilizes the Same Skills as Garment Making, but Craft Scissors, Not Fine Fabric Shears, Are Recommended. *Source:* Image credit: Kirsten Schoonmaker.

Heat, in the form of steam from an industrial steamer, was applied, setting the Fosshape in its three-dimensional configuration. Depending on the amount of heat applied, Fosshape can become quite rigid or, with less heat, retain some flexibility, and a needle can still pass through the material. While a heat gun and small domestic steamers can also be used to set Fosshape, the industrial steamer offers an even and controllable heat application, making small adjustments possible during the working process.

For this simple mount, the cutting, sewing, and heat molding of the Fosshape shape could be accomplished in less than an hour. Additional time was needed to cover the mount. In order to prevent any distracting flashes of white along the edge of the mount and to keep stray polyester fibers from migrating to the object, the support was covered with gray cotton show fabric. The cotton was secured to the Fosshape using a running stitch and a curved needle. Additional strips of Fosshape were molded and covered to support a gentle undulation of the apron ties. Installation of the apron was simple and handling of the object was minimal. The final result added a subtle lift for the apron. It should be noted

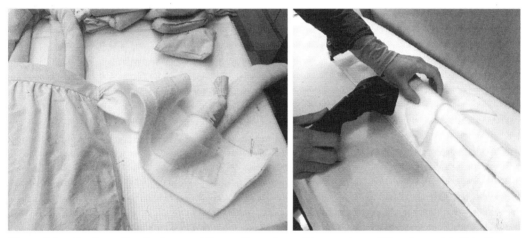

Figure 9.2. Fosshape Can Be Arranged Over a Dress Form, Mannequin, or Other Support to Take the Desired Shape. An Industrial Steamer Provides Even Heat that Allows the Fabricator to Control the Setting Process. *Source*: Image credit: Kirsten Schoonmaker.

Figure 9.3. Grandma Moses's Apron on View in the Exhibition *Grandma Moses: American Modern*, Shelburne Museum of Art, 2016. *Source:* Courtesy of the Bennington Museum.

that the Fosshape very easily supported the light weight of the apron in its horizontal installation, but further support, like carved Ethafoam, polyester batting, or internal armature, should be considered based on the needs of the installation.

Fosshape has a wide range of uses in the mounting of costumes and textiles. It can be used to create subtle support for garments on view, as shown here, but it can also be used to create everything from arms and legs in specific poses for existing mannequins to standardized shoe supports for storage. With some basic sewing skills, a willingness to experiment, and a bit of imagination, Fosshape can be used to add customized support to any garment or textile. It can add the personality and movement that make textiles so appealing. A mount that supports the constructed shape of the garment, whether simple or dynamic, can ensure that these objects don't appear lifeless or flat but can capture the imagination of the visitor, ensuring a closer look.

REFERENCES

Amnéus, C. and M. Miles. 2012. "A Method for Invisibly Mounting Costume Using Fosshape." *Journal of the American Institute for Conservation* 51 (1): 3-14.

Gamper, C. and E. Henni. 2015. "'Keeping in Shape': An investigation into the suitability of using Fosshpae for costume storage mounts at Historic Royal Palaces." Material in Motion: Preprints. 10th North American Textile Conservation Conference, New York: NATCC.

ADDITIONAL READING

Uhlir, S. 2017. "Articulated Solutions for the Mannequins in the Circle of Dance Exhibition at National Museum of the American Indian—New York." *Journal of the American Institute for Conservation* 56(1): 43-58.

SOURCES OF MATERIALS

Fosshape600
WonderflexWorld
Brentwood, NH 03833
Tel: 603-778-0190
Email: info@wonderflexworld.com
http://www.wonderflexworld.com/

10

Preparation in Action

THE OBJECT DIRECTS THE PROCESS: CREATING ETHAFOAM CRADLES FOR
THE FIELD MUSEUM'S VERTEBRATE PALEONTOLOGICAL COLLECTION

Adrienne Stroup, Collections Assistant, The Field Museum

Vertebrate fossil collections are characteristically diverse in size, shape, and composition. They are often as fragile as they are heavy, and specimens may range in size from nearly microscopic shark teeth to 7-foot long limb bones of the largest dinosaurs. Since these collections include any backbone-bearing animal that lived and managed to be recorded in Earth's rock record, which spans hundreds of millions of years, it is no wonder that preparing and handling these specimens for storage or loan require the collection staff to approach each fossil as unique, bearing its own specific challenges.

The fossilization process, where minerals replace the bone's original organic material, will increase the bone's weight, but not all fossils are mineralized to the same degree. Ice Age fossils, from the Pleistocene epoch, retain their original composition and weigh less than older fossils of comparable size because the honeycomb texture of the bone has not completely permeated with minerals, simply because they are younger in geologic age. Animal bones from this time period only had thousands, not millions, of years to fossilize.

Though mineralized and often massive in size and weight, fossils are still fragile and can be quite friable. If the fossil was exposed to weathering before it was collected, it may be flaky and prone to crumbing. Since they are the bones of animals, sometimes they can be extremely delicate—depending on what part of the skeleton was preserved. For example, vertebrae often have long, thin processes that stick out and can be easily broken off. Even the largest dinosaurs, the sauropods, have some of the most delicate, thin-boned skulls.

Some bones may be incomplete due to weathering or breakage. It was a common practice to replace the missing elements with plaster, which can be seen on many older specimens in the Field Museum's collection, especially specimens that had been on exhibit at some point. This is what is referred to as a restored specimen. Plaster elements and glued joints from previous breaks remain the most fragile parts of a fossil specimen.

Within the Field Museum's geological collections, which include meteorites, rocks, minerals, and animal and plant fossils, the vertebrate fossils are the most requested specimens for loans. In fact, the vertebrate fossil loan program is among the most active loan programs at the Field Museum overall.

When looking at trends in vertebrate fossil lending over the past 10 years via our database, there is a notable increase in loans for 3D scanning. The use of X-ray computed tomography (CT) scan data in paleontological research have become popular because this nondestructive method for analysis is more informative and increasingly accessible, largely due to the decreased costs involved even as the technology improves. CT scans allow researchers to analyze a fossil's internal structures in three dimensions, just like doctors use these data in the medical field.

With no scanner on site, the Field Museum has partnered with the University of Chicago to fulfill requests for scans of our collection using their custom-build PaleoCT scanner from General Electric. Requests of this type have driven up the number of outgoing loans in an already actively used collection. We have also worked with other local institutions that offer 3D imaging such as Argonne National Laboratory and the University of Illinois at Chicago.

Ethafoam, manufactured by Sealed Air Company is the brand name for polyethylene foam; it is often used as a proprietary eponym for polyethylene foam within the conservation field. This material is ideal for archival storage of museum collections because it is nontoxic, resistant to most chemicals, and a stable plastic that will not discolor or break down over time. In addition, its closed-cell design prevents it from absorbing water or off-gassed vapors.[1] Ethafoam can be purchased in planks or rolls of various thicknesses and densities. Most commonly used in the Vertebrate Paleo Collections at the Field Museum are rolls of 1/4-inch-thick foam cut to line cardboard specimen trays and sheets of 1-inch-, 2-inch, or 4-inch-thick foam for creating cradles for specimens that are larger than 10 × 16 inch specimen trays, which are the largest trays we use in specimen cabinet drawers.

This material is ideal because it can be easily cut with any type of knife from simple box cutters to handheld jigsaws and glued together with hot-melt glue to create supportive cradles for specimens with complicated shapes. Cradles made of Ethafoam are also lightweight and can be constructed in a relatively short amount of time compared to building a conventional wooden crate. Furthermore, this material can be used again and again—as seen below in figure 10.1, the sheets of foam were reused from an earlier shipping cradle—and cut to form the new cradle.

The easiest way to create a cavity for the bone to rest in is to use multiple layers of foam. By cutting all the way through the first layer of foam, a cavity in which the object can lay is formed. The second layer of foam will remain uncut and serve as the platform the specimen rests on. If the object is not stable on the flat layer, the easiest way to fix this is to add small wedge-shaped pieces of foam to the flat layer, nestled and glued in place to prevent the object from rocking. Alternatively, the supporting layer can be carved in to, but it is much easier to build up from a flat surface than to excavate down into the foam.

Next, determine where it is safest to handle and lift the specimen out of the cradle and cut out hand-sized holes from the top layer to provide easier access to the specimen. Creating these access points will reduce the risk of damaging the object from having to squeeze ones' fingers in between the object and the foam.

The layers can then be glued together with hot-melt glue. Take care to allow the glue to reach the optimum temperature or else the layers will peel apart easily. Waiting for the glue to ooze out of the gun a little ensures that the ideal temperature has been met. Ethafoam is also easily written on with permanent marker. Writing the orientation of the specimen can be helpful if it is not obvious which way the object should be placed.

Lastly, polyester batting can be used to line the cavity if a little extra cushioning seems necessary. However, with paleontological specimens, I tend to use a layer of Tyvek over the polyester batting. Fossils that are rough in texture are subject to flaking or plucking when nestled in thick, flocculent batting. Wadding up the Tyvek a few times helps soften it, even further allowing the material to contour to the object.

THE FIELD MUSEUM'S *TYRANNOSAURUS REX* GETS A PROPER DIAGNOSIS

The Field Museum's *Tyrannosaurus rex* specimen, known to collection staff as FMNH PR 2081, but more affectionately known as "SUE," is one of the most recognizable specimens on exhibit. This specimen is a nearly complete individual and still holds the records for being the largest and oldest *T. rex* known to science. Biggest, oldest, and most complete are not just superlatives to impress visitors; the completeness of the skeleton allows scientists to learn about SUE as an individual animal, and since it was old for its species, pathologies like arthritis, broken bones that healed, and evidence of infection are numerous.

In 2019 a team of radiologists, Charles Hamm and Rolf Reiter, visited the museum to study some of the pathological bones. Among them the left lower leg bone, or fibula, was of particular interest as it shows an abnormal mass of extra bone growth along two-thirds of the shaft. Plans were made to scan the limb at the University of Illinois at Chicago's Outpatient Care Clinic.

Since almost all of SUE's real bones are on permanent exhibit, and SUE happens to be one of the Field Museum's most popular attractions, it was agreed by both the collections and the exhibits staff that the bones should remain off exhibit for the shortest amount of time possible. The innovative mounting armature, created by Research Casting International, allows for individual bones to be removed without affecting the rest of the mounted skeleton. Most importantly, the armature supports each bone in a nondestructive way. Historically, mounted skeletons were erected by drilling holes through the bones and stringing them like beads onto a wire frame. As the technology for studying the internal structures of the bones did not yet exist, mounted skeletons were simply for display and viewing pleasure. The Field Museum prides itself on displaying real fossil material over casts, with only a few exceptions to this rule. Since these mounted skeletons are first and foremost research specimens, the design of modern armature must cater to researchers' needs as well as be visually interesting to the public. Overall, the bone remained off exhibit for only 24 hours.

The fibula, with a length of 41 inches, was too long for a preexisting cardboard box or wooden crate. If not properly supported, a bone of this length could easily break at the weakest point, usually the middle. It is unlikely that a cardboard box, with its tendency to flex and bend, would lend enough support to transport the limb bone. Furthermore, a wooden crate with metal screws could not be

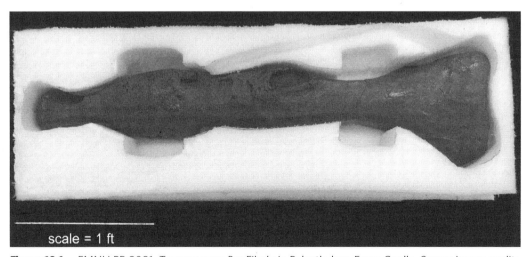

Figure 10.1. FMNH PR 2081, *Tyrannosaurus Rex* Fibula in Polyethylene Foam Cradle. *Source*: Image credit: Adrienne Stroup/Field Museum.

used due to interference that any metal would cause with the CT scanner. Therefore, a cradle was constructed from two sheets of 4-inch-thick Ethafoam to safely contain and support the bone for transport. Foam of this thickness, especially doubled up, flexes very little, creating a stable platform for carrying the specimen.

The more a specimen is handled the more likely it is to get broken, so creating foam cradles is the safest option. Not only do they aid in transportation, but they also provide support within the scanner itself. Once the specimen is wrapped up for shipping, ideally the specimen does not need to be unwrapped until it returns to the museum. Therefore, the outside dimensions of the cradle should be within the limits of the scanning bed. The rule of thumb is to make the cradle only as large as it needs to be—extra bulk does not add extra protection.

Overall, the cradle successfully supported and protected the bone on its journey from exhibit to scanner and back again. The density of the Ethafoam provided a sturdy platform that supported the weight of the bone, while being cushiony enough to pad the delicate rugose surface of the pathological lesion in question. Earlier studies of SUE's fibula suggested that the bone had fractured and healed poorly and the excessive bone growth was the result. However, the CT data show no previous break. Hamm, Reiter, and their paleontological collaborators determined that the Field Museum's *T. rex* suffered from osteomyelitis, a type of bone infection.[2] Without the ability to safely lend specimens, new discoveries like this one would remain a mystery.

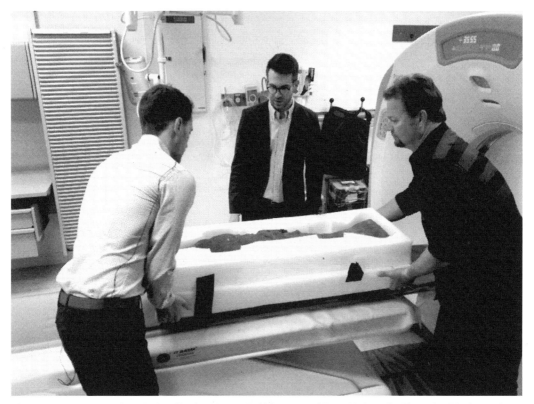

Figure 10.2. From Left to Right: Charlie Hamm, Rolf Reiter, and Pete Makovicky Place the Fibula on the Scanning Bed. *Source*: Image credit: Kate McGee/WBEZ.

LOW-TECH MATERIALS HELP ADVANCE PALEONTOLOGY IN SURPRISING WAYS

Scanning SUE's fibula was covered by the press and required a lot of logistical planning between multiple museum departments and UIC staff.[3] Most loans are orchestrated without any media attention but are just as significant.

From the iconic saber-toothed cat *Smilodon* to the lesser known but even more unusual South American saber-toothed marsupial *Thylacosmilus* and rhino-like *Proadinotherium*, the Field Museum's largest subset of the vertebrate paleontological collection is the fossil mammal collection. Though the skulls of these animals have been well studied by conventional methods, CT scanning has widened the opportunities for viewing the internal structures in ways that had not been possible in the past without damaging specimens. Prior to the invention of CT scanners, conventional X-rays were used to view structures such as the inner ear and the braincase, but the results were limited. If the rock, or matrix, surrounding the fossil is too dense, the image will not yield enough detail to be useful.

Therefore, studying the braincase of a fossil animal required an innovative but time-consuming method of producing a latex mold and plaster cast of that internal structure. This method requires pristine fossil skulls, where the braincase is not crushed, distorted, or partially missing, limiting the sample size. Furthermore, the matrix must be removed from the cavity, to allow a thin layer of latex to be poured in, coating the inside walls of the braincase. Roughly an eighth of an inch of latex, added in layers, is needed to give it enough strength to withstand its extraction from cavity. After removal from the fossil, the latex is filled with plaster to recreate the shape of the braincase.[4] The Field Museum houses a large collection of these plaster braincases called endocasts, posthumously gifted to the Geology Department by the family of the inventor of this method Leonard Radinsky. Subsequent studies have proven these endocasts are fairly comparable to CT-derived endocast models, in terms of accuracy, but it is a time-consuming method that has been virtually replaced by CT technology.

The University of Chicago's PaleoCT scanner can fit specimens smaller than 9.5 inches in diameter and 9.5 inches tall for a single scan. The smaller the specimen, the higher the scan resolution can be achieved. Larger objects can be scanned in sections and stitched together, but the specimen cannot exceed 20 inches in height or 14 inches in diameter.[5] Specimens are mounted in the middle of the scanning chamber, where a cylinder can be mounted on a stage. The best cylinder used to contain specimens is actually a clear plastic water cooler jug with the base cut off and inverted so the neck of the bottle can fit onto the stage.

Orientation of the specimen in the scanner is important and is also limited to the constraints of the cylinder in which it must fit. For getting a complete scan of the *Proadinotherium*'s braincase, the specimen needed to be arranged in the scanner vertically, so that the base of the skull rests down in the cylinder and the snout points upward. This allowed the specimen to be rotated in the chamber while the distance between the specimen and the X-ray tube remained fairly constant, and most importantly the X-rays were not penetrating through the entire length of the skull to scan just the braincase as it would be if it were positioned horizontally. Vibration, which may occur when the machine is in operation, can disrupt the scan quality as well. Therefore, creating a cradle to support the delicate skull while securing it in the plastic cylinder and absorbing any vibration was essential to addressing this issue.

Much like the cradle for SUE's fibula, the custom-made cradles for the fossil mammal skulls both cushioned the specimens for transport from the museum to the university and could be placed directly into the cylinder and scanned without being unwrapped, saving time and reducing risk to the specimens by minimizing handling. A second water jug was cut open and left at the museum to make sure the specimens and their cradles would fit. We have even packed up specimens and their

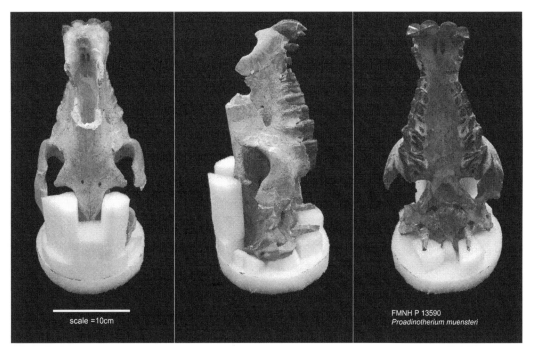

Figure 10.3. Fossil Mammal Skull, FMNH P 13590 *Proadinotherium*, in Polyethylene Foam Cradle. *Source*: Image credit: Adrienne Stroup/Field Museum.

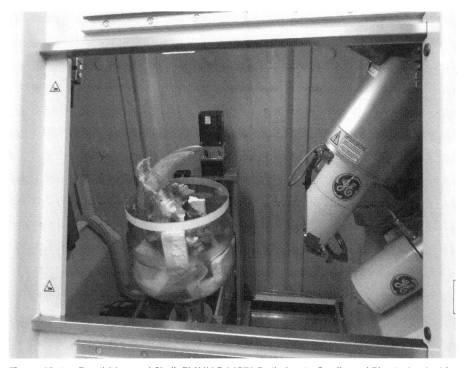

Figure 10.4. Fossil Mammal Skull, FMNH P 14271 *Smilodon*, in Cradle and Plastic Jug Inside PaleoCT Scanner, X-ray Tubes Are Located on the Right. *Source*: Image credit: Zhe-Xi Luo, University of Chicago.

cradles in the extra cylinder so that the entire package could be set up in the machine immediately upon arrival at the lab.

As technology advances, museum staff are tasked with solving unique specimen-related challenges to meet the needs of researchers studying our collections. In the end it is often the simplest materials that help carry out these requests. Ethafoam cradles have aided in the execution of scientific loans in terms of safety and efficacy. It is an easily workable, cost-effective material that can support vertebrate fossils in transit even across the variable size, weight, and fragility ranges unique to each specimen. Though these examples focus on vertebrate fossils, the materials and techniques described are applicable for any museum object that needs to be transported safely. Beyond 3D imaging, loans for study or exhibit are a major operation in many museum collections, and by using relatively simple materials, along with a little creativity to help carry out these requests, we can provide access to the Field Museum's collections on a scale that is far greater than could be achieved if limited to online access to digital collections or in-person visits alone.

NOTES

1. Chris Barber, "Ethafoam™ Polyethylene Foam," February 10, 2014, https://www.paccin.org/content.php?266-Ethafoam.
2. C. A. Hamm et al., "Comprehensive Diagnostic Approach Combining Phylogenetic Disease Bracketing and CT Imaging Reveals Osteomyelitis in a *Tyrannosaurus rex*," *Scientific Reports* 10, no. 18897 (2020): 1–15, https://doi.org/10.1038/s41598-020-75731-0.
3. Kate McGee, "Sue the T. Rex Travels across Town for an X-Ray," *WBEZ Chicago*, February 19, 2019, https://www.wbez.org/stories/sue-the-t-rex-travels-across-town-for-an-x-ray/2f5e8115-2755-4e31-b6dd-24664c1cdd35.
4. P. Thomas Schoenemann et al., "Validation of Plaster Endocast Morphology through 3D CT Image Analysis," *American Journal of Physical Anthropology* 132 (2007): 183–192, https://onlinelibrary.wiley.com/doi/10.1002/ajpa.20499.
5. The Luo Lab, "UChicago PaleoCT," Accessed June 30, 2021, https://luo-lab.uchicago.edu/paleoCT.html.

11

Installation of Objects

Once your objects have been made ready, the environment has been properly prepared, and all the puzzle pieces at play have come together, now the installation of the object can proceed. And while this may seem a straightforward act of placing the object on a pedestal or setting it in a case or hanging it on a wall, the reality of this is far more complex and deserves the same attention and consideration as handling and preparation. The thoughtful and well-conceived installation will, first and foremost, contribute to the safeguarding of objects, ensuring that the act of the installation does not create a potentially hazardous situation or damage or that the impact and outcome of being put on display or shifting the environment may accelerate or initiate lasting damage or change. Secondarily, these considerations will impact how the object is seen and interpreted by the viewer and will have monumental influence on the curatorial, conceptual, or contextual understanding that the included object is aiming to provide. Simply stated, *the way the object is presented matters*, in both practice and principle.

To holistically define these considerations, let's start with the practice. This aspect to installation will not only take into account the physical constraints and condition of the proposed object, as well as the potential hazards in relation to positioning in the environment, but also include the components of the presentation that will enhance or detract from the intended central focus, which should be placed squarely on the object or the grouping. Preliminary considerations of the installation in relation to the object would have been evaluated long before the actual installation or transition: whether the thing can be safely displayed or moved. The answers to these questions are rarely made within the bubble of the preparation staff and certainly never made without consultation by colleagues: registrars, curators, conservators, and lenders. The preparator does, however, bring insight and expertise into the methods and techniques of display that can be employed, many times a key supplemental factor in this determination. And, as so many museums, galleries, and object-based institutions are well aware, these roles often fall to a single member of a small staff. If and when the item in question has been deemed to be moved or installed, a determination of additional mechanical needs must be addressed: How will the item hang or rest? What kind of support furniture or safety devices will be used? And, most importantly, Can the object adequately accommodate (or be accommodated by) whatever device is determined? These solutions are most commonly in the wheelhouse of the preparation team or conservation specialists. Deep knowledge of appropriate hanging systems, security hardware, and mounting techniques that require a learned approach or familiarity with specialty tools or equipment falls to the preparator's responsibility and experience. Informed decision-making on the many types of hardware, materials, and methodologies to accomplish the specified task, too, is part of that assignment.

The final practical aspect of installation that requires the preparator's consideration is the designated environment. Can the new or proposed space safely and securely accommodate the object?

What needs to happen to prepare the space? What will need to be prepped, constructed, or included to support the objective? What impact will this object have on the space while in place, and how will this affect other objects or future installations once the installed object is removed? In the case of museum exhibition installation, this may include factors that will require input and collaboration from curators, exhibition designers, and educators. The curator will ultimately decide on placement as it pertains to the intended narrative; the designer is charged with interpreting that narrative into an experience within the environment; and the educator may provide input that will enhance the public's interpretation. In non-exhibition situations, a similar collaboration takes place; for private or domestic installations the same input may come from the owner or occupant, and in storage or nonpublic institutional situations direction may come from the registrar. In all of this, the preparator must consult accordingly to these voices, adding information regarding the feasibility and technical details of the project that include insight in the physical limitations or architectural details of the space and how this object will affect or will be affected by them.

This brings an important point of note: *the preparator must know their space*. They should have working knowledge of important mechanical and architectural details including the construction makeup of walls and environments they maintain, the load bearing weight of their floors, and the variances and code restrictions that may impact public access and safety. Not to say that all preparators are and should be academically expert in architectural construction, structural engineering, or code enforcement. However, the preparator should have an applied and informed understanding of these details in the spaces they maintain or the environments in which they work. Knowing how a wall is constructed, either in a museum or residential home, will most certainly impact the decisions on what kinds of tools, hardware, and devices can and should be used to properly install and ensure the safety of any object.

A note on dating the construction of your walls: Many residential and institutional exhibition spaces are finished with drywall construction. A 2012 study[1] found that high amounts of chrysotile asbestos was used not only in the production of drywall board but also in drywall accessories and products, for the inherent heat and fire resistance and high tensile strength and its ability to control shrinkage in the drying process and improved temperature stability. The asbestos content in joint compound, seam tapes, and other materials ranges from 3 to 15 percent chrysotile by weight and that in the earliest production contained 10 to 15 percent asbestos, gradually decreasing over time. The use of asbestos in drywall and drywall products was not banned in the production of these materials in the United States until 1977 by the Consumer Product Safety Commission. This means that piercing, hammering or screwing into, or sanding a wall surface constructed before 1980 may have the potential of releasing hazardous particulates into the air where the preparator/installer is working. This is commonly referred to as a "hot" wall, and any hardware installation should be conducted using appropriate safety precautions. Before the start of an installation, it is suggested that the evaluation of the environment includes the testing of wallboard for any hazardous materials and to make subsequent accommodations and adjustments to the installation process, including the contract of abatement or environmental safety teams.

In matters of principle, the context of the installation is considered: how the object's position and placement will impact or inform the space, the viewer, and other objects in the vicinity. There are standard guidelines that act as a base for this, and then there are the external factors and conceptual exponents that influence and guide the process. Is the object read and interacted with alone or is merely one element in a group of objects meant to be read as a whole? How does the method and manner in which we display the object impact how it is perceived and understood? Seemingly minor details, such as the height the object hangs on a wall and the relative distance placed around an object in the center of a space, are in reality quite consequential to the way the object is perceived, defined, and understood. The collaborative process that dictated the practical details of the installation is equally present in the account of the principle. In public exhibition or presentation, there is also a curatorial voice that influences aspects of the project: not just in the aspects of how many objects and proximity but in the inherent conceptual value of the object and how that value or meaning can be reinforced through variations of space, placement, height, or proximity. Another factor not yet considered is the maker: How does artist's intent impact how the objects are installed? This is a decisive voice in process, not only for the preparator but for almost all parties involved—how the artist or maker envisions the object to be displayed should be a primary conceptual (and physical) determination. This can be, at times, a challenging relationship to balance: while the professional staff must take the object in question into consideration as well as the impact on the physical and architectural space, the safety and interest of the public, and the other objects under their care, the artist is concerned with their work—their vision, their concept, and their object. Navigating this balance, about what can be done and what should be done in an installation, is an institutional responsibility that the preparation staff, among the entire staff, must always consider, especially when those who create the objects are contemporary to, and present in, the planning of presentation.

Another important factor in the principles of the installation of objects and interpretive material that the preparator must take into account is accessibility—guidelines of best practice standards that aspire to create an equitable experience for all viewers, regardless of variable physical ability. Like so many of the previously defined aspects of an installation, this responsibility is not the preparator's alone. Exhibition designers, content creators, educators, and even curators, all share accountability in creating an accessible experience as is possible. Outlined below are selected guidelines that are specific to the duties of the preparator, directly consequential to an installation, from the "Smithsonian Guidelines for Accessible Exhibition Design." This document is informed by the construction standards established for the Architectural Barriers Act of 1968, the Rehabilitation Act of 1973, and the Americans with Disabilities Act of 1990[2] and should act as a resource when determining the details of any publicly accessible installation:

Exhibition Items:

- *Items in exhibitions (e.g. artifacts, graphics, props) must be visually accessible to people.*
- *Items must not be placed in locations such that they create a hazard for visitors.*

Keeping the specific guidelines of viewing heights in relation to size, placement, and environment should be a consistent factor for the preparation team when installing objects. Fixed height requirements for the display base of cases, tables, and wall-mounted shelving or furniture should be, when possible, set between 36 and 40 inches from the floor, as to allow viewable access to patrons of any height or those using a wheelchair. In addition, when arranging objects on or in display furniture, consider creating an arrangement that places the smallest or most intimately detailed objects to the front, if the curatorial narrative allows.

Audiovisuals and Interactives:

- *Controls for and operation of all interactives must be accessible and usable by all visitors.*
- *Use of interactives must be from a location accessible to people using wheelchairs or other assistive devices (e.g., canes, crutches); interactives must not be blocked by furniture or other obstacles.*

While the preparation staff may not always be the content creator or technical team tasked with developing and supporting interactive displays, they will most certainly be involved in the installation and required upkeep of the presentation. Akin to the regulations previously noted about exhibition items, the supplemental elements of instruction, interaction, and context, such as informative labels, button controls, headphones, and instructions for use, should be installed at heights and positions that will provide ultimate access for any visitor.

Circulation Route:

- The circulation route within the exhibition must be accessible according to the requirements of the Smithsonian Guidelines for Accessible Design for Facilities and Sites.
- The circulation route must be well lighted, clearly defined, and easy to follow.

When planning the inclusion of freestanding casework of objects meant to be experienced in the round (such as large sculpture or artifacts that require 360° of viewable content), remember that your environment should accommodate a clear and unfettered path for any visitor and will require a minimum of a 36- to 42-inch width of pathway that circulates around the installed object. Never install an object or gallery furniture in a position that blocks or impedes access to and from the exhibit space.

Furniture:

- All cases must provide viewing access to people who are short or seated as well as to those who are standing.
- Cases and vitrines must not present a safety hazard to any visitor.
- Seating must be provided in each exhibition; 50 percent of the seats must be accessible. Single-gallery exhibitions must have seating in a nearby corridor or in an adjacent gallery space.

A preparator with a broad and continually updated understanding of the best practices and guidelines that aim to provide equitable access in our museum and collection spaces not only serves the stewardship of the objects on view but also illustrates the professional and institutional commitment to creating an experience that is unbiased and equitable to the diversity of the community.

There is a commonly shared philosophy among preparators and installers that rings true regardless of the genre of the objects or materials in question, or the specific details or circumstance of the display, storage, or rehousing. It may be best described as a clandestine approach or a form of institutional ninjutsu: the successful work done by these behind-the-scene teams should be rarely seen, if at all. The preparator's work, either in the preparation of housings, the mounts to support, prop, and position, or the fitting and security of objects in an environment, is craft and technique that when done (that is to say done well) is not immediately known or noticed. What the public is presented with is an unfettered engagement with the thing or the idea—and any interjecting evidence of the preparator's hand in that engagement is tantamount to impeding that interpretative function. At its least invasive, the literal or figurative fingerprint of an installer may merely be a visual or physical distraction from the intended curatorial or educational focus, but at the egregious remnants of poorly executed installations—marked-up or damaged walls or bases; overbearing and cumbersome mounting techniques; the unhidden chords, brackets, and hardware not inherent to the physical object, furniture, or the conceptual/contextual value—these transgressions can become unpassable roadblocks to the intended outcome of the installation.

PREPARING FOR THE INSTALLATION

Preceding chapters have outlined a carefully choreographed process that includes proper handling techniques, preparation management, and object preparation methods: all building to the apex of the project—the installation or transition of objects. Once properly prepared for their new environments with mounts, furniture, or hardware and the space they will inhabit is equally ready, cleared of all construction, finish materials, and tools, and all residue of the work has been cleaned and removed, the installation process of the object(s) can begin. This procedure will demand the same strategic approach and collaborative attention first outlined in the tenants of proper object handling, with particular emphasis placed on systematic and continuous communication among preparation team members and the larger institution or patrons.

As discussed in the chapter on preparation management, planning for the installation will require the security of a closed environment and a clear and controlled path to the active space, two factors that will many times require action beyond the preparator or installer's control. Through proper project management, installation dates should have long been clearly articulated to those impacted—in a museum, this many times creates a coordination with visitor services, security, facilities, and educational departments—as the particular footprint where the installation is set to occur should not be accessible to the public or noninvolved personnel. For smaller or singular install projects, the preparation staff will many times strategically plan to execute the task on a day when the museum is closed or, in the case of residential and commercial work, the task is coordinated for times when the patrons/ owners are not present or when the area has been identified as a low-visitation period. More complex installations, and those that will inherently require a time frame that exceeds the off-hours schedule to complete, will force a necessary shift in the access to a section, if not the entirety of the affected environment. These needs should be carefully calculated and discussed with all affected departments well in advance so all appropriate steps can be taken, specifically for the planned closure of pathways and public spaces. Last-minute, poorly communicated, or ill-conceived arrangements for installations, while sometimes unavoidable, can often result in creating potentially hazardous situations for both the objects in transition and the staff and public. If and when an urgent or immediate circumstance is necessary, all efforts should be made to ensure a controlled (if not closed) environment.

Before handling objects and moving into position, consider the following checklist:

- Objects have been completely prepped for their new environment and are ready to install.
- Coordination with all parties involved or affected (for institutions, this can include curators, conservators, registrars, and visitor services; for commercial or private projects, this may be owners, storage facilities, property management, or shipping companies) has been confirmed and approved.
- All hardware, tools, or special equipment needed to complete the installation have been identified and procured and are ready to use.
- The new environment for the object(s) has been completely prepped, all tools and materials have been removed, and all construction or repair residues have been addressed.
- Any contract work, including custodial and/or facilities maintenance, is complete.
- All necessary staff have been identified, debriefed, and informed and are present and ready to assist.
- Locations and pathways have been adequately secured and are ready for the transition of objects.
- All temporary or supplemental equipment for the project, including movable work surfaces, object transport carts, ladders and scaffold, and heavy machinery, such as vertical lifts and hoists, have been staged and are ready for use.
- When possible, corresponding hardware for object mounts have been installed in place according to layout plans (this is ideal to complete if hanging and spotting measurements can be calculated in advance of the objects being brought into the space, allowing for minimal handling or transitional rest for objects, but is not always possible).
- Lighting and environmental needs that may require additional equipment in the space have been completed or prepped for minimal interference once the object(s) have been placed.
- Once these central aspects of the project have been addressed, only then should the preparation team consider moving the object into its new environment.

TOOLS, MATERIALS, AND TECHNOLOGY

In most installation situations, there will be shared and routine requisites for basic kinds of hardware and tools that will be needed and used in the procedure. Many times, this common hardware, and its industry standard capabilities, can in fact inform the process and approach to the evaluative and prepatory phases of decision-making, adding detail to what can be possible and what is needed. An important factor in selecting the appropriate hardware for your installation will commonly be generated by both the evaluation of the object and the environment. Can the object accommodate the introduction of certain materials? What will the walls or furniture meant to support the object require to safely and securely accommodate this task? Knowing what is available, what is considered industry standard, and what can be specialized for unique situations and needs is critical to the preparation team. The following includes general tools, materials, hardware, and installation furniture that are utilized in common practice rather than an encyclopedic list of all installation materials. Specialty tools, custom hardware, and object-specific materials may be introduced depending on the particular need or circumstance—communication with conservators, curators, and collection specialists will inform these unique scenarios.

Basic Hardware

While there is a long list of specialty hardware used in professional object installation, much of what is needed and routinely employed can also be found in local hardware stores or home building supply. *Common-head brads* are a standard for most small- to medium-frame or two-dimensional hanging situations. The term "brad" refers to a wire-cut nail, often relatively lightweight and thin. The "common" or flat head of the nail makes it ideal for easily driving and capturing with a hammer and holding materials and hardware in place, as opposed to the finish nail, which does not have the same flat head structure and is meant to disappear into trim rather than hold hardware. Finish nails should never be used as fasteners for object installation. The ultimate benefit of using brad (smooth shank) nails in walls is in the mending: for display spaces or residential construction that necessitate frequent or efficient repair, the cut brads, when removed properly, leave damage that is far easier to patch and prepare than other fasteners or screws. As with any installation decision, the choice in hardware should always be ultimately informed and directed by the object's safety and security—if the scenario demands a heavier-duty fastener, the correlating damage/impact it will have on the display environment is always secondary. The common-style brad or nail will routinely accompany the basic hangers used for hanging traditional frames. *Drywall screws*, with a bugle head and course thread, can be a very effective fastener for many applications but are not meant to carry extreme weight. A standard drywall screw will comfortably accommodate 50–70 pounds of weight but will sheer if overly stressed.[3] These basic screws are ideally suited to capture and securely hold in most wall construction, especially capable for gypsum and plaster. Using screws rather than nails has both benefits and drawbacks. Using screws creates a highly secure and rigid connection and results in far less ancillary vibration radiating throughout the environment than that of a hammered nail—this can be especially relevant depending on existing objects in the space or the stability of the structural space. The removal of the screws from substrates can also be more efficient and less impactful than the physicality needed to remove nails. However, the residual damage and subsequent preparation needed to mend the wall or surface from a screw rather than a nail can be more involved and time-consuming than that of a nail hole. In addition, depending on the makeup of the surface itself, a screw may not be sufficient in creating a stable point of connection. For example, a standard interior residential wall built after the 1940s would most likely be constructed of a singular layer of half-inch drywall on studwork, and a drywall screw (not directly screwed into the wood stud frame) would not support substantial weight or pressure before the gypsum layer crumbles, breaks, or fails.[4] In these cases, an *anchor* can supply added and needed stability if the hardware must be installed on a wall surface where there is no backing support or studwork behind the drywall, plaster, or other finish board. The anchor will give a screw a stable cavity to thread into while it also supports the wall material from failing. There are two basic variations on the standard anchor: the expanding anchor and the threaded anchor. The expanding anchor is inserted into a pre-excavated hole in the surface just large enough for the shank to fit snuggly. Once the hardware is screwed into the sleeve, the anchor expands to create a pressure fitting between the hardware and the surface. Alternatively, the threaded "screw" style self-tapping anchor will bore into drywall to create a large area of reinforcement for hardware, distributing the strain of the object through the larger mechanism, again salvaging the finish material from breaking under the pressure of whatever is being supported. The expanding anchor in drywall can hold between 5 and 25 pounds before failure; the threaded anchor system can hold 25 to 75 pounds, depending on size. A recent development to the standard wall anchor is the winged design, effectively creating a toggle bolt–style support, where the anchor adds bracing through both expanded pressure through the wallboard and expanded wings behind the board, distributing weight across a much larger area than that of the hardware cavity.

All these materials can be readily purchased at most hardware or home stores without any special order or lead time—a valuable resource for any installation.

Basic Hangers

When navigating a traditional wall-based installation, the basic hanger is one of the most common pieces of hardware in the preparator's toolbox. Generally, hanging hooks will be found in two variations: the brass style and the nickel-plated style. The basic design is the same: a flat plate with a curved hook at the bottom and a hole or sleeve to accept the nail that creates the bond to the surface at the top. The very simple yet effective design allows the weight of the object to be distributed down the wall so as to not overwhelm the point where the nail pierces the hanging surface. The difference between the two is in the application: The nickel-plated hangers, which come in varied sizes depending on the weight of the object, will commonly also incorporate a larger brad or nail to correspond with the scale. The brass-style hangers, which add multiple sleeves for their steel shank brads depending

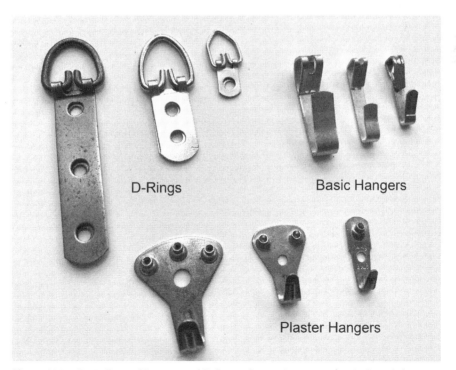

Figure 11.1. Basic Frame Hangers and D-Rings. *Source*: Image credit: Andrew Saluti.

on weight capacity, are traditionally suited for heavier-duty applications and especially for plaster walls—salvaging the finished wall surface from the damage created by the heavier girth of the larger nails of larger nickel hangers.

D-Rings

Another standard piece of hardware for installing objects that will generally accompany most wall hanging situations is the D-ring (or strap hanger). This is a pivoting metal ring (commonly shaped like a sideways "D") with a perforated bracket that allows direct connection with an additional fastener. For frames, these brackets can be the immediate connection to hangers installed on a surface or can accommodate wire for a rail system or single-point installations. These are also useful for hanging other types of objects that have support systems or construction to accommodate hardware but do not have/require independent furniture or mounts, such as canvas stretchers.

Standard Level

An essential part of the installer's tool kit is a reliable and versatile level that will ensure all reference marks for hardware and the installed objects will be square and plumb in the environment. The ideal level for purposes of installation will also have a ruled edge for measurements and will be made up of a non-marking material so as to not scar the intended presentation surface. Levels come in a variety of lengths and variations: a standard selection for most preparation teams and installers is a 48-inch, non-marring, front measuring ruled device.

Laser Level

In addition to (not supplanting) a standard level, the laser level has fast become an invaluable tool for the installation process. When mounted in a central location within the installation environment, the laser level will generate a consistent guide throughout the space that will ensure the horizon or eye-line regardless of variations or inconsistencies on the ground. The laser line will expedite measuring without leaving physical marks and, if equipped with a vertical crosshair, can also assist in verifying lateral positioning. Tip: when using a laser level during an installation, be sure to mount the unit to a stable tripod that will allow a circular rotation; this will eliminate the need to reset the laser as the installation surpasses the visible area.

Braided Wire

Also called framing wire or picture hanging wire, braided wire is a versatile tool for prepping or installing objects. Usually constructed from interwoven strands of galvanized wire to create a highly strong yet flexible line, braided wire will come in a variety of thicknesses or weights that increase the load capacity that the wire is rated to hold (e.g., a #2 braided wire comprising 12 woven strands might be rated for 12 to 15 pounds of weight, while a #8 wire made of 36 strands may be rated for 35 to 50 pounds). Variations include stainless steel wires and vinyl coated wires, making handling and manipulating the wire easier for the preparator and less abrasive to an object. Braided wire is generally used on the back of frames and objects for wall-mounted installations but can also be used for other installation needs such as rail hanging or light rigging.

Security Hangers, Hardware, and Devices

This type of hardware integrates security features into basic installation functionality and comes in a variety of styles and designs ranging from interlocking plates, to basic hangers that have a snapping latch to capture the hanging mechanism, to height-adjustable locking systems. Additional variations include specific systems made for metal sectional frames. Selecting security hardware will be informed by many factors that include the overall weigh of the object, the type of frame, furniture, or mount used, as well as the duration of installation and ease of deinstallation.

In addition to the hardware designed to mount an object in place, supplemental tools and implements can be introduced to add protection from unintended removal or movement. Security hardware can range from complex technology, such as motion sensors and audible alarms that can be integrated into the hanging systems, to simple flat metal plates or brackets to carry a fastener that will fortify the mount. The physical details of the object or corresponding furniture and mounts will inform what type of security hardware is necessary/available to use: there are various options for wood frames that affix to the back of the molding (keyhole and flat strap plates), for metal frames that utilize the channel of the sectional rails (T-screw and locking systems), and for storage cavities (such as Oz clips or mobile data loggers). Another factor in selecting the type of additional security is the details of the installation: loan objects will generally mandate additional security hardware in addition to basic installation; long-term or permanent installations may warrant a permanent or more advanced system.

Cleat Systems

One of the most stable systems for wall mounting the cleat system (also called the French cleat or mating bar) is a simple construct of two corresponding lengths of bracket that will lock together along a beveled or channeled edge. Cleat systems are very effective for flush mounting, drawing objects or

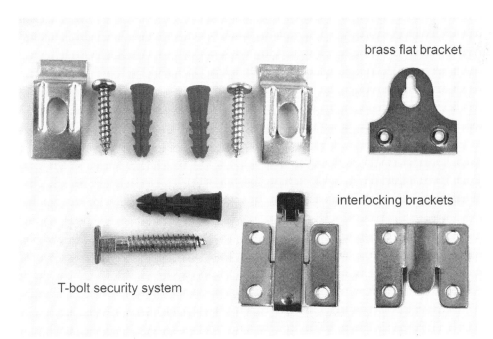

brass flat bracket

interlocking brackets

T-bolt security system

Figure 11.2. Security Hanging Hardware. *Source:* Image credit: Andrew Saluti.

materials tightly against the mounting surface. They distribute the weight of the object along the over-all length of the bracket rather than at singular points of contact or connection, such as a basic hanger, allowing for multiple points of connection to the surface for a high threshold rating for especially heavy objects. Cleat systems also ensure a consistent and stable level connection.

Rare-Earth Magnets

A popular choice for contemporary artists working on paper or two-dimensional media are elemental magnets, also called rare-earth magnets, for their strength, size, and ability to secure media without a physical connection. When installed with corresponding metal surfaces or hardware, the use of magnets can hold objects such as unframed photographs and delicate textiles in place without the need for puncture or permanent mounting devices. Magnets can correspond with common-head nails or screws to create an offset free-floating presentation and can be hidden within archivally created mounts for a wide array of objects of varying size and weight. Conservators and mountmakers have also begun to utilize rare-earth magnets for their ability to maintain a stable hold without the need for permanent fasteners. An important note when planning on using magnetics for an installation is to research the appropriate strength of the magnet, weighing the object evaluation with the pull force and shear force of the magnets used.

Museum Wax and Putty

A longtime staple to secure objects that rest on a surface from tipping, jostle, or accidental movement are museum waxes or putties. These stabilizers can be especially helpful in earthquake-prone areas and can create a nonpermanent connection to a base or shelf. Using this material conservatively is always prudent: adding small dabs of wax or making small pealike balls of putty to establish the mount is always prudent. This material should only be used on nonporous media such as ceramic and glass.

Pedestals

For dimensional objects and artifacts that require an environmental interaction or to be viewed at multiple angles, the use of pedestals (sometimes called bases or plinths) can allow for flexible posi-tioning within a presentation space. Pedestals are versatile pieces of exhibition furniture in that they can be internally engineered to accommodate objects of varying scale and weight, can be built specif-ically for a singular object or general use, and can be designed to accept acrylic case enclosure caps or create a stable surface for open display as needed. They function as both presentation tool and a secure mounting device. When planning the construction or procurement of pedestals (or any display furniture), the preparator should consider the possibility of adaptable use (rather than one-time use) as well as storage availability.

Vitrine Cases

Another standard component of display furniture is the vitrine case: a five-sided acrylic or glass "hood" that can add security to an installation, protecting sensitive or delicate objects from inappro-priate handling or contact while on public display. Vitrines commonly correspond with a pedestal or table base, fitting into a channeled groove or onto a footing that captures and secures the case in place with the addition of fasteners (this can be as simple as a base plate cut to the internal dimension of the vitrine, then mounted to the top of a preexisting pedestal). Vitrines create a closed environment and should be monitored for relative temperature and humidity, according to the objects they house and the length of time on display. When not in use, vitrines should be wrapped or protected from damage, as scratches or abrasions will take away from the presentation of the object housed therein, and the custom fabrication of these enclosures will come at significant cost.

Suction Lifters

When installing casework and vitrines, dexterity and sensitivity are vital factors in ensuring a safe and successful installation. Glass and acrylic cases can be heavy, awkward, and difficult to manipulate by hand, thereby putting the object they aim to enclose at risk during the positioning and installation. Using suction lifters gives the preparator a stable handle to operate and control what needs to be a careful, often slow placement of vitrines and cases.

Risers

A riser is a low pedestal-like platform for installations off the ground but without extreme elevation. Like their display furniture cousin the pedestal, a riser is a useful architectural element for creating safe, stable, controlled, and adaptable display conditions for larger environmental artifacts and objects. Risers can be constructed similarly to pedestals with structural support and finished edges or trim or can be as simple as a flat board or sheet with footings that denotes display space from a pathway. The use of risers can also double the security when used in tandem with pedestal or wall-mounted installations, a physical barrier keeping the public from getting too close to an unprotected object on display.

Stanchions

Another element of exhibition furniture meant for security and visitor flow is the stanchion: a system of posts connected by rope, cable, or other extending material in order to create a barrier. In collection or display settings, stanchions are commonly seen surrounding objects of high-risk or sensitivity or to denote a specific path or environment.

Digital Modeling

The use of modeling is not a new concept for the planning of installations. Physical gallery models, made from foam core or board, have been a mainstay for exhibition designers and curatorial practice for decades, and many institutions continue to use physical models in their exhibition planning. The use of CAD (Computer Aided Design) digital modeling, however, offers a far more robust experience and can be an essential tool for the preparator in planning the installation process. The digital model can allow for alterations and adjustments far more efficiently than a physical model, can be easily shared and collaborated with colleagues at any location, and can offer more intuitive views of modeled installs, spacing and measuring of objects or media, and animations of experiential walk-throughs. Beyond the exhibition process, this technology can assist in the development of storage devices according to object specifications, planning for permanent and temporary collections storage according to object dimensions, and, when used in tandem with 3D scanning and printing technology in more advanced circumstances, the design and creation of hyper-specific object mounts and bases.

The software used to create digital surrogates of a physical space has progressed to become more user-friendly and accessible to the nontechnical or digital novice. Applications such as SketchUp (www.sketchup.com) have fast become industry standards for museum and gallery modeling because of their ease of use and free and low-cost options. SketchUp also shares robust tutorial videos and classes to quickly learn the basics of the application. From the preparator's passive conservation perspective, the use of the digital model will tender the ability to plan for a variety of object-related

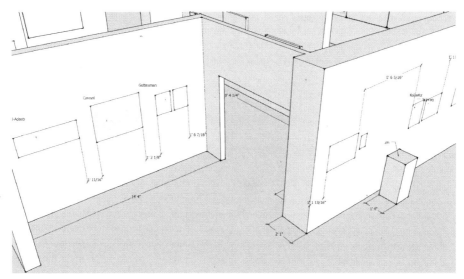

Figure 11.3. Digital Model Layout of Gallery Installation. *Source*: Image credit: Andrew Saluti.

circumstances without the direct handling of the work, such as the measuring of space for objects on a gallery wall or maximizing the storage capabilities of a given environment without having to transport or physically manipulate the object(s). The understanding and use of these tools enhance collections and exhibition practice and are essential for the twenty-first-century preparator and museum professional.

Specialty Hardware/Systems

There are a bevy of additional specialized mounts and brackets that may be required for a secure installation of objects, artifacts, and supplemental media and materials. Take the installation of musical instruments for example: while there are commercial stands and mounting devices available, museum collection objects will generally require a level of specialized mountmaking experience to reflect the particular physical structure and condition of the individual object. Ready-made brackets for artifacts such as plates and bowls are easy to manipulate and adjust to fit the need, such as acrylic or brass easels or adjustable stands. When installing media such as flat-screen monitors or digital projectors, commercially available mounting brackets not only will assist in making installation go smoothly without unexpected rigging or taking time from an object-centric focus but can also facilitate stability that will make the manipulation of the technology easier: using devices such as universal digital projector mounts (sometimes called "octopus mounts" for their adjustable bracket arms), while they may come at an initial expense, will create a far more stable and easily adjustable installation than simply positioning the device on a shelf or base (see chapter 6).

MATERIALS AND TECHNIQUES TO AVOID

In addition to the standard tools and materials used throughout professional practice, there are many materials that should be avoided when installing objects and artifacts in order to mitigate the risk of damage or danger to the objects, the environment, and the public.

Single-Point Hanging

Whenever possible, avoid a single-point hanging scenario on any wall-mounted installation. While common in residential or personal hanging situations, this method will create a less secure mount to the surface, placing all weight on a single point of connection and allowing for unintended movement and risk to the artifact. Even with the inclusion of security brackets or plates, the distribution of weight and object security is better implemented by at minimum a two-point hanging system. Note: if an object has been loaned with a single-point hanging system (such as braided picture wire), request to the lender if a multiple-point hanging system can be added in addition to the existing hardware. Once the object has been deinstalled from the lending environment, the additional hardware can be removed and the object can be reinstalled with the original mechanism.

Sawtooth Hangers

These hanging devices are commonly seen on commercial picture frames, creating a single-point connection bracket for a nail or screw to rest on. The "sawtooth" is designed to capture the head of the hardware in place but will not secure the frame or object from movement and can easily fail. Using D-ring hangers in place of sawtooth hangers is advised.

Wire Drywall/Sheetrock Hooks

A quick solution for hanging objects on unbacked drywall construction, this hardware is designed to act as both the fastener and hanger by puncturing the board without hammer or anchor. These devices will not carry substantive weight or create a secure mount, especially considering the weakness of the surface. In these circumstances, using an anchor system will establish a secure mount for the hanging hardware.

Adhesive Strips

The acceptable use of double-sided adhesive strips (e.g., 3-M Command Strips) is ubiquitous within a display environment in a myriad of supplemental applications from hanging object labels to way-finding and publication and brochure holders. However, adhesive strips should never be used to secure objects in any scenario, in wall hanging, pedestal-mounted, or display case installations. The potential for adhesive failure or the effects of the adhesive might have in direct contact with the media are not worth the risk: regardless of manufacturer specifications regarding weight ratings or clean removal. These materials, while possibly offering a simple and expedient solution, will not guarantee a secure mount or maintain a passive conservation standard that must be considered for both short-term and long-term display.

CREATING AN INSTALLATION PLAN

When planning the installation of objects, as with any collections exercise, primary consideration must be paid to the mitigation of risk. The installation of objects is (generally) the final step in a mul-tifaceted and lengthy process of research, preparation, and design. In the extremely compressed and time-sensitive portion of this timeline, the order in which objects are introduced into an environment is essential. As previously outlined, best practice dictates that no objects or artifacts should be brought into a space until they are ready to be mounted or placed in their final display environment. This in-cludes a variety of factors, both preceding the event of the installation (such as gallery preparation, patching, and painting) as well as the placement of gallery furniture (discussed in environmental installation) and an evaluation of the objects and supplemental materials to be installed. Considering an installation or display may include numerous types of media or varying dimensions and formats, as well as the possibility of large wall graphics, text panels, and object labels; the order in which these elements are introduced becomes vital to ensure object safety. A generalized approach might be to consider the order of installation in direct relation of object proximity to the installation activity and level of security once installed, starting with the supplemental finished wall elements, mounting the perimeter wall objects, then proceeding to floor or environmental objects: from the safest situations, where the objects will not be in the way of other installations, graduating to the most at risk, where objects will require the most attention and may be in pathways or workspace. This methodology is a simplified way to start; however, the tenants of handling will also play a part in this process—and the evaluation, communication, and common sense rules may modify this order. If an object requires specialty equipment or procedure that might introduce risk to the elements within the display space (e.g., the introduction of heavy equipment such as a forklift or hoist to position a large stone carving), these installations should be scheduled ahead of any other in the vicinity of the work. If the artifact is one of extreme fragility or high risk, it would be prudent to move these installations as close to the end of the process as possible, aiming to eliminate any potential hazard during the working process.

Creating a schedule of installation is another aspect of passive or preventative conservation that the preparator must articulate to and collaborate with the larger team: collection managers, registrars, and other colleagues involved—this may also include couriers. A courier is a representative from another institution that has been assigned to travel with an object being loaned—they monitor the object from the point of departure all the way through to its installed location. The courier may be an institutional registrar, a conservator, a contract handler, or a preparator. The installation plan becomes especially relevant in courier situations, as these colleagues will generally require to be present during the installation of the loaned objects and will need the borrowing institution to organize (and provide) travel and accommodations. Having a well-organized and orchestrated installation plan is a crucial aspect of the management of a successful installation.

INSTALLATION TECHNIQUES

The applied techniques and tips for installing objects have been organized into three main categories: wall installation, environmental installation, and archival/case installation. The process and practice of these divisions will correlate to the vast majority of basic institutional or private scenarios for physical objects. Audio/visual and digital component installations require specialized considerations and are addressed separately in upcoming chapters.

Wall Hanging Installations

Perhaps the most common object or artifact installation procedure, wall hanging or mounting utilizes the key component that defines the environment where our objects will reside: the walls. Not solely for two-dimensional objects, the use of a space's walls can create one of the most secure and versatile environments to display objects, unobstructively presenting items while also physically separating an object from a viewer's direct path or access. A wall hang or mount can promote the intimate inspection of small and detailed objects by installing the work at a height and manner that invites close engagement, while at the same time allowing for a monumental work or group of objects to envelope and redefine the very space where they reside. The walls of the environment can not only accommodate a linear narrative or curatorial arrangement but also physically reinforce the intended progression, depending on the design and implementation of the install. For didactic and informational display, there is not a better or more natural accessible application to insert these components into the exhibition experience than using the structural walls as that primary point of reference and direction. Using the walls of your space maximizes the physically finite resource to display objects in the most effective way.

There are, of course, limitations to using structural walls for the presentation of collection materials. First and foremost, any object that inherently demands 360° of interaction or interpretation would obviously not be an ideal candidate for a wall-based position or mount. Not that this excludes all objects meant to be seen in the round from being mounted or positioned on a wall surface, but this and other physical characteristics will dictate the decision and method. Scale most certainly plays a significant factor here, as well as the object's structural orientation and dimensional footprint. When surveying the long history of traditional wall-mounted displays, the methodology in which the objects are secured can be broken down into three categories: objects hung from a rail system, objects directly mounted to the wall, and objects resting on wall-mounted furniture.

Picture Rail System

One of the oldest approaches to hanging objects, specifically two-dimensional pictures and framed objects, is using a picture rail: a simple system that uses lengths of molding or track positioned at a high point on the presentation surface that can capture a hook or bracket to accept the hanging wire of an object or suspend a series of cables or chains that extend down the wall surface allowing for a fixed point (or points) of connectivity to position the objects in place. This system has been widely used since the fifteenth century and affords the space a flexible and reusable mechanism to install objects in a noninvasive way: where no permanent hardware is needed to puncture and scar the wall surface. The pragmatic application for these systems is especially relevant for installations in a setting where preservation is a factor, such as house museums or historic homes and buildings. They are also useful

Figure 11.4. Spotting Objects and Hardware for Installation Using a Picture Rail System. *Source*: Image credit: Andrew Saluti.

when the wall surface meant for display is not easily maintained or repaired: such as with plaster lathe or masonry construction. However, these systems are also found in contemporary display settings, chosen for the ability to accommodate a constant rotation of different objects without the impact of wall damage and repair—a factor that influences not only the ongoing condition of the structural space but also the time and budget of the installation process.

Contemporary picture rail systems come in a variety of aesthetic and mechanical styles, depending on need and use. Many systems have proprietary hardware that can be adapted to accommodate many different types of corresponding hanging hardware—often offering security devices and easily adjustable receiving hooks that aim to facilitate the installation process. There are drawbacks and limitations to using these systems. The foremost is that they are almost always visible, not easily hidden in the installed environment—this can be a significant factor for both the exhibition and exhibitor. Installing a group of objects in a designed nonlinear or conforming arrangement, one that does not necessarily coincide with a singular and consistent eye level, height, or planar position (as is common for many contemporary installations), would prove to be challenging using a rail system. Depending on the bearing load of the system in place, object's physicality (size and weight) would also potentially disqualify the use of a fixed rail.

Direct Wall Mount

The most common practice for display of objects (or media and didactic) is a direct connection to the exhibition wall. Using one or a combination of hardware or fasteners (depending on the object need), objects mounted at a predetermined height on a wall surface ensure safety and security, while at the same time enhance the intended interpretive engagement between object and viewer through a visibly uninterrupted and environmentally integrated presentation. The direct wall mount was historically considered part of the design of the room, which often incorporated the permanent installation of objects on a wall and included architectural details such as molding and trim that housed the objects, commonly portraits, to create a unified experience within the environment. As institutional presentation of objects became more temporary and ephemeral (for the ability to present objects in unique and curated contexts on a rotating basis), the direct wall mount of objects allowed for unfettered engagement with an object at a specified position and order, not confined to the restricted position or capability of the rail system. An object may be installed at any height or position in context to other objects, media, or didactic—the only restriction is the capacity of the wall itself. This method also expands the ability to include dimensional artifacts, sculpture, and other non-flat objects in a wall-mounted installation, permitting a flexibility in the fastening of object mounts and furniture to be installed in concert with other objects rather than separated by the need for environmental furniture or distanced inclusion. Wall-mounted cases and shelves, ideal for objects that cannot be safely hung or directly installed to a wall surface and that may require an enclosed, secure environment, also contribute to the benefits of mounting directly to a wall surface. Incorporating this type of furniture for objects can heighten the direct relationship and engagement between corresponding installations when appropriate and offers a more controlled or designed interaction with the viewer than that of a separated freestanding case or pedestal. The objects become an inclusive part of the environment, rather than an independent entity sitting in the environment.

Where mounting directly to the wall surface has some disadvantage to a rail system is in the repair and preparation of the wall for the next installation: with any direct mounting comes damage to the architectural wall itself. The malleability of the installation will result in the necessity to repair hardware holes, marks, and other damages that were required to securely mount the objects in position and, depending on the object need and hardware used, must be included in the preparation management installation timeline. While it is common for institutions to hire out the repair, preparation, and painting of walls to external contractors, the preparator must consider the impact that the determined means to install an object or furniture will have on the environment for the future installations.

ENVIRONMENTAL INSTALLATIONS

Even as the installation of objects on the wall structures of an environment can accommodate a large selection of various kinds of objects, there will be an equal need for some objects to be seen in the round or enclosed within independent furniture. These environmental installations often demand different considerations from the preparation staff and include additional standards, presentation furniture, and best practice methods for compliance and accessibility—well beyond just simply placing an object on a pedestal in the center of a room. In the evaluation of these installations, the preparator must now consider safety and security from multiple vantage points, without the support, protection, and inherent stability of the wall mount (both from a structural sense and from the viewable perception). Is a base required to present the object at a viewable height? Will the object be secured to the floor, pedestal, or base or will an enclosed case be necessary? How will the visitor's pathway and intended interpretation be affected by dimensional objects within the environment? If the object rests at the ground level, will a riser or stanchions be required to keep the visitor at a safe distance to prevent risk? Do the elements of the environmental installation maintain accessible pathways for the public to safely traverse?

The primary consideration when evaluating an environmental installation, like any other, is the safety of the object: stability for the object at rest, either on a mount, on a cradle, or in direct contact with a base, must be established before the object is even introduced into the space. This is made especially relevant by the fact that installation is standing independently within the environment, susceptible to risk from multiple directions as opposed to a wall-mounted object. This begins with object preparation, establishing a mount (if needed) that will carry the object in a way that does not place undue physical strain or stress on the object while on view. At the point of installation, there are common procedures that must be considered to reinforce the attention to object and artifact well-being.

Preparing Furniture

Before installing objects on exhibition furniture, part of the evaluative process is to verify that the object(s) or artifact(s) will be safely housed while on display. If the furniture includes a closed vitrine or case, object dimensions should reflect the scale of the object, at rest, on its mount (the mounted object may be elevated or presented at an angle that increases dimension). In addition, the object should not come in contact with any part of the enclosure once installed—this includes any adjustable shelving, doors, or exterior vitrine planes. A general rule of thumb is to allow for at least 2 inches of visible space between the glazed casework and the object on view: this will ensure that the preparator will have enough margin to manipulate the enclosure during the installation and deinstallation of the object, as well as creating an aesthetic presentation that does not appear to be overly claustrophobic or compressed within the case. If the object is intended to be installed in the open without an enclosure, an even greater margin is required to create the physical and visual cushion. At minimum, including 4 inches of marginal space from the object extremities to the finished edge of the pedestal or base is acceptable, but the more space that can be allotted to create that separation (without making the object on display look minimized) is ideal. In addition, if further separation between the object and viewer is warranted (consider high traffic areas, the security or condition of the objects, or the presentation of multiple elements on bases), using a low riser in tandem with pedestals and furniture can create the physical separation needed without being visually encroaching on the intended presentation.

All exhibition furniture must be set in their final position within the display environment before objects are introduced into the space. This includes any preparation that may need to happen before the exhibition: painting of bases and pedestals should be complete well before installation, allowing for ample drying and curing of painted layers. If an object will be resting directly on a base or platform, that surface (or the object) must be adequately prepped for such contact: a common installation exercise is wrapping the base in a fabric that will create both a cushion for the object to rest and a barrier from the construction of the base. The fabric wrap will also provide an aesthetic for the presentation (consideration in selecting a neutral or contrasting color or tone in addition to the surface texture should be relative to placing emphasis on the object(s) on the base).

Tip: If the object will be resting directly on a painted surface, using a sheet of polyester film that is shaped to reflect the base footprint or points of contact of the object will prevent adhesion to the painted surface, especially in situations where the installation will be long term. Create a paper template of the object footprint first; then trace the shape onto the polyester film. Place the film in the desired final location on the pedestal surface before introducing the object into the space.

Once completely prepped for the object, stabilizing the furniture in its final display location is essential and often overlooked during the installation process. Pedestals, display cases, and risers may not sit level on the ground or have proper footing to eliminate rocking or movement. Stabilizing and leveling the furniture with adjustable feet or shims and wedges must be completed and verified before the placement of objects. When leveling the furniture, test the level from multiple angles and from multiple axes. If using a pedestal or display with adjustable feet, be sure not to overextend the foot beyond the mechanism. If using a wedge or shim to level, match the color of the ground to hide the inclusion of the material if visible, and remove any excess or visible shim from view. Wooden wedges and shims can usually be purchased at a local hardware or home store, but an alternative can be mounting or mat board scrap (foam core and corrugated boards will compress over time and will not create a stable footing).

Once stabilized, and before objects have been introduced, the order of object placement is significant:

Objects should be transported into the environment, with their mounts (when appropriate), ready to be placed without the need for extraneous modifications or considerable preparation.

As previously discussed, larger objects that may require additional rigging and/or machinery and tools and would require multiple staff members involved in the handling and positioning should take precedent.

Smaller objects that require enclosed casework should be placed only when the vitrine or case is ready to be closed—do not leave objects or artifacts that require an enclosed case open in the environment.

When positioning multiple objects on a base or pedestal, consider the viewpoints according to object scale and readability and from multiple angles. Communication from the curator or collections staff may also be prudent to reinforce the intended context or narrative.

If the conditions allow, additional bases or small risers may be added to larger pedestals or casework in order to accommodate multiple objects. These added furniture elements should be prepped, installed, and stabilized during the larger furniture installation.

If brackets or attachments for didactics or labels are required, these should be installed to the furniture before the object(s) have been introduced to the space. If the installation includes an enclosed case, any printed elements that will accompany the objects within the enclosure should be ready and on hand to install at the time of object placement. Ideally the vitrine or enclosure should not be removed once an object has been installed, unless there is an urgent need for intervention.

Once objects have been positioned and secured, stanchions may be positioned for safe viewable distance. If there is additional lighting to be adjusted, stanchions may be moved or removed as needed (unless the barrier has impact on the object).

For external installations, additional factors including weather and traffic flow will need to be considered and addressed as a part of the installation planning. For the installation of public sculpture and objects, this will commonly include coordination outside the preparation staff team, with contractors employed for construction and rigging. In these cases the voice of the preparator can dictate the evaluative, communication, and common sense aspects of the process if not directly involved in the activity.

ARCHIVAL DISPLAY

The installation process is similar for archival display. The unique attributes of books, manuscripts, and other sensitive objects are carefully considered throughout the installation, as with any object-based project. Unique to many archival installations is the display furniture and methodology of installation. Enclosed display cases are the standard vehicles of display, rather than open pedestal presentation or direct wall mount. Archival cases will commonly include movable freestanding enclosed display cases as well as "built-in" casework within the environment—this may limit flexibility of the range of material that can be installed but creates a secure and stable environment for presenting special collections and manuscript materials. Often these built-in cases will negate the need for additional display furniture such as frames, pedestals, and vitrines. While the process of installing archival materials is not unlike previously described processes, there are special considerations to take into account.

Before objects are introduced into the casework or display, be sure to properly clean all glazed casework before installation. The introduction of cleaning solutions should never occur when unprotected objects are in the immediate vicinity. Especially when dealing with acrylic cases, the motion of wiping the glazed surface can cause a buildup of static electricity on the surface of the case, which can cause the attraction of loose or movable papers and media, creating potential risk. Even when using antistatic cloths and sprays, the casework should be cleaned before the objects are introduced.

When closing an archival display case (freestanding, wall, or any other) it is imperative that the process occur slowly and methodically, being extremely careful to not create a vacuum or suction of air inside the environment that may affect the loose or movable media on display (this is an important consideration when closing any enclosure with objects, especially so for archival materials).

SPOTTING YOUR INSTALLATION

Once objects have been prepped and are ready to be installed, the arrangement within the space must be confirmed before the installation of any hardware or furniture can take place. This is a process known as "spotting." The process is a collaborative one, commonly directed by a curatorial voice, though additional colleagues including exhibition designers and collections staff can also play a role in the layout. While not necessarily directing the decision-making, the preparator's control of the process is constant and relevant, from preparing the environment for the process to the directed handling and positioning of the objects as final decisions are made, and taking an active role in informing those decisions that may impact the installation. Spotting includes the order, placement, and measured spacing of objects and other elements within an environment. The process is most relevant to wall-mounted installations, where exact final measurements and distances must be determined prior to mounting; however, the inclusion of dimensional furniture and casework will inform these determinations.

The initial spotting of objects can occur well before the act of installation and object handling, through the use of physical or digital models to create preliminary layouts and positioning. Utilizing a digital model, the preparator can easily create accurate estimations of object spacing and proposed installation scenarios. Once more, modeling the installation will eliminate the need for overhandling objects within the environment—mitigating risk during the installation process. The need for physical spotting of objects for installation is almost always necessary, however, as the model (physical or digital) will rarely take the place of physically being within the environment. As accurate as a model can be, there will always be adjustments! When initiating the spotting process, the preparator should consider the following.

The environment must be prepared for the objects to be in place. For wall-mounted elements, this will mean having a stable cushion of polyethylene foam on the ground (minimum two blocks per object) to rest the objects on the intended wall. Additional padding may be needed at the top of the object or frame to protect the wall from errant marks or abrasion.

Measurements for the spotting process include the spacing in between each object or group of objects in relation to the architecture and furniture. To calculate these lateral measurements start with the overall measurement of the display area (DA). Add together the horizontal or lateral measurements of each object as well as any other furniture or didactic element (O). Subtract that compiled lateral dimension from the display wall measurement: this will be your remaining total remaining space (RS) on the wall or area. To create a consistent spacing between objects, divide that number by the total number of elements to be installed in that area plus one (remember that if there are five objects on a wall, there will be six spaces that surround the objects: one before and one after). The final equation will look like this:

$$(DA - O) / (RS + 1) = \text{space between each object.}$$

In some cases, equal spacing will not be desired: more space is given around objects of larger scale or extra space is given to areas of visual rest or "dead" or "dark" areas of the installation. These can include corners of galleries, doorways and points of egress, or any architectural impediment to the installation. In these cases, the result of the equation can act as the reference for adjustment. For example, if the final consistent spacing of four objects on a wall is 24 inches, but extra space is desired before and after the group of objects installed, the preparator can make informed adjustments without

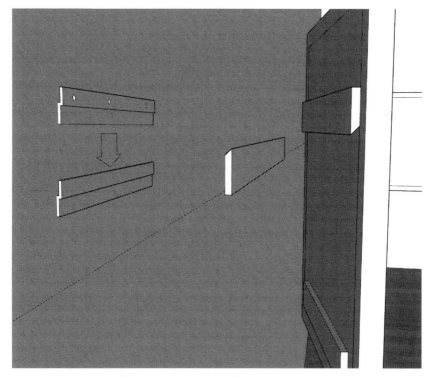

Figure 11.5. Using a Cleat Hanging System. *Source*: Image credit: Andrew Saluti.

having to physically manipulate the objects in question. If 30 inches on either end of the display area is needed, the preparator can easily calculate that the new internal spacing will be 20 inches in between each object (the overall lateral space [DA – O] minus the desired spacing [60 inches] then divided by the remaining spacing between objects [3]).

Movement of objects and elements should be done carefully, and always maintain proper handling techniques with adequate assistance—never push or slide objects to reposition. Place padding or blocks at the new location and carefully lift and place objects as needed.

The spotting process can also include the creation of grouped objects and artifacts: where multiple elements are combined into a singular entity in terms of spacing. This is a valuable visual installation resource to emphasize a context between multiple elements on display. Grouping objects in a wall hanging can also be a way to maximize the viewable area when numerous objects are meant to be installed. When creating these nested installation situations, it is important to reference not only the lateral dimensions in your assessment but also the minimized margins and spaces between the objects themselves. For example, if grouping two framed objects together side by side, one should include the desired amount of minimal space between the frames (this is an arbitrary measurement that can be determined by the overall scale of the objects. For example, a 2-inch margin would be an appropriate space between smaller frames or objects).

The key to creating the visual rhythm in these determinations is consistency: the spacing between objects within the same environment should relate to the entire experience; variation will create a distinct break in this rhythm and should be used with purpose. The lack of consistency will affect the continuity and overall experience of the intended engagement with the objects on view.

THE HANGING EQUATION

While the details, methods, and needs of wall installations can vary greatly, the equation to mount objects and groups of objects with a sense of inclusivity and interconnectedness within the display environment is constant. There is a standard mathematical equation that acts as a universal tool for the mounting and hanging of any object, any group of objects, and any curated arrangement of objects meant to be seen in unison or as independent sequential elements. This equation accounts for all the variables that the object or environment may introduce, assembling the data to offer a consistent and calculable reference that will guide the wall-hung installation. By inputting specific collected measurements, this equation can cover the totality of objects, furniture, or anything that needs to be installed on a wall:

$$H/2 - A = B + E$$

H: Overall height of the object or group. This should include the most extreme vertical measurements of the object or the total height of multiple objects including any vertical margin or spacing.

A: The distance from the top of the object/group of objects to the hanging mechanism. Regardless of what kind of hanging mechanism is being used (wire, D-ring, or cleat), this measurement should be assessed from the highest vertical point to the precise position where the object hardware meets the corresponding wall hardware or bracket.

B: The total distance from the midpoint of the overall height to the hanging mechanism. This calculation (dividing the overall height by two, subtracting the total distance of the hanging mechanism to the top of the frame) informs the measurement needed to add to the established horizontal consistent in the environment.

E: The established eye level for the environment. Also called a horizon line, this is a perceived consistent baseline measured from the ground up that all the installed objects relate to throughout

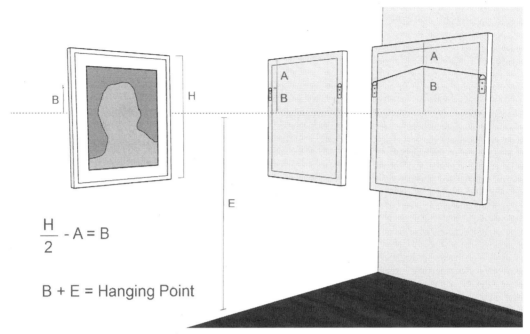

$$\frac{H}{2} - A = B$$

$$B + E = \text{Hanging Point}$$

Figure 11.6. Illustration of the Hanging Equation. *Source:* Image credit: Andrew Saluti.

the environment. The measurement (height) can be variable and is dependent on aesthetic, physical, and inherent or architectural factors within the environment or the objects installed.

The process of implementing the hanging equation is straightforward once the essential mechanisms and elements have been determined:

Step 1: Measure the overall height of the object(s) and divide by two to find the midpoint. This is where the established eye level will intersect the object once installed.

Step 2: Measure the distance from the hanging mechanism to the top of the object. Find the exact point in which the hanging mechanism will meet the corresponding hardware on the wall and use that point as the reference for this measurement. If the hanging mechanism is part of a separate mount and not on the physical object, be sure to use the compiled overall measurement (object and mount) when making this calculation. If the hanging mechanism is adjustable, such as a hanging wire behind a frame, apply pressure to the mechanism as if it was carrying the weight of the object and take the measurement from that applied position.

Step 3: Find the distance from the hanging mechanism to the center line. This is a simple subtraction of the measurement from step 1 minus the measurement from step 2. The result is the measurement that the wall-mounted hardware needs to be from the desired eye level.

Step 4: Add the remainder to the eye level for the mounting hardware height. This is the distance you will use from the ground to where the hardware must be placed on the wall to capture the object. Alternatively, if using a laser level during installation, the distance from step 3 can simply be measured from the laser line.

Step 5: Mark the height of the hanging mechanism. Be sure to reference exactly how the mechanism will be secured to the surface. In the case of most hanging scenarios, this is best done by using the point of connection as the consistent reference mark, rather than the variables of the actual hardware or system, that is, where the object mechanism will meet the wall mechanism, as is the bottom hook of a basic hanger rather than where the nail will need to be driven. This will eliminate the need for additional measurements depending on what system is in place. This mark can be placed at the center of the intended placement but is merely a height reference for the lateral spacing of the hardware.

Step 6: Measure the lateral distances between the hanging mechanisms and the horizontal edge of the object. This will determine the exact placement of where the hanging mechanism must be located on the surface for accurate placement. Using a level with a marked ruler edge will facilitate this process, allowing the preparator to reference the lateral spacing along a level line. For example, if a frame has a D-ring exactly 2 inches from the edge and the corresponding D-ring on the opposite side of the frame is 20 inches away, the marked level can be used to reference this spacing along the desired line.

Step 7: Adding hardware. Once the marks have been made, hardware can be mounted into the surface. Note: never install hardware while standing over an object. Always reposition the object away from the working area before introducing tools or action. Depending on the condition of the corresponding objects in the installation area as well as the intended mounting surface, the measurement and marking of all hardware on that wall may need to be calculated and installed with all objects removed, rather than installing objects sequentially. The vibration caused by the installation of hardware might have adverse effects on surrounding objects already installed. This will slow the installation process but will be a necessary precaution to minimize potential risk.

Step 8: Hanging object(s). With assistance from handling staff, raise the object to meet the mounting hardware. If there are multiple points of contact, articulate which handler should rest their side first and follow with an audible verification of the second mount. Slowly release the object and allow to rest in place. Double-check the level and position before moving on to the next installation. Note: if the evaluation and condition of the object or frame prevents direct contact with a level or measuring device, carefully position the level to correspond with an edge without resting the level on the surface. Alternatively, a laser line can be used to verify the level of the object without any additional contact.

Variations on Wall Hanging

Using the hanging equation provides a universal foundation for the installation of any object within a display space, creating a unified experience and connection between multiple objects. Variations on the equation are common and are easily employed when breaking down the components of the installation into elements that can be input into the equation in order to configure the desired outcome.

Variation: Salon Hanging

The hanging equation works easily with singular or few grouped objects together, but in some cases numerous objects of varying dimension are presented together, called a *salon-style* installation or *salon hanging*. This is in reference to the seventeenth-century practice of the French Royal Academy to exhibit paintings tightly positioned on a wall from floor to ceiling. In contemporary settings, the salon-style hanging is often associated with a grid-like arrangement of objects and can be an organic or geometric arrangement. The key to using the hanging equation in these cases is to consider the entirety of the arrangement as a singular object: finding the overall height of the group to determine the central placement in relation to a desired eye level. There are additional steps that will be added to the process, for example, once the overall height and final vertical apex of the grouping on the wall is determined, the installation must move sequentially down each object, finding the distance from the top measurement down to each corresponding hanging mechanism rather than measuring up from the eye level. This should be visually mapped out in advance, as with the spotting process, so the installation of hardware can commence once the overall height has been determined (the remaining measurements are fixed according to the object hanging mechanisms and the desired spacing

Figure 11.7.   Salon-style Hanging Using a Common Horizon as Reference.
Source: Image credit: Andrew Saluti.

in between each object). These installations can be complex, especially when the objects involved are inconsistent in their size and shape. The hanging equation, however, will be an important step in determining the overall position on the intended surface. Contemporary versions of the salon-style hang sometimes consider the entirety of the display surface as a singular installation, with variable objects placed throughout the space. Here, again, is where the overall determinations in relation to an eye level can be fused with a map or layout of the intended placement of objects. While these types of installations may appear to be independent of the visual rhythm, if they are to be seen in a similar or adacent environmental context, the equation should be considered.

Variation: Using a Special Reference Rather than Horizon

There are circumstances when the hanging equation should not be employed or strictly adhered. These can stem from a variety of situations but will often include the following.

Architectural references: Depending on the construction or physical details of the display space, there may be need to abandon the use of the eye level equation for other factors within the viewable area, such as wall trim and rails, fixtures, furniture, or other industrial and construction impediments. In these cases, the desired hanging should be focused on the object need and safety.

Object physicality: There are commonly situations where the scale or physicality of an object forces a change to the consistency of the objects surrounding it. This can also occur when artifacts are displayed alongside artwork or standing pedestaled objects are placed in concert with wall-mounted displays. In these cases, a break from the consistent hanging equation can reinforce the context of the object and become a powerful narrative tool while presenting the object at a desired interpretive position.

Artist's or maker's intent: If the objects are being installed by, or have the input from, the maker of the work, that intent should be considered equal to the care and safety of the object itself.

To apply these points, let's take, for example, the Italian tondo painting on panel illustrated in figure 11.8.[5] This oil on panel, thought to be from the early sixteenth century attributed to the School

Figure 11.8. Tondo Painting Being Installed. *Source*: Image credit: Syracuse University Art Museum.

of Raphael, measures 67 inches in diameter. The frame that surrounds and supports the painting is considerable, measuring a width of 12 inches, weighing well over 220 pounds, and is an early example of gilt compo (or plaster) with a hardwood underlayment. On inspection, the frame had preexisting holes for basic eye screw hardware that most likely held a heavy cross wire for single point of suspension on a surface. With no visible signs of rot or weakness the material is in fairly good condition that will accommodate the addition of contemporary hardware and won't likely cause undue stress or place the object it carries in any hazard. Before a decision can be made about what mechanism will be used to safely fix the object to the wall, the preparator must consider the ancillary wall structure. In this case, the team knows precisely how the gallery walls are constructed: a steel frame construction reinforced with a layer of 1/2-inch plywood plate beneath the final visible layer of 5/8 drywall. This combination of plywood sheet and plaster drywall is ideal to carry a heavy load without additional anchor hardware or the need to find and utilize the structural studs. With this in mind, the preparation team decides that a mating bar cleat system is an ideal hanging mechanism: allowing the weight of the object to be distributed over the long expanse of the hanging bar fastened to the wall. In addition, a second mating bar has been added, not only to provide additional and auxiliary points of support but also to prevent the object from pulling forward from the wall, a symptom of two factors—the position of the primary hanging cleat and the overall weight of the object. The upper hanging mechanism, carrying the majority of the load, must be placed relatively high in the overall dimension of the object and frame, so as to keep the newly introduced hardware added to the support frame only, not invasive to the painting's support cradle. This high hanging point relative to the overall constitution of the object and the close-fitting will many times result in the object pulling away from the wall surface, rather than resting against it. The second concern is the extreme weight of the object and frame concentrated on a section of the support wall; even though the gallery walls have been reinforced to provide overall rigid support for traditional hanging situations, this particular space does not have a hard ceiling that adds structural security to the perimeter walls, rather, a drop ceiling to conceal (but retain access to) mechanical and electrical systems. A potential risk of structural sag or lean stemming from the object's pull adds risk not only to the hanging painting but also to the environment, objects, and patrons.[6] While this second hanging mechanism adds security and stability, it also creates a far more complex installation process—the more points of connection that are incorporated, the greater the possibility of misalignment or disparity in the way the object and the hanging devices align. This illustrates why careful calculation and due diligence in reviewing all measurements and dimensions before the object is manipulated is not only the preparator's best practice but a vital aspect to the process. One final detail concerns handling: how the object will be elevated and positioned onto the hanging devices mounted to the wall. While the evaluation of the support frame suggests that the frame is stable enough to handle the tactile pressures of manipulating the object into position, the fact that this object is circular adds a new layer of challenge: Without any clear points of handling, how will the preparation team manage to safely elevate this object into position? In this scenario, because of the relatively confined space of the gallery, the prospect of bringing in rigging or mechanical equipment to assist is not possible. Therefore, the preparation team decides to use the stability and structure of the frame to their advantage, adding a set of nylon strap handles to the lower portion of the tondo, a simple pair of devices that can be hidden behind the installed hanging frame but will also be accessible in the case that the object needs immediate handling. With the hanging and handling mechanisms fixed to the support frame, the team positions the object lying prostrate on a padded cart so the object can be safely moved into position when the corresponding hanging hardware is installed.

Once these practical details have been addressed, the conceptual principles of the installation can be weighed. The team, in consultation with the director, curator, and registrar, discusses the visual impact of the object in the space, its inherent curatorial value and narrative, and the work in context to other juxtaposed objects as well as the physical environment overall. The architectural limitations of the space are the first to refine the install: with an overall object height (or, in this case, diameter) of 67 inches and a gallery ceiling height of 108 inches, using the intimate 58-inch eyeline consistent with the smaller frames and objects also planned for the gallery would not be appropriate or physically possible, bringing the center of the tondo awkwardly high on the wall. This scenario calls for an independent measurement, based on the scale of the specific work, separate from its neighbors. Placing the object centered on the wall (hung at the eyeline of 54 inches, using the standard equation) will present the work at a comfortable and engaging level for the viewer and will in turn make the object a focal point in the space. This resolution coincides with the curatorial narrative, as the object has been selected to be a visual and historical anchor in the chosen arrangement of objects. From the design/ visitor experience perspective, the installation of this monumental object has the potential to be a landmark that guides visitors into the space as they transition from surrounding galleries. To enhance this, the lateral position of the frame becomes an essential determination, one that will impact not only how the object is viewed transitionally into and within the defined environment but also the position and installation of the surrounding objects—factors that are also regulated by the fixed dimension of the gallery. The visual command of this object will augment the spacing rhythm that is otherwise consistent between other objects planned for inclusion in the space and increasing the spread from 24 inches between the surrounding frames to 30 will amply provide the needed room for the tondo. Expanding visual rest can assist in creating balance between objects of variable scale, while also placing emphasis on the selected object. Now armed with this collaborative input and direction, the preparation team can plan accordingly for the installation of the corresponding wall hanging brackets to mount the frame, as well as the placement of hanging hardware for the corresponding objects that will complete the installation of that environment.

Finally, the transition of the object, organized and controlled by the preparator, will not be able to be completed by a single staff member. Using the guiding principles of proper handling, the preparation team fuses aspects of object evaluation, communication, and common sense to prepare to manipulate the painting. The object will need to pivot 90° from its resting, horizontal position to a vertical, elevated state. The padded cart that is carrying the object in place will need to be removed as the object is lifted. The combined weight of the frame and painting demands the assistance of multiple staff to safely manipulate the object and will require coordination and in a confined and focused situation. It is determined that four installers will be needed to complete the task: two preparators will manage the vertical lift of the object using the added nylon strapping attached to the lower portion of the frame, while two additional team members will stabilize and guide the object into the planned position on the wall and onto the corresponding hanging cleats. A fifth assistant, not directly engaged with handling the object, is on hand to swiftly move the padded cart out of the way and to provide any sudden or unexpected aid while the object is in transition. The outcome of this orchestration is the safe and successful installation of a unique and challenging object.

NOTES

1. Amanda D. Phelka and Brent L Finley, "Potential Health Hazards Associated with Exposures to Asbestos-Containing Drywall Accessory Products: A State-of-the-Science Assessment." *Critical Reviews in Toxicology*, vol. 42, 1 (2012): 1–27.
2. Janice Majewski, "Smithsonian Guidelines for Accessible Exhibition Design," Smithsonian Institution Accessibility Program (Washington, DC: Smithsonian Institution, 2010).
3. A buggle is the tapered, conical shape of the screw head that allows it to self-sink into material. This can also be an effective hanging element when appropriate. The heavy threads of the screw enable a better and more secure capture of drywall and plaster substrate. The size of the shaft is indicated by the #4, #6, #8, and #10 designations. The higher the number, the thicker the shaft and the more weight it can carry before failure.
4. Drywall was invented in 1916 but did not catch on widely as a residential building material until the baby boom of the postwar. Plaster and lathe wall construction was still a popular method of finishing but became a higher-end method of interior construction. The difference between the two can be easily detected in the finish of the surface: plaster walls will have a much smoother, harder, ceramic like finish, while drywall will generally be less dense and rigid to the touch.
5. School of Raphael, untitled (Madonna and Child with the Young St. John), *c.* 1500. Oil on panel. Gift of Mr. Donald Schupak '64, L'66. Syracuse University Art Museum, 2014.0460.
6. A good analogy for this is to consider a basic cardboard box: if one puts pressure on a sidewall of the box without cover, the action causes the structure to flex. If that same pressure is applied to a box that has an enclosed and fixed top, there is structural resistance that prevents the structure from collapsing.

REFERENCES

Coleman, Brian D., MD. "Picture Rails for Period Houses." *Old House Journal*, 2012. Updated June 21, 2021. https://www.oldhouseonline.com/interiors-and-decor/how-to-hang-pictures-in-an-old-house/.

"Everything You Need to Know about Hanging Art." Christie's.com, July 22, 2019. Accessed May 2020. https://www.christies.com/features/How-to-hang-artworks-8182-1.aspx.

"Exhibit and Display." Gaylord Archival. Accessed March 2020. https://www.gaylord.com/c/Exhibit-and-Display.

Jacobs, Neva F. B., Kevin M. Towle, Brent L. Finley, and Shannon H. Gaffney. "An Updated Evaluation of Potential Health Hazards Associated with Exposures to Asbestos Containing Drywall Accessory Products." *Critical Reviews in Toxicology* 49, no. 5 (2019): 430–444. DOI: 10.1080/10408444.2019.1639612.

Mangekin, Steve. "How Much Weight Can Drywall Hold?" Alpha Inspections website, published October 13, 2020. Accessed December 28, 2020. https://alphabuildinginspections.com/how-much-weight-can-drywall-hold/.

Mikesell, Michal. "How the DAM Uses Rare-Earth Magnets with Art Installations." Denver Art Museum, June 1, 2012. Accessed May 2021. https://www.denverartmuseum.org/en/blog/how-dam-uses-rare-earth-magnets-art-installations.

"Picture Frame Hardware." United Manufacturers Supplies, 2021. Accessed December 2020. https://www.unitedmfrs.com/picture_frame_hardware_s/41.htm.

Rae, Haniya. "An Exciting History of Drywall." *The Atlantic*, July 29, 2016. Accessed December 28, 2020. https://www.theatlantic.com/technology/archive/2016/07/an-exciting-history-of-drywall/493502/.

Rowell, Christopher. "Display of Art." *Grove Art Online.* 2003; Accessed 30 December 2020. https://www-oxfordartonline-com.libezproxy2.syr.edu/groveart/view/10.1093/gao/9781884446054.001.0001/oao-9781884446054-e-7000022896.

Russell, Francis. "The Hanging and Display of Pictures, 1700–1850." *Studies in the History of Art* 25 (1989): 133–329. Accessed December 2020. http://www.jstor.org/stable/42620690.

Sawinski, Catherine. "Mr. Layton's Gallery—The Salon-Style Hang." Milwaukee Art Museum blog, April 12, 2013. https://blog.mam.org/2013/04/12/mr-laytons-gallery-the-salon-style-hang/. Accessed February 2021.

"SketchUp Free." SketchUp.com. Accessed March 2020. https://www.sketchup.com/plans-and-pricing/sketchup-free.

12

Preparation in Action

EXTERIOR SCULPTURE AT THE STONE QUARRY HILL ART PARK

Emily Zaengle, Executive Director, Stone Quarry Hill Art Park

In 2016, and every year after, Martin Hogue transforms Stone Quarry Hill Art Park into a campground. Hogue, associate professor in the Department of Landscape Architecture at Cornell University, chose four areas at Stone Quarry for his project: *Camping at the Art Park*. Every weekend in June, with just the addition of a picnic table, camping gear, and the people (the campers), these areas of existing sculpture, trees, and meadow become campsites. Participants haul in their tents and sleeping gear, while Stone Quarry staff provide a communal campfire, restroom facilities, and water. During the day, the campsites are a part of the Art Park landscape and daily visitors to the Art Park encounter these sites—the tents, picnic tables, and camping gear as art objects.

Figure 12.1. Camping at the Art Park, 2017. *Source*: Image credit: Stone Quarry Hill Art Park.

Hogue's *Camping at the Art Park* demonstrates that moment when landscape becomes an art site—a moment catalyzed by the installation process. Stone Quarry's artistic focus favors work like Hogue's—ephemeral, experimental, and experiential. However, the Stone Quarry staff also partner with artists to install art objects that are more fixed in the landscape such as metal, wood, and ceramic sculptures. In both instances, the ephemeral and the fixed, the preparator shepherds the artist, object(s), and land through the process of transforming landscape to art site.

At Stone Quarry one of the most interesting features of the landscape, and an often-challenging component of creating an art site, is the "depth to bedrock" measurement. This measurement is the amount of soil or earth that exists between the surface of the ground and the solid rock below. As the name "Stone Quarry" implies, rock is abundant and the depth to bedrock measurement is very low at several prominent locations in the park. This measurement is important when installing artwork because many outdoor pieces require an anchor system—often a pole or post in the ground. When there is a shallow depth to bedrock, it can be almost impossible to anchor a piece without drilling through bedrock (a costly process that requires special equipment). At the very top of Stone Quarry Hill there can be as little as 3-6 inches of soil sitting on top of a solid sheet of rock.

When installing the sculpture *Bucking, Rearing, Shying* by artist Esther Benedict, the depth to bedrock was an important consideration for deciding where to locate the sculpture's three metal horses. Stone Quarry selected a site with a high depth to bedrock and installed the pieces with bolts and columns of concrete. Five years later the installation had failed. The sculpture was leaning, and the legs of the horses were not bucking or rearing as designed but beginning to rest on the ground. This failure was a surprise to Stone Quarry staff. The initial installation should have worked. There was another factor at play. While Stone Quarry staff considered many characteristics of the site, including depth to bedrock, they had not accounted for the way visitors would engage with the sculpture. Visitors were

Figure 12.2. Esther Benedict, *Bucking, Rearing, Shying*, 2016. *Source*: Image credit: photo by Bob Gates, courtesy of Stone Quarry Hill Art Park.

so enamored with the sculpture that they were touching, pulling, and in some instances trying to sit on the horses. What seems apparent and unspoken rules to those trained to work with and around art objects is not as apparent to visitors encountering an art site for the first time. It is the responsibility of the preparator to anticipate and consider these interactions as a part of the art site.

Mowing patterns can help visitors read the boundaries of an art site; creating an area of gravel, concrete, or woodchips can also help expand the art site and keep visitors at a distance. For *Bucking, Rearing, Shying*, visitor safety and the integrity of the piece dictated a complete reinstallation. While it is nearly impossible to control visitor engagements with art sites in an environment as open as Stone Quarry, it was possible to improve the integrity of the sculpture to withstand the conditions. Rather than concrete piers, the three horses were anchored to a square "sandwich" of concrete and steel. Rebar was threaded from the sculpture to the bottom of the steel plate. The steel plate was buried 3 feet in the ground and layered with concrete and topped off with another steel plate. The project was completed in collaboration with a local welder and the donor that originally gifted the sculpture to Stone Quarry.

With the outdoors as the art gallery, the preparator is most helpful to the artist and art object when they deeply understand the various characteristics of a site and how these features will interact. Knowledge of the landscape is part of the creation and installation of outdoor artwork. A keen understanding of the geology of the site as well as wind patterns, hydrology, and ecology is essential, but it is also important to understand visitor behavior and tendencies. Spending time on site is an important part of building this knowledge of landscape and its visitors.

Artist and Stone Quarry Art Park founder Dorothy Riester spent decades shaping the hilly landscape of Stone Quarry, first for her private residence and then opening it to the public for other artists and visitors. Dorothy's familiarity with the characteristics of the landscape and its role in the art experience is evident in the series of shallow pools she created by scraping earth from the bedrock. The pools vary from a 3 to 12 inches deep and the bottoms are solid bedrock. When it rains, the pools fill by rainwater. During dry seasons, the pools dry up, revealing the fossilized surface of the bedrock below. The pools each have a unique ecology that support an abundance of frogs and plant life. Through artist and visitor engagement these pools become art sites.

At Stone Quarry these three things—artist, landscape, and visitor—are equal parts of the producer of an art site. The role of the preparator is to facilitate these interactions, to both anticipate and respond as art, people, and place interact over time and space.

13

Practical Basics for Lighting, Audio, and Video

Beyond the physical object–related methodologies and practice that will be a standard part of any preparator's routine, indirect or environmental practice, such as gallery and exhibition lighting, audio installation, and digital video components, will also be important and typical responsibilities depending on the size and scope of the institution. Much like the correlating relationship between preparator and the conservator, there are specialists, designers, and engineers in the museum lighting and technology field that have advanced expertise in preservation and presentation lighting—much more so than the preparator is expected to bring to the role. More common, however, are situations where the basic knowledge and principles of lighting and digital installation are necessary and are assigned or applicable in tandem with the installation of objects or exhibitions and will fall to the preparation staff to accomplish.

Drawing comparisons between the conservator's role and the preparator's role in their responsibilities and actions when working with a collection object is apropos to defining the relationship between the lighting designer/engineer and the preparator: the specialized experience, training, and knowledge of new techniques and technologies that the lighting specialist brings will most times far outweigh the preparator's own practice but would also not necessarily need to be invoked for the average scenario or routine assignment, such as a basic task of adjusting the lighting fixtures in a newly installed exhibit. And, continuing with the comparison of the conservator to that of the preparation staff, the lighting specialist (if not on staff) is often contracted or consulted when the scenario goes beyond the basic adjustment of lighting levels or fixture position. For larger capital projects and long-term display, it is far more appropriate to consign the service of a lighting specialist when designing a new lighting system and updating lighting controls, anything that may require expert intervention and external contract work. In addition, when creating display for objects with unique needs or highly sensitive condition needs, the lighting specialist should always be engaged. From the preparator's perspective, consider the relationship between passive and active conservation. A passive lighting situation may be identified as the shift of a gallery's existing fixture or the installation of a media player for digital video, reacting to, modifying, or reusing existing hardware and equipment and adapting to the current need or situation. It is in these situations that the expectation will be that the preparator will have tacit knowledge of what to do and how to do it. These fundamental elements of lighting, audio visual, and digital installations will cover a majority of these situations and will also influence and inform the collaborative process between the preparator and the specialists, designers, makers, and engineers that may be engaged when more robust and unique circumstances arise.

BASICS OF LIGHTING

For the preparator, the lighting of objects is an extension of the passive conservation and preservation methods employed throughout all the components of the practice and, like many of the preparator's activities and responsibilities, will include a multifaceted framework of requisites and outcomes that can have enormous impact for the object and the public, functionally in terms of object safety and preservation, and aesthetically and interpretively enhancing and affecting the way the viewer engages with the object or display. Controlled lighting within the gallery or presentation space will play a significant role in the effectiveness of the installation not only in regard to the safety and stability of the object but also in terms of public access and curatorial narrative. Calculated variations in lighting can heighten the experience of engaging with the object—placing more or less emphasis on any one part of a display—and can lead the viewer through a designed or predetermined path and can reinforce the wayfinding, or intended pathway, of object experiences. Proper lighting can also be a valuable tool in visitor safety and traffic flow, clearly illuminating environmental flow and egress. Parallel to the risks associated with mishandling, inadequate housings, or unsuitable installation techniques, improper or uncontrolled lighting scenarios, such has unfiltered natural light, nonspecific or unadjusted illumination within gallery and storage spaces, or overexposure, will have a detrimental effect on objects and artifacts. *Remember: the damage and degradation caused by light is irreversible.*

All objects are impacted by light, from woven fiber artifacts to bound volumes to cast bronze sculpture—though it does not impact all objects equally. Especially light-sensitive objects include textiles and dyed fabrics, natural materials such as leather and organic artifacts, works on paper, and photographs, though attention to lighting conditions for any kind of object is best practice. Like other impactful environmental factors such as temperature or humidity, light is an element that can be measured, which leads to the opportunity for control. Light units are called lumens, and light intensity is measured in *foot candles* (ftcd) (lumens per square foot) or *lux* (lumens square meter).

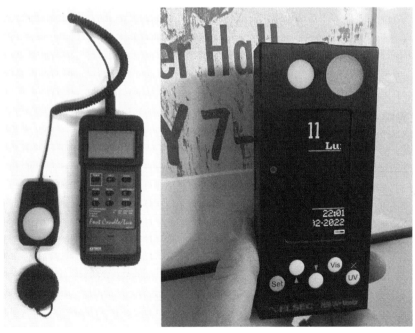

Figure 13.1.   Examples of handheld light meters. *Source:* Image credit: Andrew Saluti.

In order to document the intensity of visible light in relation to the object, a *handheld electronic light meter* will give the most accurate measurement. These devices are far more accurate than meters built into cameras or smartphone apps and will give an immediate reading compared to light-sensitive strips such as blue scales, or blue wool cards, that show the impact of light over time (though these are effective for monitoring the ongoing impact to objects). In addition to handheld light meters, there are also data logging light detectors and probes that can collect information for a specific location or display and transmit data in real time, similar to the environmental monitors that collect relative temperature and humidity. In addition to the documentation and impact of visible light radiation, the preparator must also recognize the corresponding radiation that bookends the visible light spectrum: ultraviolet (UV) and infrared (IR) radiation. Some light meters can detect and measure UV and IR levels, but this is a separate measurement from the visible light detection. Neither UV nor IR are visible, but both are damaging—IR radiation will increase the temperature of a surface, while UV will weaken and yellow materials. UV radiation carries the most amount of energy and is thus the most destructive for objects and artifacts. Not all light meters will measure the amount of UV (in microwatts per lumen) emanating from the light source, but this information is commonly included on the lamp packaging or can be found on the manufacturer's website. Mitigating the exposure to visible light and UV is crucial to the preparator's passive conservation responsibilities.

SOURCES OF LIGHT

In order to understand how to control light, it's important to first define the various sources of light that one may be dealing with. The preparator will need to have a solid comprehension of what kind of lighting system is in place, what the specific type(s) of illumination are being used, and how the lighting can be adjusted, controlled, and maintained. Some scenarios will have the contemporary systems with the latest advances in illumination ideal for preservation standards. More often, the lighting system in place will require constant attention and adjustment in accordance with changes in objects and installations. There are two main sources of visible light: natural light and electric light. Regulating the amount of light from any source is important, and there is no one type of illumination that will prevent degradation or physical change. There are, however, differences in methodology and technology to control the intensity and impact of light on objects, and it is important for the preparation staff to be informed as to what type of lighting system is present and what might be available to be changed, altered, or updated. Some basic terminology for describing and identifying the tools and methodolgies of controlled illumination follows.

Lamp: The term used to describe the actual source of illumination. Lamps can come in a variety of sizes, outputs, and specifications depending on the specific lighting need. Lamps are often incorrectly identified as "bulbs." Lamp styles will vary depending on the shape and color temperature of the light needed, the intensity of the light emitted, and the connection to the fixture.

Fixture: The vehicle that contains the lamp to deliver illumination. Fixtures can be stationary or movable, depending on the system in place. In storage settings, fixtures are generally stationary, while in exhibition or display settings, fixtures are often movable and adjustable. Second to object evaluation and need, the specific type of fixture being used will dictate many lighting decisions, including lamp style and any added adjustment accessory.

Luminaire: A source of illumination, the term used to describe the fixture with a lamp in place creating a source of light. The terms "lamp," "fixture," and "luminaire" are often used interchangeably; however, when embarking on lighting assignments, each term will describe different components of the project.

Natural light: Sunlight. Natural light contains high levels of UV radiation, is difficult to control, and will cause surfaces and media to fade. The use of natural light in collection and presentation spaces should be carefully considered and will necessitate input from collections professionals, conservators, and lighting designers to create a safe and effective illumination scenario for the objects, displays, and public access.

Incandescent lighting: A traditional source of exhibition lighting, incandescent sources generate light by running an electric current through a filament; a small amount of that energy creates visible light, while the majority is released as heat. Tungsten-halogen lamps are a version of incandescent filament inside a bulb filled with halogen gas—allowing the filament to burn brighter and longer. This style of lamp is commonly used in exhibition lighting for the quality of the color and their longevity but also give off a large amount of heat. Standard examples of these exhibition tungsten-halogen lamps include the PAR (Parabolic Aluminized Reflector) and MR (Multifaceted Reflector) styles.

Florescent lighting: More commonly used in general or commercial lighting scenarios (rather than controlled applications such as galleries or display areas), these lamps are constructed of frosted tubes filled with mercury vapor. Florescent lamps are inexpensive and long-lasting but also emit a high amount of UV radiation and can be challenging to modify or adjust for specific object needs.

LED: Light emitting diode lamps are fast becoming the ideal choice for controlled lighting situations. LED light is created through the use of semiconductors that can emit light of specific color temperatures. LED lighting is significantly more efficient than incandescent and fluorescent lamps and do not emit UV or IR radiation. They use less energy and have a longer life span than most lamps currently used in exhibition or collection settings. Museums are quickly adopting LED illumination not only for the benefits to preservation of objects but also for the environmental advantages. LED lamps come in a variety of styles retrofitted to accommodate most fixtures. In addition, new LED lamps and fixtures can be fitted to allow unique settings for color and intensity of the LED lamp on each individual unit—enhancing the ability to control lighting levels per object or setting.

Ambient lighting: Illumination within an environment that has no specific direction or focus, the general light within a space. Ambient lighting can be a byproduct of architectural elements (windows, doors, and passageways) or can be the result of light spillage from adjacent installations. Recognizing and measuring the presence (or lack thereof) of ambient light is important when attempting to adjust light levels within a controlled space.

Another element that is part of any lighting scenario is the light's color temperature. This is a visible indication of the quality light, from cool to warm, measured in units of degrees Kelvin (K). Cooler light will have a reading of 3,500–5,000 K, while warm light measures lower (2,800 K). In preservation low light scenarios, a warm light is generally preferred to the starkness of cooler temperatures—the color temperature is usually indicated on the packaging of the lamp and can also be found on distributor's websites.

It is customary for the preparation team to handle multiple lighting scenarios and systems within the same institution or setting. Short-term and rotating exhibition spaces will usually have an adjustable track lighting system in place, one that allows for malleable lighting installations to accommodate the widest possible illumination needs. Long-term and permanent display environments may employ a track system but can also incorporate fixed elements that are not intended to be adjusted on a frequent basis. Storage, office, and prepatory spaces often use general lighting to create a well-lit setting for broad use. Spaces that have been repurposed for collection or exhibition usage may not have the ideal illumination in place for the newly intended function, for example, the use of fixed fluorescent lighting for exhibition lighting or track light fixtures within preparation areas. Each of these lighting scenarios, when objects and artifacts are introduced, requires conservation considerations and attention.

LIGHTING STANDARDS AND EVALUATION

With the basic elements of light sources and systems identified, the preparator must make informed decisions as to which type of illumination is ideal for the object and the environment that the object resides. This, like all preparation tasks, will start with the evaluative process—not only for the object but also for the specific situation: How sensitive to light is the object? Will the object be on view to the public or in storage? In an exhibition setting, what types of illumination controls are in place? The preparator should be knowledgeable of the recommended light levels for object preservation and may consider consultation from conservators, specialists, or other resources for object and media specification. The following are general parameters for illumination and UV exposure.

Table 13.1. Parameters for illumination and UV exposure for the preservation of objects, by media type.

Extremely Sensitive Objects	works on paper, including watercolor paintings, manuscripts, prints and drawings, photographs, dyes, and textiles	5 ftcd/50 lux
Moderately Sensitive Objects	oil and tempera paintings, undyed leather, lacquer, wood, horn, bone, ivory, and stone	10-15 ftcd/ 110-160 lux
Less Sensitive Objects	ceramics, glass, and metals	20-25 ftcd/ 215-270 lux

UV must be filtered and should ideally emit no more than between 10 and 75 microwatts per lumen.

Handheld light meters are used for these "spot" or "incident" light readings. These devices are equipped with a photosensitive sensor dome or bulb that is housed either on the device or as a satellite attachment connected by cable. To capture an accurate measurement of how the light is impacting the object:

- Do not rest the device or the extension directly on the surface of the object; hold the meter in front of the area being measured.
- Make sure the sensor bulb is parallel to the surface that is being measured rather than aiming at the source of illumination.
- Take multiple readings around the surface in order to accurately capture the intensity of the light. Depending on the style of lamp, the adjustments made, or the size of the surface being measured, the light level may vary across the span of the object. Isolating the highest point of intensity should be used as the reference used in making additional adjustments.
- Considering the length of time the object or artifact is on view, it may be pertinent to implement routine light readings throughout the length of the installation to monitor any changes that may instigate adjustments or action.

The effect of light is cumulative: in addition to closely monitoring the intensity of the illumination, the amount of time the object will be exposed to a light source must also be documented and considered. Even at the recommended "safe" levels of intensity, light will cause more damage depending on the length of time the object is exposed. Calculating light hours provides valuable information for the exhibition planning process, guiding installation and lighting strategy, as well as informing the curatorial process in evaluating if the object is in the condition to be shown: many institutions will require the proposed light hours (or light exposure) for an object loan request. The equation is simple:

Light level (ftcd or lux) × Time (hours) = Exposure (ftcd/lux hours)

The "time" part of this equation represents the total hours of illumination—meaning the period when the object is actively being lit within the environment not the total time installed (unless illumination cannot be controlled, via natural or ambient light). This can be part of the preparator's lighting plan. If an exhibition is open to the public from 10:00 a.m. to 5:00 p.m. (period of active illumination), Tuesday through Saturday, for 6 weeks, estimating the amount of exposure for a sensitive work on paper might look like this:

$$5 \text{ ftcd} \times 210 \text{ hours (7 hours/day} \times 5 \text{ days/week} \times 6 \text{ weeks}) = 1050 \text{ ftcd hours}$$

Or, another way to think about how much light the object will be exposed to:

$$1050 \text{ ftcd} \times 1 \text{ hour} = 1050 \text{ ftcd hours}$$

Measuring the level of intensity is a primary consideration when adjusting or designing lighting scenarios but only represents half the equation. Consideration for the time exposed will also inform what initial steps and ongoing procedures the preparator might take to control the light within the environment. Total exposure limits will vary per object and will consider object condition and accrued exposure time. A conservator or collections specialist will determine the object's installation eligibility and restrictions, as well as the required time of rest.

CONTROLLING AND ADJUSTING LIGHT

Combining the information about the lighting system with the directives based on object needs will now allow the preparation team to take action in controlling the lighting within the environment. There are a myriad of ways a collections professional can control the intensity, shape, and extent of the light projected on objects and an equally large array of materials and accessories to facilitate the desired outcome. These methods will coincide with a hierarchal process that begins with the power source, then extends to the type of fixture employed, to the added accessories that alter the light emanating from the chosen fixture, and finally to the position and direction of the light in relation to the object. The environment that the object(s) will reside and how they are installed or stored will also play part in this process: lighting multiple or grouped objects as a singular element within an exhibition setting can be a useful way to reduce intensity; creating lightfast or enclosed housings will help to minimize exposure when illumination is needed to actively work within the space.

Controlling Lighting from the Source

The first place to start with lighting control is the power source—or, at least, the power switch and a lighting routine. This will vary depending on the environment's usage or function. In a nonpublic space, such as a preparation or storage space, the lighting will more than likely only have two levels: *on* or *off*. Best practice dictates that whenever an environment that contains objects is not in use or occupied, the lighting should be turned off. This can be a part of a staff guide and routine. To mitigate instances of "human error" in forgetting these practices, installing motion sensors that will automatically turn the power off once a room has been vacated is an ideal addition to general lighting in collections environments.

More advanced systems for adjustable controls will commonly be associated with a display area's track lighting system. Track lighting is a museum exhibition environment standard, given its flexibility to be adjusted and repositioned according to the installation need. These controls can be as basic as a toggled dimming switch through the use of rheostatic controllers or "dimmers" (similar to a residential switch for interior lighting). These controllers act as a resistance control for the electric current that is supplied to the lighting system. By raising or lowering the amount of power to the track, the light levels will adjust in turn. These are effective for a singular consistent level of lighting within a track but do not allow for the fine-tuned adjustment of individual, sectional, or zoned areas of the display space. For this level of control from the power source, a more robust track lighting system must be in place. These systems will commonly be equipped with a digital controller that has the ability to adjust and program preset levels for multiple zones, per space. These track systems often have two circuits per track, meaning that, depending on how the fixture is installed, the lighting may be controlled by a different zone or circuit. The versatility that these systems employ allows the preparator to program multiple lighting scenarios, sometimes on the same wall, depending on the need of the space. These complex lighting systems should be designed in consultation with a lighting engineer who will be able to propose specific systems according to the needs of the space.

Controlling Light from the Fixture

Even with the use of a robust multi-zone control system, there may need to further refine the amount of illumination on an object beyond what the zone control can offer. In situations where varying object requirements mandate customized control at the source of illumination, there are alterations and accessories that can be pursued by adjusting how the light emits from the lamp and fixture.

Starting with the lamp itself, one option in factoring illumination control is the *beam*: the overall degree of the angle that the light is projected from the lamp. A narrow spot may have a beam of 7° to 15°; broader flood lamps will have a beam of 35° to 50°. The final effect of the beam on a surface, however, will always be determined by the distance from the fixture to that surface, that is, how far the lamp is from the target of illumination will determine the final area of illumination. The beam selection must always be considered in tandem with the distance of the projection—this is generally referred to as the *throw*.

More common procedure in the selecting and adjusting lighting is the selection of the style of fixture itself. Gallery fixtures (or luminaires) are designed to emit a wide range of varying lighting level and scenarios. The three most common variations within museum exhibition lighting are the wash, the flood, and the spot.

A *wash* fixture projects light in a broad, undefined manner, without any one target or focal area. Wash fixtures are exceptional for areas where low but consistent lighting scenarios are needed, such as areas exhibiting works on paper, natural fiber materials, and textiles. The wash will not create a defined shape of light, rather, it creates a controlled ambient light within an environment.

The *flood* will provide a more refined illumination than the wash but still broad in its final impact on the illuminated surface. The flood is a common fixture used to light large areas of an installation without directing an overly intense or focused beam directly on any one object.

The *spot* is the lighting fixture that will create the dramatic and concentrated illumination that is commonly used in gallery situations. The spot fixture will usually be outfitted with a lamp that has a narrow beam that produces very little ambient light utilized to place emphasis on an object or section that requires attention. The use of spot fixture must be designed carefully, as too many spots within a controlled space may create a dangerous situation not only for the objects they highlight but also for the public's ability to traverse the environment: without enough ambient light to illuminate a clear path the gallery can become a hazardous situation.

Additional lighting scenarios, such as interior archival case lighting, must be carefully considered and measured before exposing artifacts to long periods of display. Determining the type or style of light source to inform actions for adequate control is the principal task; then, finding the method to adjust and control said illumination is second. For example, an older-style archival case may be equipped with fluorescent illumination built in; therefore, the primary step is to install UV blocking filters at minimum; replacing the system with a controllable and low-intensity LED or fiber-optic lighting system is the ideal. LED solutions offer an ideal choice, especially as archival cases represent a closed environment and must carefully regulate fluctuations in the environment, as they give off very little heat.

Spots, floods, and washes are used in concert with each other to create a balanced lighting environment but do not necessarily have any controllable effect on the intensity of the light. For this adjustment at the fixture, the preparator can add a series of accessories to fine tune, alter, or even block some of the light that emanates from the fixture. These accessories include lenses, filters, screens, and more.

The lens is a glass shield or plate that can be inserted in front of the lamp housed within a fixture to alter the light that is being projected. Plastic lenses should be avoided as the heat generated by the long periods of use can cause these accessories to fail or wear easily. There are two main types of lenses that the preparator will most commonly utilize in a controlled lighting scenario: the diffuser and the filter.

A *diffusor* is a lens with a textured surface that acts as a prism, changing the direction of the light that passes through. Diffusors can come in a variety of "optical types" and "spreads" and can be used to diminish the intensity or change the shape of a spot's projected throw, as well as enlarge the surface area of the illumination. Diffusors with a single spread have ribs that, when light passes through, will change the direction of the beam in single axis, elongating the overall throw of light (useful to illuminate multiple objects installed in close proximity to each other). Double or multi-spread diffusers will change the beam in more than one direction at the source, softening the intensity of the light and enlarging the surface area it covers. Both styles have specific functionality that make them valuable tools in further refining the shape of the light from the predetermined intensity at the source. Diffusors are not only used in track lighting fixtures but also commonly used in florescent lighting: the textured plastic cover that surrounds or rests in a florescent lighting fixture is also a diffusing element and can be purchased in a variety of spreads and levels of displacement.

Figure 13.2. Lenses and Screens Used in Gallery Lighting. *Source*: Image credit: Andrew Saluti.

Another type of lens that can be added is a *filter*, which will alter or adjust the nature of the light projected from a lamp. Filters, as the title suggests, allow certain kinds of light to pass through, while blocking or shifting others. The most common (and arguably most important) filter in a collections environment is the UV filter; a necessary inclusion to block or diminish the damaging levels of UV radiation that is inherent to many light sources. UV filters appear to be clear, but the glass lens is blocking the non-visible wavelengths of the UV spectrum. In addition to filters for gallery fixtures, UV filtering tubes can be added to fluorescent lighting fixtures, and UV blocking films can be purchased on a roll to cover exterior windows or skylights that allow natural sunlight to invade an environment. Other filters can augment the color, or balance, of the light from a fixture (these types of filters are not generally used within a museum or collections environment but can be added to modify overall hue). It is not good practice to use toned or color filters to combat a shift in the color temperature of your lamps: this change is a good indication that the lamp is nearing the end of its life and should be replaced rather than adjusted.

A *screen* is a mesh barrier that will block the visible light at different levels depending on how tightly or loosely woven the mesh is. Think about the screen door of a home and how the light is subtly blocked as it passes through. Screens are effective for those instances when a certain type of throw is required, but the intensity must be altered. When a diffusor may change and soften the shape of the light, the screen will simply knock down the intensity.

A *louver* (or louvre) is a device that controls light spillage and direction through the use of a baffle, often in a grid or honeycomb pattern.

A *snoot* is a cylindrical or conical extension that can be added to further refine the shape of the beam from the lamp and, like a louver, will help to control unwanted light spillage from the fixture.

Commonly used in theatrical stage lighting, *barn doors* are a series of hinged flaps that can be positioned to create a light blocking element in a specific shape or side from the fixture. Barn doors are especially effective when lighting moveable or temporary walls or structures that do not extend to the ceiling height or installations that are not enclosed within a controlled space, where the need to prevent light spillage near the top of the structure or beyond the targeted area is necessary.

Another approach to controlling the illumination within an environment is the physical position of the lighting fixture itself. The flexibility of a track system adds an inherent control of illumination by simply changing the location of the source of the light. There are defined methods that the preparator should consider in this approach; it is rarely as simple as moving the fixture farther away to lessen the intensity of the light, especially when one must consider a factor that may not be present during the time of installation: the viewer. Moving a fixture too far away from the intended target can result in possible reflected glare or unintended spillage and ambient light. Additionally, if the fixture is positioned behind the viewer's position, their body will create a cast shadow that may extend to the object they are engaging with. The position of the fixture should be gaged by the angle of direction: ideally between 30° and 45° from the forward ceiling, depending on track height. This will offer a foundation for the acceptable distances of the fixtures to be positioned. Additional adjustments that can be made are the lateral position of the fixture, which can be defined as direct and raking light.

Direct lighting can be defined as having the position of the fixture that is targeting an object. This is the lighting scenario that may be the easiest to position and control the interaction with the object. Direct lighting will usually create the least amount of cast shadow against the wall or beyond the object. It will also project the most intense amount of illumination and must be addressed with modicums of control and refinement. Objects of deep contrast or highly reflective varnished surfaces will not respond well to a forward-facing direct light source, and, in these situations, a variation in position may better present and preserve the object.

Raking light casts the direct light source across the object surface that is then reflected past the immediate viewable area rather than directly back at the object while still providing illumination. Think about how a ball might bounce if thrown straight at a wall target (direct) and then at the same target

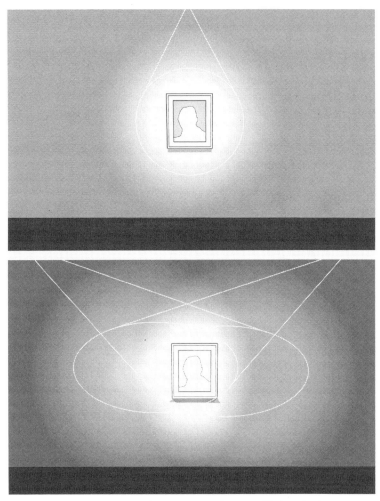

Figure 13.3. Graphic Example of Direct Lighting and Raking Light.
Source: Image credit: Andrew Saluti.

but from the side. This is how the light reacts to the surface of the artifact being illuminated. The benefit of racking light is the minimization of glare and reflection that might impede the engagement with the work, as well as the lessened intensity of the illumination, and thus, the possibility of less adjustment or action to be taken. The downside to creating a raking light scenario includes the possible need for multiple fixtures to create a consistent illumination on a single target, the potential for unintended or expanded cast shadows due to the angle of the fixture, and the unintended highlight of surface textures and irregularities that would not be visible from a more direct illumination.

Finally, for installations that involve artifacts and objects that are extremely sensitive to light and are housed within exhibition furniture or casework, a lightfast covering can be the most effective in mitigating light damage. A draped fabric that can be easily lifted by the viewer and then replaced to protect the casework and objects from illumination is a simple, traditional, and effective tool in mitigating overexposure to light.

When implementing a lighting scenario for an installation, the preparator can use the following tips to best prepare for the installation needs:

- Organize accessories and fixtures, test lamps, and have spare on hand.
- Remove the fixture from their previous position rather than attempting to adjust in place.
- Consider the object, contextual, and illumination needs (and restrictions).

CONSIDERATIONS FOR AUDIO/VIDEO INSTALLATIONS

Much like controlling the light within a collection setting, the installation of audio and video (or digital video) (A/V) can be a daunting task, especially when placed within an environment of multiple installations, experiences, and contexts. These dynamic elements are common additions to the exhibition and collections experience, adding rich content that can enhance the interpretation of complex concepts and histories. Audio and video elements, whether they are representative of a collection object or curatorial context, or are supplemental and didactic meant to enhance the experience, must be presented in a manner that does not adversely impact the presentation or interpretation of the installation in which they reside. This means that the lighting scenario for the installed objects must also consider the projected and ambient illumination given by these sources and vice versa: the placement of a projected video can directly impact the light levels of the surrounding environment.

In addition to mitigating potential impact that an A/V installation will have on the lighting in the space, there is also the consideration of sound. These impacts can be described as noise and light pollution in the installed space and can deter from the designed experience or intended interpretation of the installation. In most cases, selecting a proper delivery method for this media can offset the negative effects that pollution may have in the gallery. When considering how a particular media element may impact the gallery experience, the preparator, in consultation with the curator or exhibition designer, should suggest the following.

What will the audio/video content contain: narration, ambient music or sound, or other effects? If the media is a narration or conversation, this may interfere differently than that of an ambient soundtrack or other effects.

What is the intended coverage for the media? Is the material meant for an intimate group of visitors or a broad audience? Will the intended placement sufficiently support this intended interaction or does the media need to be moved to another location?

What is the physical proximity to other media within the installed space? Does the media compete with other audio and video installations nearby or is it the sole source of noise in the gallery?

Gathering this information will enable the installation team to plan for what types of delivery methods may be best suited for the media as well as the installation overall. The levels of audio delivery can be organized in a hierarchy of individual engagement to broad projection and can be projected through a variety of basic technological means.

Headsets may be the simplest way to control ambient audio within an installation. Headphones are inexpensive and can be readily connected to most media sources, allowing a singular visitor to experience the media. The physical mounting of these devices can be as basic as a hook projecting from a wall or pedestal where the headset rests when not in use, or can be more bespoke, with specialty mounts that carry the headset with heightened presentation. It is important to recognize that some view the public installation of headsets, and their shared use, to be displeasing. Headsets should be routinely disinfected as a part of daily gallery maintenance and, depending on the quality of the set, may need to be replaced within the duration of the exhibition.

Personal devices should also be considered, as they have the least impact on the installation. These may take the form of an audio wand that can be supplied by the institution at the beginning of the exhibition installation or a direct link or download to the visitor's smartphone or personal device. The ability to create a personal experience that is completely controlled—and contained—to the individual's personal experience can be achieved with the inclusion of a scannable code (such as a QR Code) or a sharable online resource to access the intended media for any given section directly on mounted labels within the space. This does require some ability and resources with website maintenance but easy enough to create without the need for contracted web development or production.

A more complex and interactive approach might be the installation of a *parabolic speaker system*. The parabolic speaker creates a controlled cone of sound that is restricted to a narrow physical space. Once a visitor passes through the directed area, the audio can be heard clearly and at a desired level. Once the visitor leaves that proximity, the audio is no longer perceptible. This type of audio delivery is particularly effective when there are multiple narrative elements that need to be experienced within specific areas of the installation. These units can be mounted discretely, generally directly above the area where the audio is intended to be presented. Some disadvantages to parabolic systems include the cost: each speaker will come at considerable cost compared to other solutions. The parabolic systems can also be challenging to install: the directed audio is so focused that it will often reflect off hard or polished surfaces, much like billiard balls on a pool table. However, if the exhibition space is designed to accommodate this style of audio projection, the experience can be the most seamless and immersive of all the audio delivery options.

The use of standard *audio speakers* may be appropriate, depending on the parameters of the preceding outline of questioning: if the intended audience is a large group rather than an individual experience, installing standard speakers that direct toward the group location may be the most effective way to deliver the content. This will also be impacted by the layout of the exhibition (Will there be physical barriers separating this engagement from others?) or the installation of other group-based interactive spaces.

HIERARCHY FOR DIGITAL INPUTS

In addition to the audio output, the preparator must also consider how video media is delivered to the viewable output source. This is often dictated by the original format of the media, as well as the technology on hand to display it. When working with any video format, the hierarchy of digital input/output can direct the process, maintaining the highest quality presentation possible. It is important to note that the quality of the presentation will only be as good as the original media, as well as the level of quality level of the output display. This hierarchy is relevant in that there is often choice in the selection of input/output connections, and this can inform decisions based on the factors of display technology and original media. This hierarchy is organized by highest (best) quality first, with lesser levels of quality following.

Direct media stream: A digital file is directly connected to the screen or projector. This method is preferred, though also necessitate that the equipment for video delivery have an internal media player.

HDMI (High Definition Multimedia Interface): This is the highest common connection for transferring media content, providing the highest resolution of image and audio signals to the display device.

DVI (Digital Video Interface): This is a connection that delivers a high-quality signal, generally used with computer monitors or other graphics-based devices. Unlike HDMI, a DVI connection will not carry audio—only the video signal.

VGA (Video Graphics Array): One step below the quality of a DVI is the VGA (Video Graphics Array) connection. This is the standard connection for a computer monitor or screen, commonly recognized by a blue, 15-pin serial connection. The VGA connection will not deliver a high-resolution image signal but still maintains a decent quality digital image that does not include an audio feed.

Component Connection: It is a multi-cable connection consisting of five RCA-style connectors (three for video, two for audio) that deliver an analog video signal with a stereo audio signal. These connections should only be used when the display equipment prohibits any digital input or output—a last resort in the display of media. Component connections are still common on most output display and can be effective when incorporating dated or historic media into an installation.

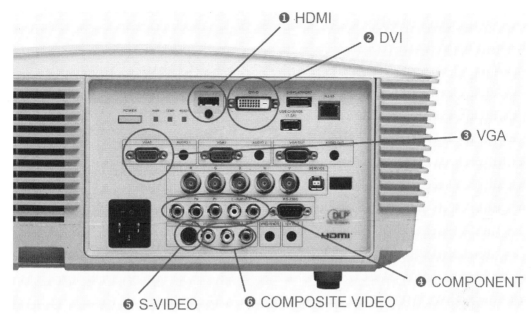

Figure 13.4. Hierarchy of Audio/Visual Inputs. *Source*: Image credit: Andrew Saluti.

The lowest forms of video output are the *S-Video* and *Composite Video* connections. These analog display connections are rarely used and are only capable of delivering a standard quality of image, far inferior to contemporary high-quality video signals.

Note: When installing any media in a gallery setting, it is ideal to utilize contemporary technology that does not incorporate any moving mechanical parts; these devices tend to wear and fail from continuous playback. This includes VHS, DVD, Blu-ray, vinyl recording, audio cassette, or CD playback: all these media types require a player that incorporates many moving mechanisms, gears, and other parts that when stressed can not only damage the player but more importantly permanently damage the original media. Whenever possible, and when budget allows, a digital copy of such media types will eliminate the need for mechanical playback and help to preserve the content for exhibition and archival preservation.

INSTALLING DIGITAL VIDEO

Once the general considerations for media have been determined, and the technology to deliver the media has been established, the preparator may be faced with one more decision: Should a video be presented on a mounted flat screen or projected in the gallery environment? The decision may rest upon the curator/exhibition designer's original intent: Will the included video act as an object within the context of other installed objects or is the video intended to be a part of the designed, physical environment? This may be the most basic way to isolate the need—if the media is an object within the curated space, a screen may be appropriate. If the media is intended to be a part of the space, a projection is a better solution if the environment can sustain that type of presentation. Additional consideration, as previously discussed, is the intended audience: if the media is meant for a broad group, the projection might be better suited. Even as these decisions are made by a curatorial voice, the preparator can provide input and insight as to how the media output may affect or be affected by the larger installation.

When mounting projectors, there are basic points to consider.

Figure 13.5. A Universal Mount for Digital Projector. *Source:* Image credit: Andrew Saluti.

A digital projector can be mounted from a variety of positions—including upside down from a ceiling. This is commonly the most effective approach for projected video, as it largely removes physical interruptions in the projected image by those who are in the physical space.

Projectors must have adequate air circulation to cool the intense heat generated by the lamp that projects the image—enclosing the projector inside gallery furniture, or suffocating the fan intake, can do irreparable damage to the projection system, often requiring costly replacements of the lamp and bulb.

Universal mounting bracket systems can be used to safely and securely mount the projector in the desired location and position. These mounting systems, often nicknamed "octopus mounts" for their adjustable tentacle-like brackets that can be shifted to the position of any projector base, will fix a projector in place, so that once the image has been correctly positioned, the unity will not shift out of the desired orientation. In addition to the position of the mount, the preparator may need to adjust the *keystone* of the image: a function of most digital projectors that corrects the lateral and horizontal angle of the projected image.

The projected video can be an impactful and immersive experience within the gallery setting but also requires a greater sensitivity to the environment and to the installation than the mounted screen. Each has characteristics that impact the viewer's engagement and interpretation of the content.

Gallery Management

One final task in the installation of media is that of maintenance. Carefully outlining the daily routines of opening and closing procedures for gallery and museum staff is an essential aspect of preserving the installed experience. Engaging the visitor services and "front of house" personnel with a walk-through of what should be happening with a media installation, as well as a tutorial in troubleshooting when something goes wrong (such as a power outage or accidental change in control), will relieve the need for the preparator to constantly intervene once the gallery installation has been completed. Documentation is essential, and proper communication with institutional colleagues (as outlined early in this text) will prove effective tools in the maintenance of the installed experience.

REFERENCES

Conn, Donia. "Protection from Light Damage." *The Environment Preservation Leaflet* 2, no. 4 (2012). Northeast Document Conservation Center (NEDCC), Andover, MA.

Cuttle, Christopher. *Light for Art's Sake*, 1st ed. (London: Routledge, 2007): 191–199.

Haas, Steve. "Effectively Managing Sound in Museum Exhibits." (2015). S H Acoustics, Stamford, CT. PDF. https://shacoustics.com/wp-content/uploads/2016/01/Effectively-Managing-Sound-in-Museum-Exhibits.pdf.

Herskovitz, Bob and Rich Rummel. "Track Lighting in Museums Part 1: Selection and Design." Tech Talk. *Minnesota History Interpreter* 34, no. 6 (November–December 2006): 3–5.

Hubner, Mary. "CONSERVA-TIPS." *History News* 35, no. 4 (1980): 46. Accessed June 21, 2021. http://www.jstor.org/stable/42649508.

Sackler Gallery & Freer Gallery of Art. "Light Duration Guidelines for Exhibited Works of Art." Smithsonian Institution (2011). http://www.connectingtocollections.org/wp-content/uploads/2011/08/hbcu-light-levels-for-storage-and-exhibition.original1.pdf.

Scottish Museums Council. "Advice Sheet: Monitoring Light and UV Radiation in Museums." December 2005. Accessed March 20, 2021. https://formacaompr.files.wordpress.com/2010/02/monitoring-light.pdf.

14

Preparator's Resources

PROFESSIONAL COLLECTIONS ORGANIZATIONS

These organizations are specific to the preparator's practice and include community groups, announcements for webinars and workshops, materials and supply resources, and direct access to skilled professionals. While some require annual membership fees, much of the content can be accessed through free registration.

American Institute for Conservation (AIC)

culturalheritage.org

The AIC and the Foundation for Advancement in Conservation work together to promote the preservation and protection of cultural heritage. The association is a national membership organization for conservators and allied professionals who preserve cultural heritage, and the foundation is a nonprofit that delivers and supports an array of programs and initiatives to protect our shared cultural heritage. The website contains excellent resources, events, publications, and directories of conservators and archival practice.

Association of Registrars and Collection Specialists (ARCS)

arcsinfo.org

The mission of ARCS is to represent and promote Registrars and Collections Specialists, nationally and internationally, to educate them in the professional best practices of registration and collections care and to facilitate communication and networking. In addition to educational opportunity announcements, job boards, and other resources and reference, the ARCS listserv is an active and responsive professional community network.

Canadian Conservation Institute (CCI)

www.canada.ca/en/conservation-institute

The CCI, a Special Operating Agency within the Department of Canadian Heritage, advances and promotes the conservation of Canada's heritage collections through its expertise in conservation science, treatment, and preventive conservation. CCI works with heritage institutions and professionals to ensure these heritage collections are preserved and accessible to Canadians now and in the future.

International Mountmakers Forum

mountmakersforum.net

The International Mountmakers Forum is an organization that exists to support the work of the mount making community. It is committed to fostering communication, promoting best practices, and disseminating current information regarding materials, tools, techniques, and solutions for object storage and display. It is a resource for tips and solutions, training opportunities, jobs and opportunities, tools and materials, conferences, events, workshops, and seminars.

Museum Trade

museumtrade.org

This website is hub for preparators, installers, and other collections professionals who are responsible for the installation of exhibitions and handling of objects to share resources and tips and showcase examples of innovative and experimental approaches.

Preparation, Art handling, and Collections Care Information Network (PACCIN)

paccin.org

PACCIN is dedicated to building a network of individuals interested in sharing the practical information and essential resources that help hands-on collections care professionals to better protect and preserve the cultural property in their care.

PACCIN provides a venue to access and participate in the critical dialogue of professionals who are interested in elevating standards of art and artifact handling and housing. Some areas of focus in these standards include packing, crating, shipping, installation, mount making, rigging, exhibition fabrication, storage methodology, and educational and employment opportunities as well as ongoing industry updates of current technical and material usage.

Storage Techniques for Art, Science, and History Collections (STASHC)

stashc.com

STASHC provides information and tools so that institutions of all types, sizes, and resource levels can learn how to create safe and appropriate storage solutions. These solutions were written by and for collection care professionals in all fields. This website includes glossaries, conversion charts and tables, and an encyclopedic resource for materials, equipment, and supplies.

Society for the Preservation of Natural History Collections (SPNHC)

spnhc.org

"The Society for the Preservation of Natural History Collections [SPNHC] is an international organization devoted to the preservation, conservation and management of natural history collections." It is an excellent resource for preparation, identification, and care of natural history artifacts. Full text leaflets, workshops, and other resources.

PROFESSIONAL MUSEUM ORGANIZATIONS

The following list of museum organizations are not strictly geared to preparators and collections practice but the larger consortium of the museum profession. This list is not comprehensive and is organized by international/national (US), regional, and state groups. These organizational resources include local community meetups and workshops, job postings, and other professional opportunities.

INTERNATIONAL

International Council on Museums (ICOM)

icom.museum/

"The International Council of Museums is an international organization of museums and museum professionals which is committed to the research, conservation, continuation and communication to society of the world's natural and cultural heritage, present and future, tangible and intangible. ICOM is a membership association and a non-governmental organization which establishes professional and ethical standards for museum activities. As forum of experts, it makes recommendations on issues related to cultural heritage, promotes capacity building and advances knowledge. ICOM is the voice of museum professionals on international stage and raises public cultural awareness through global networks and co-operation programs. ICOM is the only global organization in the museum field."

NATIONAL (UNITED STATES)

American Alliance of Museums

aam-us.org

"The American Alliance of Museums (AAM) is the only organization representing the entire museum field, from art and history museums to science centers and zoos. Since 1906, it has been championing museums through advocacy and providing museum professionals with the resources, knowledge, inspiration, and connections they need to move the field forward."

American Association of State and Local History

aaslh.org

"The American Association for State and Local History is a national membership association dedicated to helping the history community thrive. For the better part of a century, AASLH has provided leadership and resources to its members who preserve and interpret state and local history to make the past more meaningful to all people. AASLH is the professional association for history-doers.

"Today AASLH provides crucial resources, guidance, professional development, advocacy, new publications, field-wide research, and a sense of connectedness to over 5,500 institutional and individual members, as well as leadership for history and history organizations nationally. It is the only comprehensive national organization dedicated to state and local history."

Association of Academic Museums and Galleries

www.aamg-us.org

"The Association of Academic Museums and Galleries is the leading educational and professional organization for academic museums, galleries, and collections. In recognition of the unique opportunities and challenges of its constituents, the AAMG establishes and supports best practices, educational activities and professional development that enable its member organizations to fulfill their educational missions."

National Association of Interpretation

www.interpnet.com

"The National Association for Interpretation (NAI) is a 501(c)(3) not-for-profit professional organization dedicated to advancing the profession of heritage interpretation, currently serving about 7,000 members in the United States, Canada, and over thirty other nations. Individual members include those who work at parks, museums, nature centers, zoos, botanical gardens, aquariums, historical and cultural sites, commercial tour companies, and theme parks. Commercial and institutional members include those who provide services to the heritage interpretation industry."

Small Museums Association

smallmuseum.org

"The Small Museum Association is an all volunteer organization serving small museums in the mid-Atlantic region and beyond. SMA's mission is to develop and maintain a peer network among people who work for small museums, giving them opportunities to learn, share knowledge and support one another, so that they, in turn, can better serve their institutions, communities and profession."

REGIONAL

Association of Midwestern Museums

www.midwestmuseums.org

"Since its founding in 1927, the Association of Midwest Museums [AMM] has sought to connect museums across the eight-state region of the Midwest, including Illinois, Indiana, Iowa, Michigan, Minnesota, Missouri, Ohio, and Wisconsin. Our mission is to strengthen museums in the Midwest by providing nationally relevant, regionally specific programs, products, and networking opportunities. Through our programs and activities, AMM encourages professional standards for all areas of museum administration and provides cutting-edge information and resources to museums and cultural institutions in the Midwest and the greater museum community."

Mid-Atlantic Association of Museums

midatlanticmuseums.org

"The Mid-Atlantic Association of Museums [MAAM] is a not for profit membership organization, founded in 1947. Our organization represents museums professionals, organizations, institutions and museum service providers, providing a forum to enhance the image of museums and educate individuals on an array of field specific study and programs. We chiefly represent those museum interests in Delaware, the District of Columbia, Maryland, New Jersey, New York and Pennsylvania.

"We bring together the resources of the Mid-Atlantic region's museum community and make them available to our members through conferences, symposia, and workshops in your neighborhood. MAAM is recognized as a regional association by the American Alliance of Museums (AAM)."

New England Museum Association

nemanet.org

The New England Museum Association "[NEMA] is a community of museums and the professionals who work in them. They supply professional development, advocacy, thought leadership, research, networking opportunities, and other tools that cultivate their excellence as institutions and individuals."

Mountain-Plains Museum Association

www.mpma.net

"The Mountain-Plains Museum Association [MPMA] is a dynamic organization that collaborates with museums to preserve and celebrate the region's rich and diverse cultural, artistic and natural heritage. It serves its members by providing educational opportunities to assist museums to strive toward excellence in areas of collections preservation, exhibitions and interpretation. It advocates for museums and museum workers. It provides leadership in the discussion and development of strategies for the evolution of museums, and it serves as a central source of information to meet the needs of museums facing the challenges of today and the future."

Southeastern Museums Conference

www.semcdirect.net

"The Southeastern Museums Conference [SEMC], a nonprofit membership organization, is an association of museums, museum staff, independent professionals and corporate partners. We focus on the Southeastern United State including: Alabama, Arkansas, Florida, Georgia, Kentucky, Louisiana, Mississippi, North Carolina, South Carolina, Tennessee, Virginia, West Virginia, Puerto Rico, and US Virgin Islands."

Western Museums Association

westmuse.org

"The Western Museums Association [WMA] is a nonprofit, membership organization dedicated to serving museums, museum professionals, and related institutions by providing vision, enrichment, intellectual challenge, as well as a forum for communication and interaction. Through training and educational programs, the WMA empowers the diverse museum community of the West to cultivate leadership and enable institutions to remain relevant in a dynamic world. Additionally, the WMA creates opportunities for its constituents to build skill-sets to better serve their communities through their museums by providing professional development opportunities west of the Rockies, including in Alaska and Hawaii, the western Canadian provinces of Alberta and British Columbia, among others."

STATE (SELECTED)

California Association of Museums

www.calmuseums.org

The California Association of Museums' key programs and services include "professional development programs, including an annual conference and regional workshops that address best practices and trends; CAM eNews, which is distributed every two weeks to thousands of subscribers; studies and reports; an active advocacy program that monitors legislation and spearheads strategic initiatives to support funding sources; and special initiatives that provide leadership in important issues affecting the field. Much of CAM's work is led by Member Committees that actively involve members of the association."

Museum Association of New York

nysmuseums.org

"The Museum Association of New York inspires, connects, and strengthens New York's cultural community statewide by advocating, educating, collaborating, and supporting professional standards and organizational development."

Florida Association of Museums

www.flamuseums.org

"The Florida Association of Museums is the non-profit professional organization for Florida's museums and museum professionals. The mission of the Association is to represent and address the needs of the museum community, enhancing the ability of museums to serve the public interest."

Ohio Museums Association

ohiomuseums.org

"The Ohio Museums Association is the leading advocate for connecting and empowering Ohio museums and museum professionals. Founded in 1976 by members of Ohio's museum community, the Ohio Museums Association is committed to serving our state's dedicated museum professionals and institutions through career resources, professional development opportunities, networking events, advocacy on a state and national level—these are just a few of the benefits that help make OMA a vital career resource for museum professionals at every stage of their career.

"OMA works with a variety of museums, museum professionals and providers of museum services to strengthen the state's museum, foster excellence in the field and support the museum community."

Pennsylvania Museum Association

pamuseums.org

"PA Museums is Pennsylvania's statewide trade association serving museum professionals and institutions. Based in Harrisburg, PA Museums was founded in 1905 and during its long history was known as the Pennsylvania Federation of Historical Societies and the Pennsylvania Federation of Museums and Historical Organizations."

Texas Association of Museums

www.texasmuseums.org

"The Texas Association of Museums strengthens the Texas museum community through collaborations, connections, professional development, and advocacy.

"TAM serves our museum community by nurturing and training museum leaders, developing and celebrating the field, and voicing the public worth of museums."

Virginia Association of Museums

www.vamuseums.org

"The Virginia History Federation was incorporated in 1968 to promote and support Virginia's historical museums and sites. In 1978, the name was changed to the Virginia History and Museums Federation to reflect the broadening of its mission to include all museum disciplines. The name was changed once more, in 1980, to the Virginia Association of Museums (VAM) to further establish its identity as an organization whose purpose is education and support for all museums and similar cultural institutions in the Commonwealth."

ARCHIVAL SUPPLIES AND RESOURCES

The following list of international companies present the primary suppliers of archival and prepatory materials including mounting hardware and materials, tools and equipment, prefabricated storage containers, installation mounts and housings, and other essential materials used in the preparation of collection objects.

Archival Methods

archivalmethods.com

655 Driving Park Avenue
Suite #5 / Dock #8
Rochester, New York, 14613
Toll-Free (US): 866.877.7050
Outside US: 585.334.7050

Supplier of archival storage, preservation, and presentation products.

Carr McClean (CA)

www.carrmclean.ca

461 Horner Avenue
Toronto, Ontario, M8W 4X2
800.268.2123

Conservation Resources International, Inc.

www.conservationresources.com

5532 Port Royal Road
Springfield, Virginia, 22151
800.634.6932

Conservation Resources delivers high-quality conservation and archival storage materials to major institutions dedicated to preserving cultural and historical artifacts worldwide. They have developed and patented many products and constantly seek to identify needs in the conservation community and develop products to address these concerns.

Conservation Support Systems

conservationsupportsystems.com

P.O. Box 91746
Santa Barbara, California, 93190-1746
800.482.6299

Décor Moulding and Supply

www.decormoulding.com

300 Wireless Boulevard
Hauppauge, New York, 11788
631.231.5959
800.937.1055

"Founded in 1888, Decor is one of the largest wholesale suppliers to the picture frame industry. Decor Moulding supplies the industries' broadest and most up-to-date selection of mouldings, frames, ovals, and framing supplies backed by the largest inventory levels in the United States." Also an excellent resource for archival boards.

Gaylord Archival

gaylord.com

PO Box 4901
Syracuse, New York, 13221-4901
1.800.448.6160

Gaylord Archival is a leading provider of preservation and exhibit products to institutions and individuals across the globe. In addition to archival-quality storage boxes, folders, sleeves, envelopes, and more, they offer a large selection of predesigned, customizable exhibit cases, mounts, and archival display materials.

Hollinger Metal Edge

hollingermetaledge.com

9401 Northeast Drive
Fredericksburg, Virginia, 22408
800.634.0491

"Hollinger Metal Edge is a supplier of archival storage products for government and institutional archives, historical societies, museums, libraries, universities, galleries and private collectors. Founded in 1945 in Arlington, Virginia, the company worked with officials at The Library of Congress and NaArchives to develop acid free papers, storage boxes and envelopes that would allow for the proper preservation of valuable documents and photographs. The company operates manufacturing plant in Fredericksburg, Virginia."

Klug-Conservation

klug-conservation.com

Zollstrasse 2
87509 Immenstadt, Germany
+49 (0).8323.9653.30

"With over 150 years of experience, Klug-Conservation has developed the know-how to produce premium quality products, ensuring maximum permanency for the long-term preservation of cultural assets for archives, museums, libraries and picture framers." The website is an excellent resource for contemporary conservation methods and issues, as well as technical knowledge blog and newsletter.

Larson Juhl

www.larsonjuhl.com

990 Peachtree Industrial Blvd #3829
Suwanee, Georgia, 30024
800.438.5031

Larson Juhl is an industry leader in the manufacturing and distribution of custom picture frames moldings and framing materials.

Light Impressions Direct

lightimpressionsdirect.com

100 Carlson Rd
Rochester, New York, 14610
1.888.222.2054

"Established in 1969 in Rochester, NY, Light Impressions offers a large variety of fine archival storage, display and presentation materials for negatives, transparencies, CDs, photographs, artwork and documents. An excellent resource for photographic storage and works on paper preservation and presentation materials and supplies."

Preservation Equipment Ltd

www.preservationequipment.com

Vinces Road
Diss
Norfolk
IP22 4HQ
+44(0) 1379 647400

"Preservation Equipment Ltd was founded in 1986 by Cliff Gothorp to provide access to quality materials and equipment for professionals working in the field of conservation and preservation of archives and works of art and ancient artifacts. PEL has launched innovative products such as Crossweld polyester sealing machine, Museum Vac, Preservation Pencil and Conservation Work Station. They also launched the first fully online archival bespoke box service in the UK, *boxsite.co.uk* to make custom box ordering easier than ever. Exclusive partnerships include companies such as University Products, Print File, Lineco and Akachemie. The PEL brand Arcare offers access to high quality range of archival quality products suitable for professional and hobby use."

Small Corp

smallcorp.com

19 Butternut Street
Greenfield, Massachusetts, 01301
800.392.9500

"Products for the display, conservation, and storage, specializing in the design and manufacture of archival museum exhibit cases and museum quality picture frames. Wholesale customers include museums, educational institutions, artists, fine art framers, historical societies, conservators and art professionals." Their website also includes resources for archival practice.

Talas

talasonline.com

330 Morgan Ave
Brooklyn, New York, 11211
212.219.0770

Talas is a Brooklyn-based conservation, archival, and bookbinding supply company. An excellent resource for specialty fabrics and materials for archival presentation and use.

University Products

universityproducts.com

517 Main Street
Holyoke, Massachusetts, 01040
Phone: 1.800.628.1912

University Products offers a wide selection of high-quality library supplies and museum-quality archival materials, tools, and equipment. It is an excellent resource for cleaning and preparation tools in addition to archival display and storage solutions.

Museum Services Corporation

museumservicescorporation.com

385 Bridgepoint Way
South St. Paul, Minnesota, 55075
United States
651.450.8954

"The Museum Services Corporation (MSC) designs, builds, and sells art conservation, restoration, and preservation equipment."

INSTALLATION AND EXHIBITION SUPPLIES

The following resources are suppliers of exhibition, installation, and framing materials; tools; and equipment. Included are fabricators for specialty mounts, gallery hanging systems, and museum-quality frames.

888 Manufacturing Corporation

888mfgcorp.com

62 South 2nd Street, Suite H
Deer Park, New York, 11729
888.338.3318

Manufacturer and distributor of picture frame and installation hardware.

Absolute Products (the United Kingdom)

absoluteproduct.com

The Hub, Pathfields Business Park
Station Road, South Molton, EX36 3LL
United Kingdom
+44 1769 572389

Designer and manufacturer of products and materials to display, protect, and interpret objects, in addition to wayfinding and crowd guidance supplies.

Art Display Essentials

www.artdisplay.com

2 West Crisman Road
Columbia, New Jersey, 07832
800. 862. 9869

Online resource for prefabricated mounts, displays, hanging systems, cases, and other furniture.

Benchmark Mountmakers

benchmarkcatalog.com

P.O. Box 214
Rosemont, New Jersey, 08556
609.397.1131

"Since 1980, Benchmark has worked to augment the capabilities of museums, galleries, historical societies, corporate and private collections, through custom mountmaking and on-site artifact installation for exhibition. Benchmark is known for its on-time, on-budget work done by knowledgeable and good-natured mountmakers." Direct resource for the customizable Butterfly Bookmount.

Case[Werks]

www.casewerks.com

1019 Cathedral Street
Baltimore, Maryland, 21201
410.332.4160
800.810.2852

"Case[werks] was founded in 2001 by Reinhard Nottrodt and Matt Malaquias in Baltimore, Maryland. The two combined experience in design and the manufacture of archival casework to a partnership with Vitrinen- und Glasbau REIER GmBH of Lauta, Germany. REIER has grown into one of the leading display case manufacturers with successful projects for cultural institutions all over the world."

Grainger

grainger.com

Grainger is one of the largest sources for MRO (maintenance, repair, and operating) supplies and industrial products. Grainger offers over 1.5 million products from thousands of trusted MRO suppliers. It is a source for installation tools and equipment.

MasterPak

masterpak-usa.com

145 E 57 ST 5th FL
New York, New York, 10022
USA
800.922.5522

"Masterpak is an excellent source for the materials needed to safely package, ship and store fine art. Masterpak provides art packaging products to artists, auction houses, galleries and museums around the world, serving as the sole purveyor of OzClips® as well as the TitanStrongBox™ worldwide."

Metropolitan Picture Framing

www.metroframe.com

6959 Washington Ave South
Minneapolis, Minnesota, 55439
952.941.6649
800.626.3139

Metropolitan Picture Framing is a family-owned manufacturing business located in Minnesota. They custom mill and finish North American hardwoods to make contemporary museum-quality wood molding, frames, and support strainers.

Museum Hanging Systems

museumhangingsystems.net

2 West Crisman Rd.
Columbia, New Jersey, 07832
908.496.4946

Mechanical systems and solutions for hanging art in museum, galleries, and institutions. Also offers custom mount making.

Picture Hanging Systems (Netherlands)

www.picturehangingsystems.com

Esp 245, 5633 AD Eindhoven—The Netherlands
P.O. Box 1049, 5602 BA Eindhoven
Distributor of the STAS rail hanging system.

United Manufacturers

www.unitedmfrs.com

300 Wireless Boulevard
Hauppauge, New York, 11788
800.795.1589

United Manufacturers advertises itself as "Your one source for all your picture framing needs." From supplies to tools and equipment, they have an extensive selection of framing and installation supplies.

PROJECT MANAGEMENT APPLICATIONS

The following list of project management applications and platforms are an important tool for preparators and exhibition staff in the administration of collections-based projects.

Airtable

www.airtable.com

Airtable is a customizable platform for managing data and projects through a cloud-based system. Pricing is based on project or staff/user needs.

Curia

curia.com

"Curia is the first collaborative exhibition planning app designed exclusively for the needs of the museum community." This application is especially designed to provide an out-of-the-box, cross-platform collections and exhibitions project management system.

Gantt Project

www.ganttproject.biz

Gantt Project is a free, open-source downloadable application that will allow the user to create effective project management tables and workflows.

Wrike

wrike.com

CONSERVATION CENTERS

Conservation Center for Art & Historic Artifacts (CCAHA)

ccaha.org

264 South 23rd Street
Philadelphia, Pennsylvania, 19103
215.545.0613

"CCAHA is a nonprofit, full-service facility with experts in a range of disciplines. They have been providing conservation and preservation services since 1977. Their mission is to provide expertise and leadership in the preservation of cultural heritage. Their conservators repair and stabilize books, photographs, and documents. Preservation services staff actively work in the field, providing education programs and helping institutions plan for the future of their collections. They also offer digitization services, fundraising assistance, framing."

Midwest Art Conservation Center

www.preserveart.org

2400 Third Avenue South
Minneapolis, Minnesota, 55404
612.870.3120

"The Midwest Art Conservation Center is a non-profit organization for the preservation and conservation of art and artifacts, providing treatment, education, and training for museums, historical societies, libraries, other cultural institutions, artists, and the public."

NorthEast Document Conservation Center (NEDCC)

www.nedcc.org

100 Brickstone Square
Andover, Massachusetts, 01810
978.470.1010

"Founded in 1973, NEDCC was the first independent conservation laboratory in the nation to specialize exclusively in treating collections made of paper or parchment, such as works of art, photographs, books, documents, maps, and manuscripts. Today, the Center offers conservation treatment, digital imaging, and audio preservation services, as well as preservation training, assessments and consultations, and disaster advice on collections."

Index

Occupational Safety and Health Administration
(OSHA), 16
Oddy test, 97
offset clip (z bracket), 72, *72*

pedestals, 5, 8, 21, 23, 83, 86, 118-19, 125-27
Permalife, 56
PERT chart (Program Evaluation Review
Technique), 35
Phifer, Thomas, 40
picture rail, 123-24, *123*
Plexiglass, 84
polyester sheet, 57, 61-62, 66, 84, 86, 89
polyethylene strap, 77-78, 84, 92

Reiter, Rolf, 103-4
Research Casting International, 103
Riester, Dorothy, 139
risers, 119, 126

sawtooth hanger, 121
Schapiro, Miriam, 98
screen, lens, 149
senior preparator, 8
Shelburne Museum, 98
Silbert, Susie J, 40
silica gel, 68
Smartsheet, 35
snoot, 149

spot, lighting, 147
stanchions, 119, 125-26
stands, 4-5, 7, 84, 94, 120
Stone Quarry Hill Art Park, 137-38
suction lifters, 119
Syracuse University Art Museum, 89, 133

taxidermy, 2, 8, 80
templates, 35, 79, 83-84, 87-89
templates, book cradle, 77, 90-91, *90*, 93, *93*
templates, footprint, 89, *89*, 126
templates, tools, 88-89
triple constraint method (tcm), 31
Tyvek, 66, 102

Ultra Low Penetration Air (ULPA) vacuum, 81
University Products, 97, 166
utility cart, 23

velcro, 94
video, installation, 153
vitrines, 112, 118-19, 127
Vivak, 77, 84

wash, lighting, 147
Washington State Historical Society, 36
wheat paste, 56
Wonderflex World, 97

About the Author

As a faculty member and the program coordinator for Museum Studies at Syracuse University, **Andrew Saluti** engages in consistent collaboration with the diverse community voices and cultural heritage collecting institutions that populate both academic and professional sectors of the Central New York region. Together with his colleagues, faculty, and students Saluti considers equity, inclusivity, and accessibility core and vital aspects to museum practice and pedagogy. This commitment is reflected in the broad scope of teaching, mentoring, curricular design, and professional practice that he facilitates, as well as through an ever-expanding network of emerging and established museum professionals from around the globe.

Before stepping into the role of program coordinator for Museum Studies at Syracuse University, Saluti was the chief curator of exhibitions, programs, and education for the Special Collections Research Center at Syracuse University Libraries and the assistant director of the Syracuse University Art Galleries and Collections. He continues to be an active member of numerous museum boards and advisory committees. Saluti's dedication to and experience with museum governance and leadership, in concert with almost 20 years of professional practice in both archival and object-based collecting institutions, informs ongoing research and pedagogy that comprises both curatorship and collections, with specific interest and focus on the practical installation and design, as well as the role of institutional responsibility, stewardship, and sustainability of academic collection building.